# Recovered Memories of Abuse

# Recovered Memories of Abuse
## ASSESSMENT, THERAPY, FORENSICS

Kenneth S. Pope    Laura S. Brown

AMERICAN PSYCHOLOGICAL ASSOCIATION
WASHINGTON, DC

Published by the
American Psychological Association
750 First Street, NE
Washington, DC 20002

Copies may be ordered from
American Psychological Association
Order Department
P.O. Box 92984
Washington DC 20090-2984

Printer: Kirby Lithograpic, Arlington, VA
Typesetter: Innodata Publishing Services Division, Hanover, MD
Cover designer: Berg Design, Albany, NY
Technical/Production Editor: Sarah J. Trembath

**Library of Congress Cataloging-in-Publication Data**

Pope, Kenneth S.
    Recovered memories of abuse : assessment, therapy, forensics / by Kenneth S. Pope and Laura  S. Brown.
        p.    cm.
    Includes bibliographical references and index.
    ISBN 1-55798-395-X
    1. Adult child sexual abuse victims.      2. Recovered memory.
    3. False memory syndrome.     I. Brown, Laura S.     II. Title.
    RC569.5.A28P67      1996
    616.85'8369—dc20                                                        96-33009
                                                                                    CIP

*Printed in the United States*
*First Edition*

# Contents

# Acknowledgments

This book would never have been possible without the hard work, unwavering support, helpful editorial guidance, and exceptional skills of APA Books staff. We would like especially to thank not only Gary VandenBos, Julia Frank-McNeil, Mary Lynn Skutley, Paula Whyman, and Sarah Trembath, but also APA as an organization devoted to addressing the issues discussed in this volume carefully, honestly, scientifically, and effectively.

One example of APA's commitment to this area is the Working Group on Recovered Memories that it established. Laura's colleagues on the Working Group, especially Judith Alpert and Christine Courtois, have been endless sources of inspiration, information, and support, and their influence is reflected throughout this guide for therapists.

We would like to thank APA for agreeing to let us waive royalties for this book so that it might be made more affordable.

Ken Pope would also like to thank Ray Fowler and Melissa Warren for their editorial guidance and support in regard to his *American Psychologist* article "Memory, Abuse, and Science: Questioning Claims About the False Memory Syndrome Epidemic," which was adapted for chapter 3 of this book.

Specific thanks are due to Laura Anderson, who once again performed wonders of organizing references and ensuring that important details were not missed. She will be greatly missed as she heads off to a doctoral program.

We would like to thank our clients, who have generously called us to account when we have made mistakes; our friends and colleagues, whose criticisms and support have been essential to our decades of work in this area; those who remain opposed to our work, whose challenges have helped us learn and rethink; and our loved ones, whose caring, lives, and example have added joy and meaning even at the worst of times. Some men and women who must here remain unnamed have allowed the authors to be present during their experience of recovering delayed memories of trauma. Also unnamed are the women and men who have shared their narratives of having been abused and exploited by previous therapists. Each group in its own way has raised the authors' awareness about the potential for harm and healing present in human connections and in particular the therapy process.

Among those who generously agreed to read the manuscript in draft form and provide comments are Yossef Ben-Porath, Brandt Caudill, Phil Erdberg, Mary Harvey, Seth Kalichman, Gerry Koocher, Karen Olio, Kathy Pezdek, Joyce Seelen, Jerome L. Singer, Janet Sonne, and Onno van der Hart. We greatly appreciate their wisdom, expertise, and work, especially on such a difficult topic.

Laura Brown would like to thank Ken Pope, first and foremost, for his having suggested the idea of this book. Without his willingness to take the first step and then to spend to time to shape the initial idea into a workable form, this volume would not have been written. Ken's openness to this difficult topic and his capacity to grasp a range of apparently conflicting ideas have brought clarity at many difficult points in this writing process. Ken Pope treasures Laura as a wonderful friend and colleague unafraid to question the prevailing wisdom and take nothing for granted, and to openly and nondefensively discuss and critique her own work, evidence, reasoning, and doubts. We both appreciate the inventors of the file-transfer program, which allowed us to write together while being thousands of miles apart.

# Sexual Abuse, Delayed Memories, and Therapy: An Introduction

I magine that a woman in her thirties shows up in your office for her first session of therapy, sits down, and almost immediately begins to cry. Two months ago she lost her job in a massive company lay-off—the most disruptive event of her adult life. Two days later strange dreams began to trouble her sleep. In the dreams, she is young. Her father is doing something awful. She cannot get the dreams out of her mind, no matter how hard she has tried. Scenes of herself in bed with her father became more vivid while she was awake. She seemed to remember something for the first time in over 20 years: Her father had had intercourse with her beginning when she was 9 years old. She had tried to talk herself out of believing this, but she knew "in her gut" that it was true. She has had "funny feelings" about her father for years. She has been vaguely unhappy for as long as she can remember, and outside of her dedication to her work, has had little by way of success in her emotional life. But she does not want this terrible thing called incest to have happened to her. She feels as if she cannot continue to live if it is true. She asks the therapist, "Did that really happen? Am I crazy? What should I do? Can you help me? Do you believe me?"

This and similar scenarios are not unfamiliar to many psychotherapists: An adult enters treatment in the wake of what appear to be overpowering intrusive memories—once unavailable and now inescapable—of a painful childhood experience.

Research suggests that most therapists are likely to see at least one client[1] with "recovered memories" in their professional careers, and that some may see many such clients (Pope & Tabachnick, 1995). As controversy continues to rage around the issue of recovered memories of childhood abuse in the midst of the 1990s, it is common knowledge that this scenario may be a source of potential challenges for the therapist. This volume seeks to provide information and guidance helpful to clinicians, expert witnesses, and others when recovered memories are at issue.

## Contextual Factors

Judith Herman (1992), psychiatrist and trauma researcher, suggested that the study of trauma is inherently political, given that any discussion of trauma requires the uncovering of abhorrent social realities that a society may wish to minimize or deny. The literature has explored the social, cultural, and professional politics as they influence changing understandings of not only science, assessment, diagnosis, and therapy more generally (e.g., Caplan, 1995; Feldman-Summers & Kiesler, 1974; Fidell, 1970; Goffman, 1961; Guthrie, 1976; Gynther, Fowler, & Erdberg, 1971; Hollingshead & Redlich, 1958; Mednick, 1989; Pope & Vasquez, 1991; Scarr, 1988; Szasz, 1970, 1994; Tavris, 1992) but also the specific topics of child abuse, trauma, and memory (e.g., Armstrong, 1994; Freyd, 1994a; Goodyear-Smith, 1993; Loftus, 1995b; Myers, 1994; Ofshe & Watters, 1994; Pendergrast, 1995; Pride, 1986; Salter, 1995; Wakefield & Underwager, 1993, 1994; Wassil-Grimm, 1995; Whitfield, 1995). Clinicians and expert witnesses may, of course, agree or disagree with any specific claim, hypothesis, or interpretation of social, cultural, or professional politics made by the authors cited, or in this volume. However, awareness of these conflicting attempts to make sense of the

---

[1] A note on terminology: The terms *client* and *patient* have sometimes been used as synonyms, and sometimes to represent different theoretical orientations and approaches. In this book we use them as synonyms.

political context, their assumptions and implicit values, their relationship to the full range of information and events, and the uses to which they may be put can be helpful and perhaps essential to the practitioner in working with clients when recovered memories of abuse are at issue.

Two social movements have taken center stage on this issue. One (hereafter referred to as the *incest recovery movement*, a somewhat loosely organized social phenomenon that has no central organizing group or official leadership) was founded by adults who describe themselves as survivors of childhood sexual abuse; the other (hereafter referred to as the *false memory movement*, best represented by the False Memory Syndrome Foundation, which coined the concept of false memory syndrome [see chapter 3] and has taken active leadership on this issue) was founded by adults who describe themselves as having been falsely accused of commiting such abuse. These social movements uncovered and crystallized controversies within the mental health field regarding the nature and effects of child sexual abuse, as well as the scientific basis and standards of care for clinical and forensic practice. Each of these social movements—singly and in interaction with the other—has influenced psychotherapy and psychotherapists. Both have relied on mental health and behavioral science experts as the authority for central beliefs. Both have in turn put themselves forward as authoritative sources informing the practices of psychotherapists who work with adults when recovered memories of abuse are at issue.

## Litigation

In recent years an increase in litigation and formal complaints has intensified the heat and light of the political milieu—adults suing those whom they claim to be perpetrators, accused parents suing or bringing complaints against therapists, experts suing other experts who disagree with them and/or professional organizations that refuse to support their stance, and, most recently, clients who believe that they have been harmed as a result of the implantation of false abuse memories suing therapists for malpractice. This increasingly litigious context may influence how therapists respond to those seeking help when, as the scenario opening this chapter exemplied, recovered memories of abuse are at issue.

## The Politics of Sexual Abuse

Another contextual factor affecting the therapist in this scenario is our society's ambivalent relationship to knowledge about sexual abuse of children. Since Freud first began to write of his patients' stories of sexual abuse, then to retract and revise his findings, therapists have confronted questions of how valid such complaints might be and, if valid, how damaging they are to the child over the long term. Moreover, we find ourselves encountering questions of whether sexual abuse of children is a frequent enough event to be of concern to mental health experts.

Sexual abuse of children is a highly charged topic seeming to create impatient social demands for instant clarity that may be superficial, misleading, or downright wrong, rather than the patient tolerance needed until ambiguities can be carefully, adequately explored. While many kinds of adult actions can harm children and create the risk of mental health problems throughout the lifespan (Kendall-Tackett, Williams, & Finkelhor, 1993), this culture tends to perceive sexual abuse as particularly heinous, as evidenced by the fact that while in many jurisdictions it remains legal for an adult to hit a child (e.g., to practice corporal punishment), call a child names, or in various ways treat a child unhelpfully, in none is it legal to have sexual contact with a child, even when the child offers no apparent protest to what is happening. In an atmosphere of pseudocertainty, information as sparse and fragmented as presented in the vignette above becomes sufficient for conclusions to be drawn that may not, in the end, turn out to be accurate. The pull to arrive at this sort of pseudocertainty is strong when the issue is childhood sexual abuse.

Some professionals will be affected by strong demands to deny or affirm the presence of current or former sexual abuse without sufficient information. Some will be moved by strong demands to proclaim that such an act inevitably caused the most profound, pervasive, and lifelong damage to the child who inevitably responded with a particular set of feelings (thus sparing clinician, forensic expert, and others from considering the uniqueness of the particular interaction). Conversely, there may be pulls on the clinician or expert witness to assume that the experience would not have happened if the child had not on some level wanted, invited, or benefitted from sexual contact with an adult. There is an absence of consensus, as the following review will reveal.

## Questions About the Base Rate of Child Abuse

Historically, the sexual abuse of children has been considered an extremely rare event. Questions of the frequency with which such abuse occurs and what constitutes sexual abuse have also been a part of the epistemic framework of the current debate. A scholarly text published a little over 40 years ago, for example, reported that incest affected only about one or two people per million United States citizens each year (Weinberg, 1955). More recently, one of the most widely read professional texts— *Comprehensive Textbook of Psychiatry*—reported that the incidence rate for incest was about 1.1 to 1.9 per million (Henderson, 1975).

Since the late 1970s, however, investigations into childhood sexual abuse by Louise Armstrong, Sandra Butler, David Finkelhor, Florence Rush, Diana Russell, and others have challenged those figures. If the phenomenon is broadly defined to include all exposure to unwanted or uncomfortable sexual contact with adults or significantly older children, researchers have reported rates as high of 38% of female samples for sexual abuse prior to age 16 (Drajer, 1988; Russell, 1986). The National Committee to Prevent Child Abuse reported in 1994 that in this country 3.1 million children under 18 were reported to be victims of abuse or neglect (Levinson, 1995). The Committee reported that 1.4 million of these 3.1 million cases could be confirmed (which does not per se prove that the other reports were necessarily in error, because some reports of abuse of children cannot be completely confirmed due to lack of physical evidence). The confirmed cases, according to the Committee, represent a base rate of about 16 abused children per every 1,000 children in the United States. The Committee's data suggest that almost 90% of all child abusers are parents or other relatives (Levinson, 1995). This research suggests that sexual abuse is not rare.

Whereas these more recent research-based figures suggest that sexual abuse, both within and outside of families, affects significantly more than 1 or 2 children per million, some popular books on the topic that have emerged from the survivor movement sometimes seem to present even larger estimates without discussing in adequate detail the research or reasoning on which the figures are based. Popular press author and psychotherapist E. Sue Blume (1990) claimed, for example,

> The statistics are disturbing; the most commonly cited is that 25% of all American women have been sexually molested in childhood, most by someone they knew and trusted. Newer research, done more carefully and accurately, indicates that as many as 38% of women were molested in childhood. There are many acknowledged problems with even this research, but the greatest is this: what is not remembered cannot be reported. It is my experience that fewer than half of the women who experienced this trauma later remember or identify it as abuse. Therefore it is not unlikely that *more than half of all women* are survivors of childhood sexual trauma. (p. iv; italics in original)

Other writers have taken issue with this sort of assertion, arguing that it represents an overly broad and inaccurate rendering of the meaning of the available statistical data. Pride (1986), for example, asserted a starkly different set of claims:

> Why is there so much noise about child abuse when there is so little actual abuse? Why do people garble the facts about child abuse so badly? Why are the statistics inflated, the terms redefined, and the whole problem blown out of proportion?
>
> Statistically we see that child abuse does not even begin to approach an epidemic. Only one child out of 72,000 dies from child abuse; less than one out of three thousand is seriously harmed each year. Sexual abuse affects only about one in a thousand children, and most of these cases do not involve the natural parents. Reports of abuse and neglect are increasing, but so is the malicious use of child abuse hotlines by ex-spouses. Actual severe physical abuse is even reported on the decline. (p. 41)

Such extremes of viewpoint on the matter of child sexual abuse illustrate the potential influences of this cultural debate on clinical work or on forensic evaluations because even the matter of the phenomenon's actual base rate appears to be under contention. Beliefs about baseline rates of child sexual abuse will likely influence the manner in which a mental health professional proceeds with assessment, psychotherapy, or forensic testimony because of the influence that such knowledge may have on a professional's decision to credit or question a client's report of sexual abuse.

## Questions About the Base Rate of False Accusations

In light of such variation in estimated frequency of child sexual abuse, it is not surprising that there are also contrasting beliefs about how often *false* claims of child sexual abuse occur during an individual's childhood. Meacham (1993) reported an interview in which two frequent forensic experts in the field of childhood sexual abuse, Ralph Underwager and Hollida Wakefield, suggested "that there may be as many as nine false accusations of sexual abuse for every accurate accusation" (p. 78). Some individuals and organizations (see chapter 3) claim scientific evidence of a false memory syndrome (FMS) epidemic (e.g., M. Gardner, 1993). On the other hand, others maintain that, aside from reports arising in the context of contested custody, few reports by children themselves are entirely inaccurate, although some may represent confusion and ambiguity in an interpersonal situation (Berliner, personal communication, October 1995). Mental health professionals who hold "believe the children [as always accurately describing sex abuse]" as a central injunction may approach their work in a way that significantly differs from those who assert that the research demonstrates that 90% of all claims of child abuse are false (see chapter 5).

## Can Adult–Child Sex Be Pleasant or Beneficial?

In addition to the debates over frequency of sexual abuse of children and the credibility of reports of abuse, there is also debate about whether sexual contact with an adult is per se unpleasant and harmful to a child. Some mental health professionals make the assumption, based upon their readings of the available literature, that sexual abuse is harmful to children and has long-term negative mental health consequences (Beitchman, Zucker, Hood, daCosta, & Ackman, 1991; Kendall-Tackett et al., 1993). Others, however, discuss potentially positive aspects, suggesting that the experience may be either pleasurable or beneficial, and lacks traumatic elements. For example, in *The London Times* interview with an FMSF founder, Ralph Underwager, the *Times* reported that Underwager asserted

> that "scientific evidence" showed 60% of women sexually abused as children reported that the experience had been good for them. He contended the same could be true for boys.
>
> He confirmed that he had approved the article in the journal *Paidika*, subtitled the *Journal of Paedophilia*, before publication. In it he stated: "Paedophiles need to become more positive and make the claim that paedophilia is an acceptable expression of God's will for love and unity among human beings." (Lightfoot, 1993, p. 2)

Ceci, Huffman, Smith, and Loftus (1994) wrote, "It is not clear that fondling or even fellatio are experienced by infants and young children as assaultive; they may at times be pleasurable or neutral, thus not carrying the psychic trauma needed for repression" (p. 403). In the title of their article, McMillan, Zuravin, and Rideout (1995) referred to some of the resilient coping strategies developed by children in the face of this experience as the "perceived benefits of child sexual abuse." In *True and False Allegations of Child Sex Abuse,*[2] Gardner (1992) notes that adult–child sexual activities "are *not* necessarily traumatic. The determinant as to whether the experience will be traumatic is the social attitude toward these encounters. . . . In short, there are many women who have had sexual encounters with their

---

[2]For a discussion of the scientific and legal aspects of Gardner's Parental Alienation Syndrome, readers are referred to Woods (1994).

fathers who do not consider them to have affected their lives detrimentally" (p. 670). Krivacska (1994), in a review of Li, West, and Woodhouse (1993), highlighted the debate about positive or negative consequences of child–adult sexual contact, a purposefully neutral term.

## Empirical Evidence on the Effects of Abuse

Briere (1992) has correctly noted that many of the earlier studies in this literature suffer from methodological problems, largely those reflecting nonrandom samples and absence of adequate comparison groups. He also noted that as more data on sexual abuse have emerged, these concerns are being addressed, and the convergence of results appears to be the same. That is, studies reviewing literature on both sexually abused children and adult survivors of sexual abuse find that childhood sexual abuse tends to be associated with a wide range of psychological, psychosomatic, and interpersonal difficulties, although there is also immense individual variability, representing differences in the experience of abuse and the resources of the abuse victim.

Kendall-Tackett et al. (1993) in a comprehensive review of the literature on children who have been sexually abused, note that this group is more symptomatic as a whole than either nonsexually abused child psychiatric patients or a comparison group of "normal" children. Beitchman, Zucker, Hood, daCosta, and Ackman (1991) consider other possible sources of distress, including more general *family dysfunction*, and note that sexual abuse may be a risk factor, if not a direct cause, of adult emotional distress. Similarly, Chu, Matthews, Frey, and Ganzel (in press) reviewed studies regarding a relationship between childhood sexual abuse experiences and adult psychopathology, and reported that in almost all instances there was a positive, although not clearly causative, relationship. Polusny and Follette (1995) reviewed research from 1987 onwards on the long-term correlates of childhood sexual abuse, and found that persons with this experience were overrepresented in a variety of diagnostic categories, and also had excess reports of abusive and sexually assaultive adult life experiences.

Reviews of literature on various clinical groups or specific diagnostic categories demonstrate a rate of sexual abuse survivors well above the supposed population base rates in such diverse diagnostic groups as depressed patients (McGrath, Keita, Strickland, & Russo, 1990), patients with chronic pelvic pain (Walker, Katon, Harrop-Griffith et al., 1988), patients with irritable bowel syndrome (Walker, Katon, Roy-Byrne, Jemelka, & Russo, 1993), and patients with generalized anxiety disorder (Burnam et al., 1988; Sorenson & Golding, 1990). Even when such "obvious" diagnoses as PTSD (see Briere, 1996, in press; Courtois, 1991; Gidycz & Koss, 1989; Salter, 1995), borderline personality disorder (Bryer, Nelson, Miller, & Krol, 1987), and dissociative identity disorder (Kluft, 1990; Putnam, 1989) are ruled out of the analysis, the overrepresentation of sexual abuse survivors in both medical and psychiatric patient groups is a frequent finding, suggesting to some that, contrary to some claims, child sexual abuse may be generally harmful.

Certainly, childhood sexual abuse cannot be defined as a sole causative factor of any particular diagnosis, given the current state of evidence. There are no psychological factors that are pathognomic of childhood sexual abuse, in part because the many possible interactions between types and duration of abuse, and age and developmental stage of the abused child can predispose to a large number of possible outcomes. However, in one study where participants did report that they perceived "no negative effect" from a known history of sexual abuse, and then were compared with those reporting a perceived negative effect and with a random sample of nonabused women, the authors found that while the "no effect" group was less symptomatic and more functional than the "negative effect" group, the "no effect" group still scored in the pathological range on standard psychometric measures when contrasted with a matched sample with no sexual abuse histories (Tsai, Feldman-Summers, & Edgar, 1979). This intriguing finding suggests that there may be great variability of effects of sexual abuse in childhood, and that other factors must be taken into account when understanding whether and how sexual abuse may have been a risk factor for childhood or adult distress.

## Controversies About Memory

Still another variable in the social, intellectual, and political milieu surrounding the therapist is the state of the research on memory and, specifically, memory for trauma (see chapter 2). This is a topic charged with controversy, with some scientists arguing the position that memory is memory, and that all memories are subject to the same rules (Loftus, 1993; Ornstein, Ceci, & Loftus, 1996), while others claim that memories for trauma, while still little studied and poorly understood in the laboratory setting, may be biologically and thus cognitively an entirely or partially different phenomenon (D. Brown, 1995a, 1995b; van der Kolk & Fisler, 1994). The question of "truth" or "falsity" of a memory of sexual abuse, particularly a long-delayed memory, has become central to the current debate.

The use of the terms "false memory" and "true memory" are problematic in light of research and theory about memory. Most paradigms seem to suggest that "true" and "false" are naive or misleading labels when applied to memory, which tends toward a mixture of the accurate and inaccurate. Additionally, a review of the research on this topic finds a confusion of meanings; a "false memory" in one study refers to the inclusion of the wrong word in a list (Roediger & McDermott, 1995), while in another might describe a complex series of interactions that have been deceptively suggested to a research participant by a family member or friend (Loftus, 1993), or by a researcher who represents the information as coming from the research participant's parents (Hyman, Husband, & Billings, 1995). In the popular literature, such terminology often reflects the standpoint of the writer, and the writer's assumptions about whether a reported memory is valid or not. In such instances, the label "true" or "false" may have little or nothing to do with the validity or invalidity of the reported memory and reflect instead the writer's response to the political pressures in this area. Such flawed labels as well as competing paradigms of memory form another aspect of the context in which clinicians and forensic experts carry out their work in responding to scenarios like the one at this chapter's opening.

# What Can Therapists Really Know About the Validity of Recovered Memories?

With all of this as context, how can the therapist in our hypothetical opening scenario respond to this client's questions—"Did that really happen? Am I crazy? What should I do"? What, exactly, does the therapist know at this point that would enable her or him to answer the desparate client's questions in a manner that will help, both in the short and long term? The questions asked by our hypothetical client might form a projective test for a field in conflict over the question of trauma and how it is remembered. They open a window onto the assumptions and inferences made by therapists, not always backed by either experience or empirical data, in response to clinical presentations. Some of these therapist assumptions and conclusions are likely, based on our review of the literature, to encompass the following:

☐ Some would say that the woman is clearly an incest victim. Why would anyone make up a story about something so horrible? We must always believe claims of abuse; for the therapist to do otherwise would constitute revictimization.

☐ Some would say that she is clearly not an incest victim. Memories of important events in our lives do not hide for years and then suddenly pop up again. If something so horrible had happened to her, she would have remembered it. To believe her would be to encourage dangerous confabulation and harm to her father.

☐ Some would say that the memory may not be literally true but that her father, or someone like her father, must have done *something* to her. If the event she describes is not literally true, it is a necessary fiction covering up an even more traumatic event in her early life. Where there's smoke, there's fire.

☐ Some would say that she manifests a distinct clinical syndrome frequently described in the popular press (see chapter 3). Her demographics, the recovered memory, and her general profile clearly show what has been termed the *false memory syndrome* (FMS).

☐ Some would say that the therapist should begin using a variety of techniques suggested in clinical literature to determine whether the memory is true and to perhaps assist in the recollection of more memories.

☐ Some would further say that the therapist has a duty to investigate whether the memory is objectively true before proceeding with treatment. The therapist must gather all available records (e.g., school records, former assessment or therapy reports, medical and hospitalization charts) and schedule interviews with family members, including the accused perpetrator.

☐ Some would say that the therapist has a duty to file a formal report of suspected child abuse with local child protection or law enforcement agencies.

☐ And some, following the British Empiricist school in examining and questioning even the most basic assumptions, might wonder if she is actually a patient or whether she might be a pseudopatient secretly recording the session in order to cast doubt on the therapist.

✛ ✛ ✛

The therapist's profound responsibility to help the suffering client in such a highly ambiguous and charged situation may constitute a crisis for some therapists. A misstep in any direction can potentially bring about very painful, destructive consequences. Lacking adequate support, and facing skepticism or disbelief from the therapist, clients may turn away from therapy, convinced that no one will believe them. Just like our hypothetical client, many of those who struggle with this seemingly intolerable psychic pain may think that suicide is the only solution for their distress.

But an immediate, impulsive rush to validate the "truth" of clients' experiences can *also* be the first step towards possible harm. Misled by the therapist's seeming authority, patients may mistakenly jump to a quick but erroneous conclusion that the "memories" must be true and focus treatment around them. Patients may go on to file civil or criminal charges against the alleged perpetrator, but years later decide that the "memories" were untrue and recant—a chain of events that may be painfully destructive to all participants and might have led to the incarceration of an innocent person.

Ideally, of course, therapist and client arrive at a treatment plan in which the client comes to terms with and integrates these new and frightening experiences for whatever they are, perhaps as cognitions that do not reflect a history of abuse, perhaps as memories of abuse that actually happened, perhaps as metaphor for other painful experiences, perhaps as something else. In this ideal scenario, the client as an adult makes decisions about maintaining or changing relationships with the alleged perpetrator or other family members that are based on the client's own values and judgment. Ideally, the outcome of this scenario will be one of healing for the client in question.

## Risks to Therapists: Are They Omnipresent?

Even in one of the possible ideal scenarios, however, the current climate of charges and countercharges against therapists is one in which many difficulties may develop for a therapist. Assume that the therapist chooses steps that allow, enable, or help our hypothetical patient to discover and decide for herself what actually occurred. Imagine that she comes to decide, on her own and with no suggestions from the therapist, that she was sexually abused, and imagine that, operating from her strong belief, she reveals this "fact" to her family and confronts her father. Assume that she is pleased with this course of events and outcome. Even so, the therapist in our scenario may be subjected to formal complaints to be adjudicated by civil courts, administrative law judges, or ethics committees. This may happen because, regardless of the quality of the clinical services and no matter how many safeguards the therapist takes to protect and support the autonomy of a client, third parties may view these practices as inadequate based on the conclusions arrived at by the client, or may consider the therapist's methods insufficient to withstand formal scrutiny in a court or regulatory hearing.

Or, the autonomous decisions of the client may sufficiently anger third parties that the therapist's complicity in this outcome is assumed, and she or he becomes the target of complaint. With increasing frequency, therapists have been the recipient of regulatory and legal complaints by their clients' parents even when the clients themselves have been pleased with the outcome of treatment and believe strongly in the truth of their own recollections of abuse and their decisions based on those memories. In one instance, a father wrote to confirm his adult daughters' memories of incest but later brought charges against the therapist for apparently crediting her clients as well as his later-retracted letter, and called the therapist's actions a failure of the standard of care.

Or, the therapist's theoretical approach to treatment may be viewed as lacking essential elements of competent care, and he or she may be accused of per se malpractice. Psychiatrist Paul McHugh, who teaches continuing education workshops on the standard of care with recovered memories for the FMSF ("American Psychological Association approves FMSF as a sponsor of continuing education programs," 1995) and serves on the FMSF advisory board, stated (1993b, p. 1), "To treat for repressed memories without any effort at external validation is malpractice pure and simple; malpractice on the basis of standards of care that have developed out of the history of psychiatric service . . . and malpractice because the misdirection of therapy injures the patient and his or her significant others."

Therapists may also face ethics complaints if any aspect of assessment or treatment is based on the hypothesis of repression resulting from trauma. The Oregon Psychological Association, for example, published an ethics statement, authored by an FMSF Advisory Board member, addressing this topic: "The Ethical Principles state that psychologists must base their work on valid and reliable scientific knowledge based on research" and "[t]he idea that trauma represses memories cannot be supported" (Pankratz, 1995, p. 8).

The range of potential responses to our opening vignette illustrates that virtually *any* approach may viewed as wrong by *some* professionals. Those who condemn the particular approach chosen by the therapist may appear as expert witnesses in formal hearings against the therapist or file a formal licensing, ethics, or civil complaint against the therapist. The therapist may feel in an infinite bind: there are seemingly countless steps that might be taken, but each seems capable of making the situation worse, as does delaying or declining to take any substantial step.

## Effects of Conflict and Ambiguity on Therapists

The lack of clear, simple, instant answers and universally accepted, easy-to-follow, one-size-fits-all rules in the midst of pressing responsibilities, ambiguous situations, and potentially explosive consequences is a harrowing prospect for many clinicians. It is a context that is less than conducive to one element often necessary to promote good therapy: a trusting working alliance between therapist and client, in which the sole focus is on the client's improved well-being and functioning (Fox, 1995). The overt intrusion of the social and political milieu into the therapy office can be problematic, especially when the therapist does not practice from a theoretical model that has already taken social and political factors into account (Brown, 1994) and that might ease the therapist's way into making sense of this conflation of personal and political agendas in the therapy hour.

The therapist facing a distraught client, a client's furious parent, or a lawyer's cross-examination can flee uncertainty, complexity, and ambiguity as a sailor jumps a burning ship. Any simple assertion or simplistic rule appears like a life-saving raft in an endless sea of trouble. The therapist can then appear to be forceful, confident, and authoritative. The simple, albeit completely mutually contradictory assertions summarized earlier in this chapter (e.g., all reports of recovered memories are essentially valid; a person never forgets major sexual assault; all people who believe recovered memories are valid are witch-hunting dogmatics; all people who disbelieve recovered memories are pedophiles or pedophile-supporters; all reports of incest are wish-fulfillment fantasies) serve a function. They appear to cut through confusion, discomfort, and doubt, creating the illusion of certainty for the therapist and, perhaps, the client as well. The therapist and others need not reason, examine data, ask difficult questions, or collaborate in authentic exploration with the client of what might be real. Pseudo-knowledge and pseudo-unanimity (e.g., "Scientists know that . . ."; "Traumatologists agree that . . ."; "Cognitive psychologists believe that . . ."; "Abuse specialists understand that . . .") form a substitute for critical thinking and transform openness to possibilities into certainties about realities at which the therapist was never present. This flight from ambiguity and from careful assessment of context and information can lead to problems for clients and therapists alike.

## The Nature and Purpose of This Book

Now that some problematic issues confronting clinicians and expert witnesses have been introduced, a discussion of chapters addressing specific topic areas and touching on special subjects relevant to therapists and expert witnesses responding to reports of delayed memories of childhood sex abuse follows. The topic areas explored in this volume encompass an exploration of science, memory, and trauma; a discussion of recent claims about false memories and the methods used to promote them; preparation for the work; assessment and intervention; and forensic work. The idea behind each chapter is to identify significant concerns, suggest questions that might help clinical and forensic practitioners approach those concerns, and present examples of research findings, hypotheses, and interventions relevant to the concerns. We have tried to avoid the tempting illusion of final, settled "truth," unquestionable assumptions, and one-size-fits-all interventions. The rapidly evolving research in this area should prompt greater openness and questioning rather than premature closure. There is no fixed set of rote steps for responding to reports of delayed memories. But an attention to data can be a helpful strategy for coping with the powerful pulls of the public debate on this topic. Additionally, an awareness of the social and professional contexts shaping the attitudes and values of clinical and forensic practitioners helps each one assess his or her own responses to this difficult problem.

This book was written to help clinicians and expert witnesses respond knowledgeably, competently, and effectively when they encounter clients who report recovering memories of child abuse. The authors have sought to encourage and help clinical and forensic practitioners to endure the terrible ambiguity, intense pressures, and confusion of claims in this area while remaining open to relevant research findings and professional responsibilities. *Recovered Memories of Abuse* focuses on some of the major questions in clinical and forensic work with what trauma researcher and therapist Mary Harvey refers to as the "remembering adult" (1996). As with previous works by both authors, we hope to encourage autonomous thinking and decision-making by the clinician or forensic expert rather than promulgating a set of invariant rules.

If assessment, therapy, and expert testimony are to take adequate account of both empirical findings and clinical reality (i.e., the client's shared group characteristics as well as unique aspects), clinicians must remain abreast of emerging research findings and avoid relying on insufficient, stereotypical, isolated data in informing their understandings of each client. The reader will find in this book a brief summary of and introduction to some major issues, reminders of relevant research, and suggested approaches to clinical and forensic responsibilities. We do not intend this to be an exhaustive tome providing encyclopedic coverage. We write from the assumption that the reader knows how to conduct an assessment and provide therapy (or is in training to obtain these skills) and, if planning to testify in a legal context, has at least some initial familiarity with the role of the professional who must render expert testimony and the ethical and professional norms governing forensic practice (e.g., Pope, Butcher, & Seelen, 1993). We do not review all the scientific literature or revisit the basic clinical skills, but rather suggest crucial questions that the practitioner needs to ask when conducting this work as well as strategies and resources for addressing these questions. We attempt to reference our comments so that interested readers may turn to other sources for further study of a particular topic.

In this volume, we cover topics that we consider to be critical to effective and competent practice. In the intial chapter, we have attempted to introduce our readers to some powerful social contextual variables that shape clinical practice on this topic. Because it is seldom that a psychotherapeutic issue has been the focus of such intense debate, both in the popular media and in the professional literature, we believe it important for our readers to develop a heightened awareness of how this discourse may influence a clinician's attitudes, values, and clinical practice.

# Premises of This Book

*A major premise of this book is that the issues in this area are poorly addressed if clinicians feel they must make a forced choice between car-toonish stereotypes of "clinical" and "scientific" approaches, or between the artificially created categories of "true" and "false" memo-ries of trauma.* We have found no convincing evidence that a forced-choice dichotomy is accurate or that it necessarily leads to more valid and useful conclusions. We find it problematic when advocacy groups for whatever perspective come to be perceived as the authoritative sources on this complex and still-developing scientific and clinical issue. For readers who disagree, we invite you to consider this premise on a heuristic basis and remain open to what it might yield.

*Another major premise of this book is that science and practice in this area must not proceed in ignorance of each other but must adequately inform one another if either is to claim intellectual integrity. Neither can be considered without the other, and neither should be viewed as more important than the other.* Currently, this synergy of science and practice seems infrequently to be the rule. Hypnosis researcher Daniel Brown (1995a, 1995b) suggested that while many clinicians have little familiarity with research on memory, few researchers in the field of memory are familiar with the nature and parameters of trauma. This mutual ignorance has been a fertile field for the growth of stereotypes and misinforma-tion in all directions.

*A third major premise of the book is that current turmoil in this field distorts mental health professionals' awareness of empirical findings, scientific history, and the clinical needs of individual clients; makes us less aware of our own biases and limitations; and may overshadow fun-damental clinical and forensic standards and responsibilities. We must therefore become more aware of the heritage of these issues, both clini-cally and scientifically, so as to respond to them ethically and effec-tively.* Certain topics may become especially problematic, as we have already begun to describe. Recognizing and understanding these problem topics are crucial to competent and effective work in this area. Ignoring these factors can lead to disastrous conse-quences for clients, therapists, the therapy process, families, and so many others. Unnoticed or misconstrued, such factors can block the most well-intentioned efforts to provide scientifically based, effective clinical and forensic services. They can lead to anxiety in both therapist and client that may ultimately be countertherapeutic. Awareness of how these problem topics can undermine the effectiveness of clinicians and expert witnesses increases the possibility that practitioners will be able to engage in reflective and thoughtful, rather than reflexive and anxious, strategies for responding to reports of delayed recall of childhood sexual abuse.

*The fourth major premise is that mental health professionals must always ask: Is this assertion, instrument, or intervention supported by (or at least consistent with) empirical findings? And to what degree are such findings limited in their usefulness or generalizability in this particular instance?* Whereas various assertions made by authors on the topic of recovered memories may seem intuitively or clinically appealing or resonate with one's prior beliefs or biases, they may also be erroneous to a degree that could lead to harm to clients. Even assertions that seem to represent common sense, a logical inference or deduction, an assertion by a renowned authority, or a consensus of the field warrant careful and constant questioning. Many of the absolute statements on the topic of childhood sexual abuse may rely upon strongly held beliefs, clinical experience, a collection of anecdotes, an appeal to authority, an unsound generalization from specific experiments, or countless other justifications. But accompanying the assertion with evidence of empirical validity allows a more scientific approach; therapists who are developing strategies for assessment and treatment of clients who have alleged memory recovery must pay careful attention to developing a scientific foundation for their work and to whether attempts to apply specific experiments or hypotheses to a specific individual in a specific context are scientifically and logically sound.

*Still another fundamental premise of this book is that, in light of the current state of scientific data and knowledge, each report of recovered memory of abuse must be carefully and fairly evaluated on an individual basis.* No claim can be reflexively assumed to be valid, invalid, or somewhere in between prior to an informed and unbiased review of the data surrounding that assertion. The most plausible, coherent, and compelling report of abuse, even when it does not involve a period of forgetting, may describe something that never occurred in the life of the narrator. The most implausible, internally contradictory, and unpersuasive story, based on memory recovered after a long delay, may reflect abuse that actually was perpetrated on a person. Those who assert that recovered memories of abuse are all completely false or all completely true, or that there are characteristics of the reported memories that will *prima facie* reveal with absolute and total certainty whether the memories are valid or invalid— perhaps with the best of motives—have raced away from what is currently known based on empirical research.

## A Brief Overview

In this introductory chapter, we have tried to lay the contextual foundations that inform our choices of topic for the remainder of this volume. Each of the matters that we touched on briefly in chapter 1 will become the topic of an extensive and in-depth review and discussion in succeeding chapters.

In chapter 2, we review in detail relevant research regarding memory, including controversies within the field regarding such issues as suggestibility and malleability of memory. We discuss the interaction of trauma and memory, and present findings from the emerging research on the neurobiology of memory and trauma. We also review a variety of models of forgetting and delayed recall that may provide explanatory heuristics for clinicians.

Chapter 3 offers an analysis of the proposed false memory syndrome (FMS) and other recent claims about false memories, as well as a discussion of some of the methods used to promote these claims.

In chapter 4, we discuss the domains of competence and knowledge necessary for practice with adults recovering memories, and describe findings of current research on trauma and its impact on adult functioning. We offer readers a model for exploring whether and when they should approach clinical work with a person remembering sexual abuse, and the manners in which a clinician can help ensure ethical and competent practice.

We also review the process of informed consent to treatment and provide a model of empowered consent as a paradigm for the sharing of power in the clinical relationship.

Chapter 5 highlights specific clinical issues in work with the remembering adult, and introduces readers to a model for the empowerment of clients as active and autonomous participants in the therapeutic process. We focus on a perspective of clients in crisis as continuing to be competent adults who can and should actively collaborate in their own care and treatment planning.

In chapter 6, we address forensic issues, both for treating therapists and forensic expert witnesses, although our primary focus will be on the role of the treating therapist when faced with a forensic situation. We will explore the issues that emerge when the client becomes a plaintiff or witness in a criminal case, when a therapist is the target of complaints or litigation, either by third parties or aggrieved former clients, and the problems inherent in conducting therapy in the context of litigation. We will also, although more briefly, discuss the matters that need to be considered by a forensic evaluator in cases involving claims of delayed recall of childhood sexual abuse.

Finally, we offer a series of appendixes that we believe will provide useful reference materials for our readers. These include model consent forms for treatment and evaluation, sample cross-examination questions, and a state-by-state listing of laws regarding delayed recall and statutes of limitations for civil personal injury cases.

# 2

# Science, Memory, and Trauma: A Brief Overview

W hen delayed memories of abuse are at issue, ethical practice requires clinicians and expert witnesses to have and use carefully an adequate knowledge of research and theory about memories. Practice that is founded upon science is more likely to be helpful to our clients. But science is itself always in flux as new data and information constantly become available and hypotheses are tested, falsified, and subjected to replication and extension. This chapter highlights some representative data and concepts from the science of memory and presents a model for informed and critical review of that material by introducing readers to some of the historical and emerging trends, disagreements, and quandries in this field.

## The Interaction of Research and Theory

At first glance, the field of memory may baffle, overwhelm, and discourage practitioners, particularly the many who have long ago forgotten their introductory coursework in cognitive psychology. A subsequent, more thorough examination of the field may also baffle, overwhelm, and discourage if the practitioner is in search of definitive answers and certainty. This complex, evolving field frustrates the search for quick concepts that would safely generalize to virtually all cases. Sometimes the most seemingly basic, uncomplicated questions may elude adequate answers for well over a century. It is little wonder that the very difficult question of delayed recall of trauma is one for which answers appear complex and often conflicting. It is helpful for mental health professionals searching for a useful scientific explanatory model for clinical observations to be aware of this complexity and diversity of viewpoints within the science of memory and of the continuing evolution of these viewpoints. As the Supreme Court recently observed: "Scientific conclusions are subject to perpetual revision" (*Daubert v. Merrell Dow Pharmaceuticals*, 1993).

## The Decade of the Brain, or Learning What We Could Not Know

Innovations in noninvasive imaging technologies, improvements in electroencephelography, and advances in psychopharmacology have led many to focus on the brain as both lock and key to understanding memory, psychopathology, and treatment. The brilliance of recent discoveries has, for some, tended to blot out all other sources of information and has led others to assume that current brain studies emerge from a long history of ignoring the brain. The history of psychology, however, suggests that various sources of information, such as brain research, seem to take their turn periodically as the primary, almost exclusive focus of study, promising to provide the simple, easy path to understanding human experience and behavior.

The mental health professional will find it useful to be familiar with the history of brain research and, thus, revisit the site of undergraduate courses in the psychology of learning to recall some of the foundational work on memory. One of the most interesting lines of research began in the 1920s and stretched over the next few decades. Karl Lashley devised a series of experiments to find out where the brain holds memories. He began by training rats to run a maze. He assumed that because rats could run the maze faster after they had learned it, they must be remembering the maze and the memory must be physically manifest in the brain. He called these memory traces in the brain *engrams*.

Lashley's strategy was to take rats that had already learned the maze, cut out a tiny part of their brain, and see if they ran the maze slower. If so, then he would have located that tiny part of the brain in which the engram was held. With his first experimental subjects, it seemed he had uncannily located exactly where the engram was maintained: the rat ran the maze much slower. But more rats led to more confusion. It seemed that no matter where he removed a tiny part of the brain, the rat tended to "forget" at least part of the maze as measured by the time it took for the rat to finish the course.

What decades of research taught Lashley was that he could not find that part of the rat's brain that held the engram. Taking a tiny piece out of almost any part of the rat's brain would tend to cause the rat to run slower. The larger the piece removed, the slower the rat ran the maze. It was as if there were no single location for the memory.

In 1950, Lashley looked back on his decades of frustrating research and, with good humor, observed, "I sometimes feel, in reviewing the evidence on the localization of the memory trace, that the necessary conclusion is that learning [or memory] is just not possible" (1988, p. 62). Whereas subsequent research using sophisticated imaging techniques can suggest at least partial answers to Lashley's questions, his comment reveals that at times the available research paradigms and instrumentation may not allow adequate understanding of an observable phenomenon. This, of course, does not mean that the phenomenon in question (e.g., learning or memory) does not occur. Lashley's joke simply acknowledges that science has frequently failed to discover or describe the ways in which the brain enables a particular phenomenon to occur.

## Cognition and Consciousness

If the brain is not a recent discovery, it may seem to some that the recent cognitive revolution marked the beginning of scientific focus on consciousness. Like the brain, consciousness and cognition seem to emerge periodically, as if they had just been discovered, as a primary focus of scientific inquiry. Some early behaviorists, such as Pavlov, continued to view subjective experience as important. He wrote, "Psychology, in so far as it concerns the subjective state of man [sic], has a natural right to existence; for our subjective world is the first reality with which we are confronted" (1927, p. 329). But much of the study of consciousness and cognition as exemplified by James, Titchner, and Wundt gave way in the United States to a focus on observable behavior. As Roger Brown (1958) wrote, "In 1913 John Watson mercifully closed the bloodshot inner eye of American psychology. With great relief the profession trained its exteroceptors on the laboratory animal" (p. 93). As late as 1975, B. F. Skinner dismissed as trivial psychology's "diverting preoccupation with a supposed or real inner life" (p. 46).

Clinicians and expert witnesses who forget the wealth of memory research conducted before the current cognitive revolution cut themselves off from important theoretical perspectives and research data and from a historical and scientific context with which to understand more recent findings. Here is a passage from Kurt Koffka's 1935 *Principles of Gestalt Psychology*:

> If now we look back on the picture we have sketched of mental dynamics and of behaviour in general, we find that this picture represents a continuous sequence of organizations and reorganizations. New events happen practically every moment, events new by virtue of their organization. These new organizations are brought about by the forces arising through the relation between the organism and the environment and through field forces originating in the trace system. The function of the latter is, in our picture, primarily that of making new appropriate organizations possible, and not that of repeating what was experienced or done previously. Thus we are in full agreement with Bartlett, who says: "In fact, if we consider evidence rather than presupposition, remembering appears to be far more decisively an affair of construction rather than one of mere reproduction. . . ." (p. 646)

The idea that memory is not like videotape was a part of psychology long before the "cognitive revolution" of the last 20 to 40 years. Much of the research during this recent period that seems so new echoes or replicates earlier research; just as the brain seems to be "rediscovered" on a periodic basis, new research brings about a rediscovery of principles about memory that had apparently been forgotten.

## Models of Memory: Uncertainties Remain

As an example of the difficulty of arriving at a clear, simple explanation for a frequently observed phenomenon, consider a frequent finding in memory research concerning the apparently straightforward phenomenon of *serial recall*. Clinicians who have conducted a mental status exam have likely read aloud progressively longer strings of digits, asking the client to repeat as many as possible. Research tends to show that when a seemingly random series of numbers or letters is read aloud to another person, the person's probability of recalling each item falls into a slightly bent U. Imagine the following hypothetical experiment. The experimenter reads aloud this series of three-letter "chunks" while the participant listens:

1) xny
2) nzh
3) rpl
4) wqb
5) pdg
6) ckw
7) slr
8) vif

After all eight chunks have been read, the participant tries to recall as many as possible. The following chart presents each of the eight chunks across the horizontal axis and the probabilities (expressed as a percentage) of recall down the vertical axis. The plotted probabilities fall into a somewhat misshapen U.

There is a high probability of recalling the first (and next few) items. This is termed the *primacy effect*. The probability of recalling the end of the list is also high, reflecting the *recency effect*. The fifth and sixth items in this eight-item test (i.e., those just past the halfway mark) have the lowest probability of recall.

This basic observation of an asymmetrical U-shaped curve describing this form of serial recall has been with us well over a *chunk*

| percentage | xny | nzh | rpl | wqb | pdg | ckw | slr | vif |
|---|---|---|---|---|---|---|---|---|
| 91–100 | • | | | | | | | |
| 81–90 | | | | | | | | • |
| 71–80 | | • | | | | | | |
| 61–70 | | | | | | | | |
| 51–60 | | | | | | | | |
| 41–50 | | | • | | | | | |
| 31–40 | | | | | | | | |
| 21–30 | | | | • | | | | |
| 11–20 | | | | | | | • | |
| 0–10 | | | | | • | • | | |

century. The phenomenon has been observed repeatedly, and is widely acknowledged. Stigler (1978), who reprinted Nipher's 1878 experiments in this area, observed that

> Nine years before the publication of H. Ebbinghaus's (1885) book on memory, an American physicist, F. E. Nipher, published brief accounts of his own investigations on this topic. . . . Nipher, who used series of numbers rather than nonsense syllables as the meaningless material to be memorized, . . . found 2 memory curves; a binomial relationship for the distribution of memory errors within 6-digit numbers, and a logarithmic relationship for the decay of memory over time. (p. 1)

Thus, the phenomenon has been observed to appear consistently for more than a century. However, even so seemingly simple, well researched, and robust a phenomenon as the off-center U in serial recall, Murdock (1995) notes, is one for which

> *we still have no completely satisfactory theory or model to explain.* . . . Nipher himself . . . applied a simple binomial model for these data, the same type of probability model one would use for . . . coin tosses. . . . However, such a model is more descriptive than explanatory, and cognitive psycholo-

gists would like to know what mental processes underlie the "coin tosses." (p. 110; emphasis added)

It appears that many phenomena in memory are similar; they are well observed, and there are various theoretical models available to explain each one. But, like models for human distress and psychopathology, no one model of memory appears to have achieved universal acceptance by researchers in the field.

Murdock, author of *Human Memory: Theory and Data* (1974), describes a characteristic of the study of memory:

> How do we study memory? By using the standard scientific approach—collecting some reliable data, constructing a simple theory or model to explain it, collecting more data to test the model, revising the model in the event of unexpected findings, and so on, with the continuing interplay between theory and data. *Unfortunately, in the memory area, theory development has lagged far behind data collection.* We have more than enough experimental data, but still no generally accepted theoretical framework. (1995, p. 110; emphasis added)

Any absence of relevant, useful, testable, and generally accepted (on the basis of its ability to explain or at least illuminate the results of empirical hypothesis-testing) theory in the area of memory creates special risks for the clinician and expert witness who looks to science for definitive answers as opposed to helpful questions. The great array of isolated findings, each seeming to demonstrate *something* in the absence of theoretical context, offers such a rich assortment from which to choose that those attempting to put research data to clinical or forensic use may make—however unintentionally—a biased selection, choosing only those findings that fit a personal prejudice or political end and failing to notice those that contradict. The selected pattern of data may seem to present an inexorable path to certainty, but the selection is similar in some respects to looking at the relationships among the numerous measures of a single experiment and only then deciding which relationships to analyze statistically.

Additionally, just as memory should not be mistaken as in essence an infallibly accurate videotape of experience, published accounts of experiments should not be mistaken as an infallibly accurate videotape of what took place. Friedman (1967), for example, studied experiments as they were carried out and observed:

> Psychological experiments are supposed to be standardized, controlled, replicable, objective. The experimental sessions were unstandardized, uncontrolled, different, heterogeneous. Psychological experimenters are supposed to be inflexible, mechanical, "programmed," standardized in their behavior. These experimenters improvised and ad-libbed and were nonconforming, different, variable in their behavior.
>
> The resemblance between this experiment as observed and the experiment as it is usually reported is at best a likeness between distant relatives in an extended family.
>
> What seem to be standardized are our collective illusions about the "standardized" experiment and the "standardized" experimenter. (p. 106)

## Perception: An Active Process

The idea that the mind is like a videocamera, passively recording the scenery and storing the tapes in a vast storage bin, hangs on with a dogged persistence in popular parlance, perhaps in part because it seems to appeal to common sense (which also seemed to suggest that the sun revolves around the earth and that the earth is flat). However, the environmental information that does make it into the mind does not enter a motionless warehouse, and the mind "is not static, not a large storage bin nor a passive blank slate; it is an organ of activity, process, and ongoing work" (Pope & Singer, 1978a, p. 106; see also Pope & Singer, 1978b, 1980).

Consciousness and memory are active processes handling not only environmental information but also internal information such as proprioceptive cues, fantasies, and anticipations. Experimental studies conducted by Pope (1978), for example, examined the flow of consciousness, attention, and memory in light of such variables as gender, solitude, posture, and affect. The research findings suggested that "[t]he flow of consciousness seems predominantly oriented toward long-term memory and future fantasy: On the average, only about a third of the time was spent with consciousness primarily focused on the 'here and now.' Physical movement or the presence of others, however, led both to greater [attentional] discontinuity (more shifts of thought) and also to more focusing on the immediate situation" (pp. 282–283).

It is important to note that the research suggests something more than that the mind is not a static or passive storage bin or videocamera and actively works on the information it receives from perceptions of the environment. The accumulated research provides strong evidence that perception itself is an active, selective, constructive process.

Cognitive psychologist Jennifer Freyd conducted a series of experiments to explore the complex coding processes by which perception actively identifies and attempts to recognize visual information. She found that certain static stimuli (e.g., a photograph of a basketball player in midair) imply motion. This implied movement or *representational momentum* significantly affects both perception and memory (Freyd, 1983; Freyd & Finke, 1984, 1985). Freyd and her colleagues found that people tend to misremember some static visual images or stimuli—such as drawings of people in motion or stop-action photographs—as if they were farther along the path of frozen motion than they actually were. The memory distortion tends to be systematically related to the actual motion *implied* in the stimulus. An "oberver's memory for position can be distorted in the direction of implied motion and . . . the degree of shift is a function of the rate of implied motion" (Freyd & Finke, 1985, p. 446; see also Freyd & Johnson, 1987; Freyd, Pantzer, & Cheng, 1988). The effect occurs not only with visual but also with auditory perception and memory (Freyd, Kelly, & DeKay, 1990). This line of research suggests that "event perception and event memory [are] influenced by anticipation of future action. More specifically, even perception and memory are influenced by anticipation of the future direction of action" (Freyd & Miller, 1992, p. 7). The findings also have implications for the understanding of how brain functions are related to perception and memory.

The degree to which perception is an active, selective, constructive process becomes obvious in the research focusing on attention and perception. Hernandez-Peon, Scherrer, and Jouvet (1956) conducted experiments illustrating the profound power of attention to allow an organism to register a stimulus. They presented a metronome's rhythmic clicking to cats. The auditory nerves of the cats produced a strong, steady series of impulses. However, if a cat saw a mouse or smelled a fish, the auditory nerve impulse dropped almost to zero. It seemed as if the cat no longer heard the metronome, more than just failing to attend to what it was hearing.

# Types of Memory

The following sections describe some special topics in the area of memory that are generally relevant to clinicians and expert witnesses when reports of delayed memories of abuse are at issue.

## Autobiographical Memory

Autobiographical memory is sometimes called *episodic memory* because it is often used to refer to the memory of episodes in the person's life. It consists of our personal narrative of who we are and what has happened to us, as well as our knowledge of how to do what we do. Sometimes *autobiographical memory* (e.g., "I remember how much fun I had at my birthday party last year.") is contrasted with *semantic memory*, which focuses on more contextually free facts, ideas, or similar knowledge (e.g., "There are 12 inches in a foot and 3 feet in a yard.").

As with other key concepts in the area of memory, scientists define the concepts in different ways. Butters and Cermak (1986), for example, have a more expansive definition of autobiographical memory that embraces both episodic memory and some forms of procedural memory, such as how to drive a car or ride a bicycle.

Bartlett (1932) provided a major contribution to scientific research in the area of autobiographical memory, although it was Neisser's (1982) taking the study out of the laboratory and into lives in progress that seemed to prompt a renewed interest in this area during the last 2 decades. Bruhn (1995) concludes:

Autobiographical memory research has been done largely within a schema theory paradigm. Although memory researchers have traditionally sought to eliminate variables related to personality in studying the operation of memory, schema theory provides the ideas bridge between memory and personality. Ross (1991) has commented that "the major rationale of schema theories is that knowledge is not carried piecemeal but as an integrated set of related representations of actions" (p. 138). . . . [R]ecollections of one's early life are particularly susceptible to this process as each major lesson extracted from life's experiences can be processed and superimposed upon the corpus of one's [early memories]. (p. 281)

A seemingly obvious concept such as autobiographical memory may be defined differently by various investigators; even when the "content" of autobiographical memory remains constant across certain various research studies, the meaning may differ significantly depending on such factors as whether the memory is viewed in isolation or as part of a formal schema. Clinicians must thus exercise caution and critical judgment in their reading of this literature, and give particular care to how terms are defined.

Especially important are questions of when autobiographical memory begins; in other words, when do we begin to remember our own story? There continues to be disagreement among researchers as to the outer limits of autobiographical memory, with variations around the age of 2, or at the time when a person has some verbal abilities and a sense of self. Howe, Courage, and Peterson (1994), in a review and discussion of this issue, noted that children seem to be able to recall and recount (and thus incorporate into their earliest autobiographical narratives) experiences that occurred close to the onset of verbal expressive language use around age 2, but not those events happening significantly earlier in life.

## Short- and Long-Term Memory

Most of us use short-term memory when someone asks us to see if the mail has arrived. We don't tend to write down the request. It resides in *short-term memory* (and may be understood to initially enter into short-term memory as immediate memory) as we get up, walk down the hallway, approach the mailbox, and look inside. If someone asks us about this several days later, we may be unable to remember it. We will be more likely to remember it if it passed into *long-term memory process* and either the other person's question or our own search strategy provides adequate cues for us to retrieve it from storage. Or, this particular series of events may have become part of a script, a sort of generic "going-to-get-the-mail" memory in which one episode of getting the mail is poorly differentiated from other such episodes, as commonly occurs with repeated behaviors.

What influences whether information passes from short-term into long-term memory? The factors are seemingly many but not well understood. One of the most common is *repetition* or *rehearsal*. If people silently repeat a new acquaintance's name again and again when initially introduced, the memory is more likely to become a part of long-term memory. Repetition often improves memory storage. The state of *arousal* may play another role in the passage of material into long-term memory. For those who have undergone surgery and were fairly nervous about it, certain details such as the look and smell of the operating room as they are wheeled in on the gurney may be quite memorable years later. Similarly, but conversely, the terror and numbness of a "near-miss" car accident may lead us to have little or no recollection of what happened due to the hypoarousal that occurs. The notion of state dependency refers to the impact of level of arousal on the capacity to learn and retain. High arousal, such as occurs around the time of trauma, appears—at least in some instances—to be helpful in placing a memory into long-term storage (Christianson, 1992).

The *structural properties* of the information itself may influence the likelihood of transition into long-term memory. A short stanza of doggerel sung as part of an ad campaign may pass unwanted into long-term memory so that, weeks later, people discover themselves listening to the song from memory as part of their stream of consciousness. *Congruence with a familiar schema* may also play a role. Consider the following array: 10–9–8–7–6–5–4–3–2–1. If readers were asked about the array several weeks from now, it is likely that many would be able to recall it because it is similar to an extremely familiar sequence of numbers and may be encoded in ways that take advantage of that familiarity, such as visual (i.e., "seeing" the numbers in the mind's eye), acoustic (i.e., "hearing" it in the mind's ear), abstract linguistic (e.g., the numbers 1 through 10 backwards), or linguistically associated (e.g., the countdown for a space launch). The relative *attention* people accord to something also influences the likelihood that they will be able to recall it a long time later. Most readers have probably had the experience of taking a stroll through a dull environment while deep in thought. A few hours later it may be impossible to remember much of anything at all about the surroundings, but the sequence of thoughts experienced during the walk may come back with relative ease.

*Emotional states* may influence the degree to which information is registered, encoded, processed, and later made retrievable from long-term memory. Christianason (1992), for example, reviewed both laboratory and "real-life" studies, and found that they suggested that

> emotionally stressful events may receive some preferential processing mediated by factors at early perceptual processing (e.g., factors related to arousal, the distinctiveness or unusualness of an event, and attentional or preattentive factors) and factors at late conceptual processing (e.g., poststimulus elaboration). . . . [and that this framework may explain] why central detail information is better retained from emotional events compared with neutral counterparts. (p. 304)

The presence or absence of *social support* also appears to affect the capacity to recall that which has been retained (Goodman, Quas, Batterman-Faunce, Riddlesberger, & Kuhn, 1994; Tessler & Nelson, 1994), suggesting that factors in the interpersonal environment can affect what a person reports to have remembered. When people are offered social support at the time of an event and at the time of recall, they may be more likely to both store and retrieve the information.

## Memory Chunks

At any given moment, people tend to have an almost infinite number of aspects of environmental information as well as a rich diversity of potential internal stimuli (e.g., plans, wishes, purposeful thoughts, emotions, impulses, internal bodily sensations) available for short-term memory. How much of what is available at any given moment can enter short-term memory? The line of research and theory flowing from Miller's (1956) classic paper "The Magic Number 7, Plus or Minus 2" suggests that short-term memory typically can accommodate around six or seven chunks of information at a time. The data are divided up into a manageable number of manageable chunks. Consider the following example: A group of people listen to a sequence of 10 random digits. They then perform some easy mechanical tasks that allow a minute or two to pass and cause a reallocation of attention (so that something beyond immediate memory is involved), and then try to retrieve all 10 digits in order. If each digit were a chunk, it would exceed many people's channel capacity. More commonly, however, calling directory assistance for a phone number, hanging up, following the procedures on a pay phone to arrange a long-distance call, and then retrieving the number from short-term memory in order to dial it is made possible by perceiving the number as three separate chunks: (a) the area code, (b) the prefix, and (c) the remaining 4 digits.

Additionally, storage in memory is not a fixed or static process (Loftus, 1988). New life experiences, new information, and the very process of remembering itself all can change what we have represented in memory, and, in some models of memory, erase and replace prior memory traces with new, sometimes inaccurate, information. The passage of time also tends to weaken or erode what is stored in memory when opportunities to rehearse and thus re-store the original memory trace are absent.

In applying this information to reports of delayed recall of childhood abuse, it is helpful to consider that many people describe such memories as fragmentary and incomplete, lacking in detail, and often quite general (as in "I remember him sticking his penis in my mouth, but no, I don't know if he was circumcised or not."). This fragmentariness may represent not simply, as some clinicians have believed, the difficult nature of what is being recalled, but also the capacity of the remembering adult to have retained more than a few chunks of the memory in long-term storage at the time that the events occurred (Alpert, Brown, & Courtois, 1996).

"Searching" for more memory may be futile, because not everything that happens is remembered, and not all important details become part of what is either stored in or retrieved from memory. Few, if any, people experience child sex abuse as if it were a sort of test material that must be memorized flawlessly in all its complexity, detail, and sequence. Many people who have continuous recall describe their fervent attempts to ignore what was happening—a coping strategy that may impair memory storage. Psychotherapeutic techniques based on the assumption that an adult who was sexually abused as a child must retrieve a comprehensive, detailed, sequenced memory of the event in order to heal from its effects can be misguided at best, given the vagaries of memory, and in some instances can also be extremely harmful when they bring to mind materials that a survivor knows that he or she not wish to know.

## Declarative and Procedural Memory

Computer science, particularly artificial intelligence, suggests a distinction between declarative information (e.g., articulable facts) and procedural or implicit information (e.g., sometimes indescribable knowing how to do something). Our name and address, the current president of the United States, whether it is day or night, and the sum of 2 plus 2 are facts that we can (usually) state or declare. The complex set of muscular movements needed to walk and chew gum at the same time is something that we may never be able to state. Nonetheless, most of us have this procedural memory: We remember *how* to do it.

## Varieties of Sensory Input

The information that we remember comes to us in different channels that may, in turn, influence how that information is stored in and later retrieved from memory. Information may come to us through one or more of the senses. Information from a given channel may be processed in various ways. For example, a person may use the visual channel to look at landscapes or to read a book on landscapes. For many people, processing of the spatial information and memory seem to be linked more to the right hemisphere of the brain, while processing of the verbal information and memory seem linked more to the left hemisphere of the brain. Other senses such as the sense of time provide information that may pass into memory. Temporal information is often an important aspect of the various kinds of memory. For example, readers might be able to retrieve easily from memory the sequence in which they perform a complex set of behaviors (e.g., an elaborate dance or aerobics routine, a morning ritual of hygiene–dressing–cooking–eating); it may be much more difficult to retrieve them in reverse temporal order.

In addition to direct sensory input into memory storage, there are also internal sources of information such as fantasies, plans, and anticipation. For highly fantasy-prone individuals, a fantasy that has been frequently imagined and experienced in a symbolic sensory manner can become sufficiently "real" that it passes into long-term memory as if it had been an actual event.

## Memory Production and Retrieval

Memory can also emerge through various channels and through various methods of retrieval, though again, different researchers and theorists define and describe these characteristics of emergence in different ways. *Recognition*, for example, tends to indicate the use of memory to identify a stimulus as one that has already been encountered. *Recall* tends to indicate an active retrieval of a specific memory (of facts, episodes, etc.) without external cues. *Recollection* tends to indicate retrieval of a specific memory aided at least to some degree by external cueing. Recollection appears to be enhanced by conditions in which the presence of certain retrieval cues creates a circumstance resembling those present at the time of the original event now being recollected (Tulving & Thompson, 1973; Howe & Brainerd, 1989).

The capacity, usefulness, and effectiveness of memory may be influenced significantly by these channels and methods. In a fascinating article titled "Learning 10,000 Pictures," Standing (1973) reported that participants were able, with a relatively low error rate, to quickly identify whether they had or had not seen a specific photograph. He kept increasing the number of photographs presented and then re-presented at a later time until he concluded that the channel capacity of recognition of such visual stimuli was virtually unlimited. He also found that

> (a) memory capacity, as a function of the amount of material presented, followed a general power law with a characteristic exponent for each task; (b) pictorial material obeyed this power law and showed an overall superiority to verbal material; (c) when the recognition task was made harder by using more alternatives, memory capacity stayed constant and the superiority of pictures was maintained; (d) picture memory exceeded verbal in terms of verbal recall; comparable recognition–recall ratios were obtained for pictures, words, and nonsense syllables; and (e) verbal memory showed a higher retrieval speed than picture memory. (p. 207)

Each approach to measuring or using memory has strengths and weaknesses. For example, therapists and expert witnesses may assess a person's overall capacity to retain and report memories using standardized psychometric tests that assess memory capacity, such as the Wechsler Adult Intelligence Scale—Revised (WAIS-R) or the Wechsler Memory Scale (WMS). Or, attempts may be made to elicit information regarding specific kinds of memories via the use of various self-report instruments, such as the Impact of Events Scale or the Trauma Symptom Inventory, which request information on the frequency of certain types of posttraumatic experience, including both intrusive recall and posttraumatic amnesia. Clark (1988) summarized some potential difficulties that may occur when people try to indicate the frequency with which they have experienced certain memories or similar cognitions. Rather than indicating the frequency of the experience, the individual's responses may indicate the importance of the experience, the emotional meaning of the experience, the occurrence of similar though not identical experiences, and so on. Thus, what people report that they recall may reflect the salience of the recalled material, as well as how well it has been stored in and retrieved from memory. What people remember is thus a version of, but not the videotape of, what happened in which the version is mediated by a lengthy list of variables.

Such diversity of content, channels, processes, and measures underscores the complexity of the field and is consistent with Murdock's statement, cited earlier, that "in the memory area, theory development has lagged far behind data collection. We have more than enough experimental data, but still no generally accepted theoretical framework" (1995, p. 11). New specifics emerge that severely limit, qualify, and bring into question inviting simplicities in the description of memory. Brewin, Andrews, and Gotlib (1993), for example, reviewed the literature and compared how accurately adults and their parents recalled the adults' childhoods, and concluded, "The available data on the accuracy of memories for early experiences are inconsistent and do not offer unequivocal support for either a copy or reconstructive theory of memory. Rather, they suggest that accuracy depends to a large extent on the characteristics of the event or events to be recalled" (p. 93). Strikingly, they note that adults have a better recall of their own childhood than do their parents when events are corroborated against external sources of validity. Parents, according to these researchers, recall a happier childhood for their offspring than the collateral data would account for, whereas adults recall their own childhoods—misery and all—with greater accuracy. Such research findings may be important when critically evaluating research paradigms in which a parent's claim that an event in a child's life did not occur is used as sufficient evidence that the child's memory of an event must be a false memory resulting from spontaneous confabulation or implantation of a false memory.

## Memory and Suggestibility

One model of how people remember and misremember events comes from research on how eye-witness memory appears vulnerable to certain kinds of suggestion. Loftus has contributed heavily to this stream of research, which traces to early in this century (Loftus, 1979; Loftus & Davies, 1984; Loftus & Hoffman, 1989; Loftus & Loftus, 1980). Loftus elaborated ways in which postevent misinformation can change, or even hypothetically erase and replace, the original memory trace with an inaccurate or false memory. In her standard paradigm, Loftus has research participants view a video of, for example, a car accident in which a "yield" sign appears. Participants in the experimental condition are then given postevent misinformation in the form of the suggestion that this was, in fact, a "stop" sign; consistently, more errors in the direction suggested are made by the experimental group than by the control group that does not receive the misinformation. Loftus's research on the misinformation effect has also examined such aspects of eye-witness memory as the ability to accurately recall and describe the face of a "thief" in a simulated purse-snatching. Although these findings indicate a consistent ability by researchers to deceive participants as to a small portion of the memory, these findings do not indicate that people replace memories of an accident with, for instance, memories of an assault scene. Central details appear to remain intact.

Loftus and her colleagues' findings are apparently robust in the lab, but have been questioned by other researchers who note that actual forensic eyewitnesses—that is, people who are witnesses to a real crime and called upon to give testimony in actual criminal proceedings—are likely to be less suggestible and appear more resistant to misinformation than are research participants (Yuille, 1993; Yuille & Cutshall, 1989). These critics suggest that more than memory is a factor in understanding how suggestible people are likely to be and that, when the social and interpersonal characteristics of a situation raise the stakes related to incorrect memories, people may be more accurate, less suggestible, and more cautious. Spanos and MacLean (1986) argued that the apparently changed memory is actually a changed report, reflecting the desire of the research participant to comply behaviorally rather than reflecting any changes to memory. Other researchers have suggested that memories associated with strong affect are less vulnerable to suggestion, and more resilient, than more neutral memories such as those tested in experimental settings (Christianson, 1992; Reisberg & Heuer, 1992; Yuille & Cutshall, 1992).

Similar research on the suggestibility of children's recollections has examined whether and to what degree children's memories of events are affected by postevent suggestions of misinformation or outright attempts to create pseudomemory through repeated suggestion. This line of research has led to some interesting but often conflicting findings. Children studied by Steven Ceci and his colleagues (Ceci, Ross, & Toglia, 1987; Ceci et al., 1994)—particularly children younger than age 4—are described as being relatively vulnerable to repeated suggestions by researchers. Ceci et al. (1994) reported that they have been able to implant pseudomemories of having a finger caught in a mousetrap in children aged 3 through 6 by exposing children to 12 weekly repetitions of this story, and found that these pseudomemories were, in some children, resistant to debriefing. There were, however, interesting variations in response patterns: The 3- to 4-year-olds became less willing to accept the pseudomemories over time, and the 5- to 6-year-olds became more willing to do so. Because suggestibility is hypothesized to decrease with age, these findings raise questions about the influence of other factors (e.g., perceived social desirability of complying with the suggestions of adults).

Other researchers, most notably Zaragoza and her colleagues (McCloskey, & Zaragoza, 1985; Zaragoza, 1991; Zaragoza, McCloskey, & Jamis 1987), have demonstrated somewhat different results, finding their child research subjects a good deal more resistant when exposed to the same sorts of suggestions used by Ceci and his colleagues. Other researchers (Goodman et al., 1994; Pezdek & Roe, 1994) find that children's resistance to suggestion is partially a function of age, partially a function of whether something is experienced personally as distinguished from simply observed, and partially a function of the nature and quality of interpersonal support available to the children. In one study in which children were touched on the nose and helped into and out of a clown costume over their own clothing, both child participants and child witnesses were quite resilient to suggestions and leading questions about this procedure that attempted to elicit sexualized misinterpretations of the procedure (Goodman, Bottoms, Schwartz-Kenney, & Rudy, 1991). Readers who wish to more thoroughly acquaint themselves with the literature on this topic are referred to the edited volume by Doris (1991) on the suggestibility of children's recollections and Ceci and Bruck's (1995) book on children's testimony in sexual abuse criminal cases.

Overall findings from this research present a mixed picture. Various factors influence the suggestibility of both adults and children. Equally various are the factors that influence the storage, strength, and staying power of a memory, as well as a person's capacity to retrieve it with or without external cuing. Mental health professionals attempting to draw on this literature will need to be aware of the various limitations to its generalizability, as well as the varying results found in different research labs. A further exploration of a new line of research which derives from the studies of suggestibility of eye-witness memory, in which older family members are utilized as confederates in attempts to experimentally create pseudomemories in younger family members, will be described next.

## Experimental Analogues for False Memory Syndrome

Since the invention of the concept of a false memory syndrome (FMS) in 1992, there have been several attempts at creating a useful experimental analogue to study the implantation of false autobiographical memories for experiencing serious trauma. This enterprise arose in response to some critics' belief that while it might be possible to create false memories regarding stop and yield signs, it would be impossible to create a false autobiographical memory for experiencing a complex traumatic event. This body of research, while still comparatively new, has yielded findings that are provocative and often controversial.

Beginning with Loftus's (1993) creative landmark research study known as "The Chris Experiment" or "Lost in the Mall," experimental findings suggest that an older family member can manipulate the autobiographical memory of a younger relative (see chapter 3). Loftus recounts in her book how she encountered the challenge: A colleague said to her, "But its just not possible to implant in someone's mind a complete memory with details and relevant emotions for a traumatic event that didn't happen." She replied, "But that's exactly what we did in the shopping mall experiment" (Loftus & Ketcham, 1994, p. 211).

Loftus's student, Jim Coan, "created a false memory in the mind of his 14-year-old brother, Chris" (Loftus, 1993, p. 533). According to Loftus, the implanted pseudoevent was hypothesized to be greatly feared and mildly traumatic. Those conducting the research "developed a paradigm for instilling a specific childhood memory for being lost on a particular occasion at the age of 5. They chose getting lost because it is clearly a great fear of both parents and children. . . . The technique involved a subject and a trusted family member who played a variation of 'Remember the time that . . . ?' " (Loftus, 1993, p. 532). This research and that which followed appeared to demonstrate the extent to which an older family member could tamper with a younger family member's autobiographical memory about a traumatic event. As Loftus (1993) emphasized, "The lost-in-a-shopping-mall example shows that memory of an entire mildly traumatic event can be created" (p. 532). Of note is that when Coan attempted to induce the same memory in his mother, she was unable to generate a memory of her younger child being lost in the mall, although she did express distress at being unable to remember (Loftus, 1993).

In a more recent report of an expanded version of the study, Loftus and Pickrell reveal that relatives were able to implant a false memory of an event in 25% of the 24 subjects:

> Subjects also rated how confident they were that they would be able to recall additional details at a later time, using a scale from 1 to 5. We examined the confidence ratings for the subset of subjects embracing the false event during the first interview and who provided two sets of confidence ratings. In general the confidence ratings were low, but lower for the false event than the true ones. The mean confidence rating for the true memories for this set of people was 2.7 during the first interview and 2.2 during the second interview. The mean confidence rating for the false memory was 1.8, then 1.4. . . . All five subjects had mean confidence ratings for their true events that exceeded the confidence rating for the false one. Most of the subjects gave the same low confidence rating during the two interviews. (Loftus & Pickrell, 1995, p. 723)

Other experiments pursuing this ingenious line of research have included suggestions that the subject was awakened in the night by a noise, then fell back to sleep, and suggestions that the subject, while a child, had an ear infection during the night and was taken to the hospital (Hyman et al., 1995). Hyman and his colleagues presented stories to college students. Some stories had actually been written by the participants' parents—some of which were the proposed pseudomemories and all of which were represented to the participants as true accounts gleaned from the parents. In these studies, which represent a replication and extension of Loftus's original paradigm, similar results emerged; approximately 20% of the target subjects responded to suggestions alleged to be written by family members that such events had occurred. However, 80% of target research participants failed to develop the pseudomemories.

Pezdek (1995; Pezdek, Finger, & Hodge, 1996) has conducted another replication and extension of this paradigm with interesting results that bear on the question of what sort of memory may be implantable. In her study, confederates (consisting of graduate students in psychology) read, on two consecutive days, three accounts to a younger relative who was at least 15 years old at the time of the study. Two of these accounts were truthful ones about the target's childhood, and one was not. Two different false events were suggested: being lost in a shopping mall, which had previously been empirically determined to be a high-frequency experience in a pilot study population, and receiving a rectal enema, which had similarly been shown to be a low-frequency event. In this study, while 15% of the target subject "remembered" being lost in the mall, none was willing to accept the suggestion that they had received a rectal enema. According to Pezdek, "The typical response of participants after hearing the enema scenario was, 'I don't believe you, Jesus Christ. Did she give me an enema? Geez, I don't remember ever getting an enema.' Also, 'Absolutely not. I have no memory of that. It doesn't even sound true to me. It never happened.' " (p. 15). Pezdek suggests that her findings indicate that it may be more possible for family members to implant pseudomemories of common than of uncommon events. Overall, these research findings are provocative but inconclusive (see chapter 3).

# Repression

The term *repression* has gained enormous popular currency as a mechanism used to describe how it is that people subjected to traumatic experiences in childhood might forget and then recall these events. Loftus and her colleagues have presented some of the most interesting descriptions of repression, as well as empirical data about the frequency with which repression—especially apparently complete amnesia for memorable events—may occur. One of her earliest descriptions focused on pain and suffering:

> Memories that may cause us great unhappiness if they were brought to mind often appear to be "forgotten." However, are they really lost from memory or are they simply temporarily repressed as originally suggested by Freud (1922)? *Repression* is the phenomenon that prevents someone from remembering an event that can cause him [sic] pain and suffering. One way that we know that these memories are repressed and not completely lost is that the methods of free association and hypnosis and other special techniques used by psychotherapists can be used to bring repressed material to mind and can help a person remember things that he [sic] has failed to remember earlier. (Loftus & Loftus, 1976, p. 82)

More recent work on *motivated forgetting* examined both single and multiple traumas. Loftus described a documented study of a college professor who became unable to remember a series of traumas but a long time later was able to recover memories of the traumas:

> Eventually, R. J. was able to remember all of her traumatic experiences. . . . Even though the return of her memories made her wiser, she was also much sadder. More than most of us ever will, R. J. understood the true meaning in Christina Rosetti's words in "Remember": "Better by far you should forget and smile than that you should remember and be sad." (Loftus, 1988, p. 73)

Discussing an example of response to a single trauma (i.e., unlike R. J.'s response to multiple traumas), Loftus concluded, "After such an enormously stressful experience, many individuals wish to forget . . . and often their wish is granted" (p. 73).

In some of her most recent research on this topic, Loftus and her colleagues noted that they studied poor African-American and Hispanic women who were in their first week of sobriety from drugs and/or alcohol, and inquired of them whether they had ever had an experience of childhood trauma that had once been forgotten but now was recalled. Some of the data emerging from this sample about the frequency with which temporary but total amnesia for an event occurs led the investigators to observe, "There is a reason to believe that the 19% figure we obtained in the current study may actually be an overestimate of the extent to which repression occurs" (Loftus, Polonsky, & Fullilove, 1994, p. 81) and note that "One could argue that this means that robust repression[1] was not especially prevalent in our sample" (p. 80). Loftus and her coauthors argued that perhaps the experience of sexual abuse had simply been forgotten during a period of time in the lives of their research participants when more pleasant events, such as a vacation in Europe, commanded attention.

There has been much valuable and intriguing work on the nature of repression. Kihlstrom and Hoyt (1990), for example, discuss the process of repression in relation to dissociation, declarative knowledge, consciousness, and preconsciousness:

> The postoedipal child who is unaware that he loves his mother desperately and the rape victim who blocks out all memory for her assault have both lost access to some piece of declarative knowledge—some empirical or believed-in fact about the world. Both concepts—repression and dissociation—would permit unconscious procedural knowledge, differing qualitatively (i.e., in terms of its representational format) from declarative knowledge and inaccessible in principle, under any circumstances, to direct introspective access. Within the domain of declarative knowledge, then, it remains to make further distinctions between conscious, preconscious,

---

[1]*Robust repression* is a term recently invented to describe temporary but complete amnesia for traumatic events; see Ofshe and Singer (1994) for the origins of this terminology.

dissociated, and repressed mental contents (Kihlstrom 1987a, 1987b). (p. 201)

They emphasize that

> both the operation of dissociative and repressive skills and the products of their skills may be inaccessible to consciousness. It is an open question whether dissociation and repression even become fully automatized in this sense; in fact, there seem to be cognitive costs associated with both processes.... Nevertheless, the information-processing approach to attention and cognitive skills suggests a mechanism by which the act of repression itself could be rendered unconscious—as Freud required it to be and, indeed, as it must be to serve as an effective defense. (p. 202)

Despite such valuable and intriguing work, the term *repression* causes considerable confusion and misunderstanding, and is probably best discarded in favor of more precise language. There are three major reasons to use more detailed, scientific wording. First, some scholars, particularly David Holmes (1990), have presented an analysis of the research and asserted that "at the present time there is no controlled laboratory evidence supporting the concept of repression" (p. 96). Holmes's assertions have by no means gained general acceptance (see, e.g., D. Brown, 1994; Erdelyi, 1990), and seem to have represented a minority view at the conference at which he presented the paper (Singer, 1990). Gleaves (1996a) presents a critique of Holmes in which he demonstrates that there is abundant (depending upon definitional factors) evidence available; at a minimum, this evidence suggests that the concept of repression defined as an intrapsychic mechanism of defense as postulated by psychoanalytic theory is a controversial one in some scientific circles, despite its entrance into the common discourse.

Second, in the long history of the term *repression*, a confusion of both professional and popular meanings of the term have emerged. A brief paragraph by Matthew Erdelyi (1990) illustrates the age and just a few of the professional understandings of the term:

In 1885, about a decade before Freud introduced the concept of repression into modern psychology—strictly speaking, reintroduced it since Johann Herbart had used the concept as well as the term more than half a century before—Ebbinghouse published the first experimental study of repression, demonstrating that repression produces amnesia. Thus viewed, Ebbinghouse's research may be thought of as the first laboratory demonstration of what is commonly known today as "directed" or "intentional forgetting." (p. 1)

The rich, branching history of the term unfortunately works against clarity and precision. As the scholar and practitioner Karen Olio (1994) noted, "The use of the term 'repressed,' with its popular meaning 'to forget,' creates confusion in a clinical context between the possible mechanism (repression) and the existence of the phenomenon itself (psychogenic amnesia)."

Third, an event that seems to indicate repression may in fact represent some other cognitive process leading to absence of recall. Bower described the behavior of Sirhan Sirhan, the person who assassinated Robert Kennedy:

> Interestingly, Sirhan had absolutely no recollection of the actual murder, which occurred in the small kitchen of the Ambassador Hotel where he pumped several bullets into Kennedy. Sirhan carried out the deed in a greatly agitated state and was completely amnesiac with regard to the event. [Forensic psychiatrist Bernard] Diamond, called in by Sirhan's attorneys, hypnotized Sirhan and helped him to reconstruct from memory the events of that fateful day. Under hypnosis, as Sirhan became more worked up and excited, he recalled progressively more, the memories tumbling out while his excitement built to a crescendo leading up to the shooting. At that point Sirhan would scream out the death curses, "fire" the shots, and then choke as he reexperienced the Secret Service bodyguard nearly throttling him after he was caught. On different occasions, while in trance, Sirhan was able to recall the crucial events, sometimes speaking, other times recording his recollections in automatic writing, but the recall was always accompanied by great excitement.
>
> The curious feature of the case was that material uncovered under hypnosis never became consciously available to Sirhan

in his waking state, and he denied that he committed the murder. Moreover, he denied that he had ever been hypnotized by Diamond, denied that it was his own voice on the tape recorder, and denied that it was his handwriting—he alleged that Diamond must have hired an actor or a handwriting specialist to mimic him. Sirhan eventually did accept the theory that he must have killed Bobby Kennedy, rationalizing it as an act of heroism in the cause of Arab nationalism. But his belief was based on "hearsay," much as is my belief that I was born on a Wednesday evening—I must have been there but I sure cannot remember it. (1981, pp. 129–130)

There are doubtless many who would understand this vignette as a classic example of repression (or, given the circumstances, simple lying in the attempt to avoid responsibility for a heinous act), but Bower used it to illustrate another phenomenon, *state-dependent remembering*: "Memories acquired in one state are accessible mainly in that state but are 'dissociated' or not available for recall in an alternate state. It is as though the two states constitute different libraries into which a person places memory records, and a given memory record can be retrieved only by returning to that library, or physiological state, in which the event was first stored" (p. 130). Police officers who shoot to kill in the line of duty often report a similar phenomenon (Baker, personal communication, August 1993), in which the state of hyperarousal occurring at the time of the shooting seems to preclude the capacity to freely recall the event when the officer is in a calmer state.

Whatever the differing views on the strength and replicability of state-dependent memory, by setting aside the term *repression* or, rather, by examining other possible explanatory processes, Bower encourages and models the sort of continual process of rethinking of a construct that clinicians and expert witnesses should find useful in protecting the integrity of their own work. He notes the differing effectiveness of potential retrieval cues, suggests that "long-lost memories can be retrieved by using systematic strategies involving associative retrieval cues" (1990, p. 229), and cautions that clinical anecdotes may not be persuasive evidence for the mechanism of repression. Recent research by Constance Dalenberg and her colleagues (Dalenberg, Coe, Reto,

Aransky, & Duvenage, 1995; Duvenage & Dalenberg, 1993) has demonstrated another aspect of state-dependent learning relevant to the present discussion. Her research findings suggest that state-dependency may be a characteristic of the individual that is influenced by early experiences such as exposure to violence in childhood, and that it appears to covary with high scores on a standard measure of dissociation. The latter finding is consistent with other research on dissociative tendencies in college students with a history of abuse (Carlson & Putnam, 1993). In other words, the more a person was abused as a child, the more state-dependent his or her memory becomes, and the more likely that he or she will recall certain events only when the emotional and contextual variables closely resemble those of the actual original learning experience.

The research reports of Loftus and colleagues (1994) and Dalenberg and colleagues (1995) suggest that something resembling repression occurs and may be understood to vary systematically according to specific facts such as state-dependency, whereas the work of Bower (1981), Holmes (1990), and Olio (1994) suggests that the term and concept may be misleading and require more precise definition or terminology. In light of the diversity of work in this area, it may be best to search for and use more precise language. In consequence, we will use in this volume the behaviorally descriptive terms such as *delayed memory* or *delayed recall* when discussing this phenomenon, so as not to imply that the current understanding of what is clinically observed can be supported by any one theoretical model of memory.

## Trauma and Memory

Consider the following two passages. The first is by Elaine Mohamed, self-described as a single Coloured woman, who was arrested in 1981 in South Africa for distributing banned literature and was held in detention and solitary confinement for 7 months.

> I would sit for hours pulling the hairs out of my legs by the roots. The continual activity with my fingers and nails kept

me occupied. The hairs on my legs don't grow anymore because of this. (as quoted by Russell, 1989, p. 41)

✝

When I was released, my parents took me straight to my doctor. He said my arches were severely damaged and asked me what had happened to them in prison. He said that this kind of damage happened to people who were force-marched for days or had weights dropped onto their feet. But I can't remember anything happening to my feet. As I mentioned, I can't remember an entire week at the beginning of my detention. I blank out traumatic experiences. (as quoted by Russell, 1989, p. 43; see also Pope & Garcia-Peltonieme, 1991)

The second is by Primo Levi (1988), an Italian man who was arrested as a member of the anti-Fascist resistance and deported to Auschwitz in 1944.

I intend to examine here the memories of extreme experience, of injuries suffered or inflicted. In this case, all or almost all the factors that can obliterate or deform the mnemonic record are at work: the memory of a trauma suffered or inflicted is itself traumatic because recalling it is painful or at least disturbing. A person who has been wounded tends to block out the memory so as not to renew the pain; the person who has inflicted the wound pushes the memory deep down, to be rid of it, to alleviate the feeling of guilt. (p. 24)

Regardless of whether one believes that it is possible to block out long series of traumatic experiences or obliterate the mnemonic record of repeated torture during imprisonment, these accounts underscore why attempts to experimentally study the effects of trauma on memory in laboratory settings are fraught with difficulty. Most of such research, even when empirically sound, cannot be experimental. One simply cannot randomly assign people to hypothetical conditions of *trauma* and *no-trauma*. Although some may assume that life conducts such roughly random assignments of risk, much of what is known about memory for traumatic events is obtained through retrospective reports rather than experimental or prospective naturalistic research. Consequently, most of what is known about how memory appears to be affected by trauma comes from clinical literature and post-hoc studies. Additionally, inferences are drawn in this literature from research on how affect and level of arousal affect the capacity to both retain and recall events. Scholars in the field of trauma have tended to agree that the social, interpersonal, and contextual meanings of an event may also affect how the details of a trauma will be retained in memory, and whether or with what difficulty they will be able to recall.

Understanding how trauma affects the capacity to remember has been of interest to traumatologists for many years because of the observation that trauma appeared to distort memory in a variety of manners. The development of workable and testable hypotheses regarding the specific effect of trauma on memory is still relatively new, and there is debate among scientists about whether memory for trauma is governed by the same or different rules as memory for normal events. Trauma researchers have been at the forefront in the development of models for understanding the neurobiology of trauma, which might assist in understanding effects of trauma on memory (van der Kolk & Saporta, 1991; Yehuda, 1994; Yehuda, Kahana, Binder-Byrnes, Southwick, Mason, & Giller, 1995). The models that derive from the overall study of the neurobiology of trauma suggest that the changes to the organism—particularly to brain functioning— that are the result of exposure to traumatic stress are likely to have an effect on how traumatic events are recollected. These models will be discussed later in this chapter.

## Results of Exposure to Trauma

Exposure to traumatic stressors can have varying impacts on each person. Not all people exposed to trauma will develop any or all of the range of commonly identified posttraumatic responses. A variety of hypotheses have been advanced to explain this variability, including premorbid temperament, interpersonal resiliency factors, and the presence or absence of preexisting or concurrent psychopathology (American Psychiatric Association

[APA], 1994; Davidson & Fairbank, 1993). Some commentators have analyzed the ways in which continuous exposure to constant low-level traumatic stressors such as racism (insidious trauma) might either inoculate a person or increase his or her vulnerability to more obvious traumatic stresses (Root, 1992).

A number of psychological phenomena have shown significant association with a posttraumatic response; many are included in the diagnoses of posttraumatic stress disorder and acute stress disorder in the *DSM–IV* (APA, 1994). The trauma response is conceptualized as having three main components: numbing/avoidance, intrusion, and excess autonomic arousal. More recently, dissociation has been posited as a common aspect of the traumatic response pattern, and some evidence suggests that *peritraumatic dissociation* (dissociation occurring at or around the time of the traumatic event) is linked to the development of severe but delayed intrusive symptoms and changes in the capacity to recall the traumatic event (Foa & Riggs, 1993; Marmar et al., 1994).

Clinically observed data suggest that exposure to trauma often has two kinds of effects on memory for the traumatic event—effects that parallel and are in context to the overall trauma response. One common effect of trauma on memory, apparently related to the intrusion component of trauma response, is intrusive hyperamnesia for the trauma in the form of *flashbacks*, which can be described as brief dissociative episodes during which the trauma is reexperienced in sensorimotor form or as intrusive cognitive recollections. However, another common and frequently observed effect of trauma described in the research literature is the presence of disruptions in memory or even a complete nonorganic posttraumatic amnesia in which, for some period of time, all or part of the traumatic event is unavailable to recollection or is recalled in a fragmentary and vague manner (Alpert et al., 1996). This effect is assumed to be related to the numbing component of the trauma response.

Although it is as yet unclear how much of posttraumatic amnesia may be simply an artifact of normal variations in storage and retrieval of memory—noted earlier in this chapter—there is a clinical literature describing cases in which traumatic events, long unavailable to memory, become consciously recollected and are then independently corroborated. Some of these cases involve traumas that do not involve sexual abuse (Elliott & Briere, 1994; van der Kolk & Kadish, 1987). Other cases are specifically those in which the trauma was sexual abuse, including repetitive sexual abuse, in childhood (Briere & Conte, 1993; Herman & Schatzow, 1987; Fitzpatrick, 1994; Loftus, et al., 1994; Stanton, 1995). Frequently, a trauma survivor experiences both hyperamnesia and posttraumatic amnesia as the individual cycles in and out of the numbing and intrusive phases of the posttraumatic response pattern.

## Models of Traumatic Memory

The cognitive mechanisms by which posttraumatic amnesia may occur are poorly understood at best. Although the concept of repression has commonly and frequently been used to describe the manner in which memories are lost from and retrieved to conscious knowledge, this paradigm is somewhat problematic for the reasons previously discussed. More recently, attempts have been made to develop models for understanding posttraumatic memory phenomena that are more empirically based and less theory bound. Many of these models use the concept of dissociation as a factor in both storage and retrieval problems of memory for trauma.

Yates and Nasby (1993) have suggested that dissociation, rather than repression, provides the best possible explanation for temporary loss of access to memory for traumatic events. They argue that dissociation, because it is an empirically demonstrable phenomenon with physiological correlates that has been empirically linked to the trauma response, is the mechanism which is most likely to account for posttraumatic amnesia. Drawing upon Bower's model for the influence of affect on memory, they propose a mental mechanism, supportable by current cognitive science, by which memories for trauma may be neurologically and cognitively inhibited from conscious access until a person is exposed to specific, disinhibiting retrieval cues. Their model finds agreement in the work of Dalenberg and her colleagues (1995), whose research suggests that exposure to *rare associates*—specific and unusual cues for the retrieval of memories—is associated with the sudden onset of intrusive recollection of previously unavailable traumatic materials.

More recently, cognitive psychologist Jennifer Freyd (1995, 1996) has proposed a social–cognitive model for understanding posttraumatic amnesia and return of memory in the specific case of childhood sexual abuse, which she terms *betrayal trauma* (BT). She suggests that there is an evolutionary adaptive function in the storage of memories for repeated sexual abuse by caregivers, particularly parent figures, so that they will be inaccessible to conscious recollection until adulthood. She posits that while the child remains dependent upon the abuse perpetrator for care, this betrayal of trust cannot be known by the child if the child is to elicit the nurturance necessary for survival. The capacity to later recollect this betrayal is then linked to the now-adult's capacity to know of the abuse without risking survival, as well as to the adult's capacity to construe what was done as a betrayal of the child. In this model, knowledge of the experience is made unavailable by means of social cognitions.

## Current Research Findings on Memory for Trauma

There have been some attempts to study the effects of trauma on memory through means other than the retrospective reports of adult trauma survivors. Goodman and her colleagues (Goodman et al., 1994) have studied children who must undergo a painful medical procedure in which they are catheterized without anesthetics and are required to urinate on a table in front of medical personnel. This procedure, the *voiding cystourethrogram* (VCUG), may closely approximate certain aspects of sexual abuse for a child (e.g., genital exposure, penetration and pain, activities possibly experienced as shameful, and coercion and physical force by adults). There are also several important interpersonal elements that are different, including the fact that children receiving a VCUG are given ample social support, encouraged to talk about the procedure, and carefully debriefed both before and after. Goodman finds that those children most likely to recall accurately the VCUG are those with the most maternal emotional support. However, her research participants are still young enough that their long-term capacities to recall or not recall this event have yet to be studied.

Other research has attempted to study the ways in which adults recall trauma. However, it may be difficult for mental health professionals to generalize from these findings, because the definitions of trauma in the field of memory research vary from those used in trauma literature. For example, in Christianson's (1992) study of memory for trauma, trauma is defined as viewing a videotape of an auto accident in which blood and injuries are visible. This "trauma" resembles closely materials that can be viewed nightly on television police dramas and "true-life" shows. Other studies of memory for trauma include those of so-called *flashbulb memories* of such public events as the *Challenger* disaster or the death of President Kennedy (Ussher & Neisser, 1993)—events that are manifestly distressing to hear about, but perhaps not severely traumatic to an observer. These definitions of trauma contrast with those used by traumatologists, which include (a) the *DSM–IV* definition in which a traumatic event is defined as an experienced or witnessed event, subjectively perceived as life-threatening or possessing a threat to physical integrity, in which the person felt fear, terror, or helplessness (APA, 1994), or (b) the research definition developed by social psychologist Ronnie Janoff-Bulman and her colleagues (1992), which defines trauma as an event that shatters a person's expectations of safety and justice in the world. Although the definitions posed by traumatologists may not necessarily be more precise, they do capture the disruptive and terror-inducing aspect of traumatic events.

Recently, some prospective research findings on memory for trauma have become available. In such studies, individuals who have experienced a known traumatic stressor in childhood are followed later in adult life to ascertain their capacity to recall the trauma. Williams (1992, 1994) conducted a follow-up study of women during a period 17 to 20 years after they had been treated as children in an emergency room setting for sexual abuse. She found that 38% of this group of almost 200 women were unable to recall the index event, although these same women could sometimes recall other episodes of sexual abuse. In one instance, the participant had a memory of a covictim's experience, but specifically denied her own experience of having been sexually abused that occurred at the same time as did the other victimization. Williams reports that those who were younger at the time of the abuse and who knew the abuser personally were less likely to recall the abuse. An intriguing finding of this prospective research suggests that memories of abuse that emerge after many years may not differ significantly, as a group, from memories of abuse that are uninterruped:

> The women's memories did not come from therapy, but through environmentally triggered cues. The women reported a gradual process of remembering, often initially characterized by vague and fragmentary images. Many said these images were contained in dreams. Although the women who recovered memories were often not highly confident about their memories, when their accounts of the abuse were compared to earlier documentation of abuse, they were accurate. In fact, *their memories were as reliable as those of the women who had always remembered the abuse.* (Berliner & Williams, 1994, pp. 382–383; emphasis added)

In a recent review of the topic of memory for trauma, Koss, Tromp, and Tharan (1995) indicated that a comprehension of such memory requires a complex model that integrates understanding of neural phenomena, the meaning of the trauma for the individual, and the relationship of the traumatic experience to the overall personal context. They report that currently available evidence argues against a paradigm of memory for trauma as highly malleable or easily subject to suggestion.

Burgess, Hartman, and Baker (1995) reported data underscoring the need for a model that does justice to the complexity of the data. They found that "of 19 children, where the median age was 2.5 at the time of disclosure, 11 had full verbal memory, 5 had fragmented verbal memory traces, and three had no memory 5 to 10 years following day care sexual abuse. [The findings] suggest the nature of children's memory is four-dimensional: somatic, behavioral, verbal, and visual" (p. 9).

The reviewer of this field is left with a mixed and still unclear picture of how trauma affects storage and retrieval of memories. Mental health professionals wishing to apply this information to their practice with adults who are reporting delayed recollections need to be cautious in generalizing from the limited current findings, and to be clear that each person will have had a different capacity to store the memory, as well as unique abilities to forget and remember it.

## Hypnosis and Memory Retrieval

People who experience delayed recall of childhood abuse sometimes report having requested or experienced hypnosis as an aid to recall. However, because hypnotic technique can enhance suggestibility and lead to the development of pseudomemories in some individuals, its use as a memory-enhancement or memory-retrieval strategy seems questionable at best. Although the supposed hypnotic state or trance has been the focus of much attention in popular fiction and pop psychology as a mechanism through which Svengalis can implant false memories—some even claim that they have the ability to tell when another person is or is not hypnotized—the research presents a more complex and puzzling picture. The focus has tended to shift from a special trance state to other factors. Specifically, recent reviews of this issue suggest that suggestibility and hypnotizability are factors with wide individual variability, and that not every person's memory will be similarly affected by exposure to hypnosis. According to Brown,

> It is now quite clear that *hypnotizability* [our emphasis], not a formal hypnotic induction, contributes significantly to [pseudomemory] production; pseudomemory rates are about the same in high-hypnotizable subjects, whether or not a formal hypnotic procedure or waking instructions are used (Barnier & McConkey, 1992; McConkey, Labelle, Bibb, & Bryant, 1990; Spanos, & McLean, 1986). There is little data to support the claim that hypnotic procedures per se contribute much to [pseudomemory] production. . . .
>
> With respect to type of information, most studies on hypnotic [pseudomemory] production have been limited to peripheral details and have not suggested important events. . . . Several studies have concluded that [pseudomemory] production in hypnosis is best seen as an interaction between hypnotizability and social influence, and that social

influence substantially can increase [pseudomemory] rates in
hypnotizables. . . . (D. Brown, 1995a, pp. 6–7)

One of the most fundamental questions to be asked about
research suggesting that hypnosis, a certain kind of therapy, or
any other method produces false memories is, to what extent did
the research control for suggestibility?

## Neurobiological Aspects of Memory for Trauma

Just as primarily cognitive or behavioral aspects of memory
resist easy, simple, universal generalization, the physical or neuropsychological aspects of memory tend to cascade into complexity. However, as more sophisticated technologies become
available for observing brain functioning and measuring neurochemical and neurohormonal outputs, data have begun to
emerge that have finally moved biological models of trauma past
earlier and more primitive animal models. What this new body
of experimentation suggests is that trauma changes the functioning of the brain in ways that are very likely to affect both memory storage and memory retrieval.

McGaugh (1992) and his colleagues (Cahill, Prins, Weber, &
MacGaugh, 1994) report that neurohormones released into the
brain at the time of a stressful event enhance the brain's consolidation and storage of emotionally laden events. Yehuda and her
colleagues (Yehuda, 1994; Yehuda, Kahana, Binder-Byrnes,
Southwick, Mason, & Giller, 1995) reported that there are neurohormonal deficits, specifically changes to the ambient cortisol
level, in the brains of persons with both a verified history of
trauma and reports of absent, fragmented, distorted, or incomplete memories for that trauma. Van der Kolk (1992) has shown,
via PET scans, changes to the limbic system and amygdala on
trauma survivors when compared to a matched normal population. Southwick and colleagues (1994) have presented preliminary experimental data suggesting that trauma survivors'
noradrenergic response system varies from that of people without a trauma history. Some research (Yehuda, 1994) finds that
increased REM phasic activity is associated with either the presence of posttraumatic stress disorder (PTSD) or increased PTSD

severity, which indicates a change in brain neurophysiology in response to trauma. Wright and colleagues (1994) have demonstrated diminished EMG and GSR reactivity in survivors of known repetitive childhood trauma. Geise and colleagues (1994) demonstrated impaired gating of the P50 auditory evoked response and evidence of central nervous system noradrenergic dysfunction in a group of trauma survivors with severe PTSD. Shalev and Peri (1994) demonstrated heightened conditionability in people with PTSD compared to a control group without PTSD. Bowers (1994) noted that emerging models of cognitive neuroscience point to the presence of parallel subsymbolic processing of noncognitive material in various sensory and nonverbal modalities, which suggests that information can be known and retained in a dissociated manner in one or another neurological subsystem. Bremner and colleagues (1995) reported changes to the hippocampus of people subjected to various kinds of corroborated traumatic stressors.

In a fascinating prospective study, Putnam (1994) has found profound biological alterations of the brain stress response systems in a group of sexually abused girls aged 6 to 15. This line of research, which is still in its early stages, suggests that there are neurochemical correlates of certain kinds of intense emotional experiences. Such neurochemical changes are posited to affect memory storage and retrieval. At this time, such assertions are still in the early and heuristic stages, but they appear promising because the results appear to reveal lines of convergence.

Some recent research on brain function during the process of remembering suggests that different kinds of memory activate different parts of the brain (Bremner et al., 1995; van der Kolk, 1992; van der Kolk & Saporta, 1991). Specifically, these researchers, using both animal models and recently developed noninvasive brain-imaging techniques to study human brains in action, indicate that strongly affectively charged memories, include memory for trauma, may be stored in the brain structures of the limbic system and amygdala. Other quite recent information suggests that in individuals with a known history of trauma, the hippocampus shows decreases in size, although the specific implications of this finding for how trauma is remembered are by no means clear.

## Memory Theory Prior to FMSF and FMS

The next chapter discusses claims made by the False Memory Syndrome Foundation (FMSF) and others about false memories. Before concluding chapter 2, it is useful to draw together some of the historical themes relevant specifically to false memories. As some of the literature reviewed earlier in this chapter demonstrates, the notion that until the last several years psychology tended to view memory as a near-perfect recording device finds no historical support. A review of the literature reveals a long history of exploring *how*—rather than *whether*—memory could be fallible, malleable, and suggestible. As Olio (1993) noted, "Memory does not function like a camera to preserve an exact replica of our past. All memories contain inaccuracies and distortions in the details which are recalled" (p. 3). Psychology's fascination with memory's imperfections dates back at least to the founding of the American Psychological Association, which provides a vivid example. In a historical documentation of the association's first 38 years, Fernberger (1932) described the memorable meeting on July 8, 1892, among Association organizers Stanley Hall, George Fullerton, Joseph Jastrow, William James, George Ladd, James Cattell, and Mark Baldwin (p. 2). A decade later, he described his attempts to verify accounts of that meeting, including his contacting two of the alleged participants (Cattell and Jastrow), both of whom denied having attended. He concluded, "There is really no evidence that the meeting was ever actually and physically held . . ." (Fernberger, 1943, p. 35).

Two years before this supposed meeting, William James (1890) wrote:

> False memories are by no means rare occurrences in most of us. . . . Most people, probably, are in doubt about certain matters ascribed to their past. They may have seen them, may have said them, done them, or they may only have dreamed or imagined they did so. . . . The most frequent source of false memory is the accounts we give to others of our experiences. Such accounts we almost always make both more simple and more interesting than the truth. We quote what we should have said or done rather than what we really said or did; and in the first telling we may be fully aware of the distinction.

But ere long the fiction expels the reality from memory and reigns in its stead alone. This is one great source of the fallibility of testimony meant to be quite honest. . . . It is next to impossible to get a story of this sort accurate in all its details, although it is the inessential details that suffer most change. (pp. 373–374)

Müensterberg's (1908) studies of how people imperfectly remember experimentally staged events, Bird's (1927) demonstration of how postevent information can influence recollection, and Bartlett's (1932) analysis of how telling a story from memory (as in the game of "gossip" or "telephone") reveals distortions are but a few examples of the rich and diverse history of research in this area.

The fallibility of memory and even perception itself, which furnishes so much of memory's content, resulted in part from the creative action inherent in memory and perception. Long before Hubel and Wiesel (1962a, 1962b, 1979) investigated the neurophysiological construction of perceptions, Koffka (1935) reviewed extensive studies of how stimulus properties, contextual forces, and observer variables could bring forth misperceptions such as Wertheimer's phenomenal movement (or phi-phenomenon), the classic optical illusions, and the phantom limb phenomenon. The mind did not passively receive and store perfect perceptual representations; it actively constructed representations of varying correspondence with external events, and continued to work on the constructions. In rejecting the static, passive, storehouse model of perception, memory, and mind, Koffka—whose work is cited earlier in this chapter—emphasized, "what a strange store-house we find it to be! Things do not simply fall into those places into which they are being thrown, they arrange themselves in coming and during their time of storage according to the many ways in which they belong together. And they do more; they influence each other, form groups of various sizes and kinds, always trying to meet the exigencies of the moment" (p. 518). This valuable and often neglected history of research and theory is an essential context for evaluating current claims about false memory formation, syndrome, and epidemic.

# Conclusions: What We Do and Don't Know

What conclusions can we draw from this review of some salient topics and data? First, that the science of memory offers a range of provocative findings that are of importance to mental health professionals who encounter clients reporting delayed recall of childhood sexual abuse. However, these findings are not always in agreement, nor, in a sound science, should they be. This requires careful reading and critical thinking by clinicians in the application of the available information, as well as openness to new data as they emerge. Second, that diverse models available to explain the underlying mechanisms for certain frequently observed phenomena of memory are likewise still in a state of development and offer a variety of possible paradigms.

Bauer's review article, "What Do Infants Recall of Their Lives? Memory for Specific Events by One- to Two-Year-Olds" (1996), provides but one example of the continuing emergence of surprising findings that reveal flaws in widely accepted models of memory, resulting in continuing alteration of those models. She noted,

> As recently as a decade ago, it was widely believed that the answer to the question posed in the title of this article, "What do infants recall of their lives?", was "essentially nothing." . . . Rather than being shaped by an empirical body, the field was shaped by a tenacious and influential assumption that children in this age range simply were unable to remember the events of their lives. The assumption held sway in large part because of a methodological impediment: Infants are unable to participate in the paradigm of choice for memory researchers, namely, verbal recall. With the development of a nonverbal analogue to verbal report, my colleagues and I began to examine the assumption that infants are unable to remember the past. We found it an unwarranted assumption. . . . Even 13-month-olds demonstrate the capacity to recall events over extended periods of time. . . . The challenge ahead is to identify the factors that maintain the accessibility of early memories over the transition from infancy to early childhood. (pp. 29, 39)

The research, theory, and history reviewed in this chapter suggest that the science of memory is itself not a static storehouse of established truths that are beyond question. For clinical and forensic work to be adequately informed by the science of memory, therapists and expert witnesses must consider a wealth of research findings, assumptions, hypotheses, and models. They must consider the emerging, evolving, sometimes conflicting attempts to acheive a scientific understanding of human memory, especially as it is relevant to trauma. They must consider the full range of this literature, including not only that which supports, but also that which refutes or challenges, their current beliefs. Therapists and expert witnesses must be prepared not just to read claims about the science of memory, but to question them carefully and effectively. It is this process of scientific questioning that is the topic of chapter 3.

# 3

# Clinical and Forensic Work as Questioning: Considering Claims About False Memories

This book's approach is not to provide a simplified set of supposed answers or support a sense of certitude, but rather to suggest that an essential task of therapists and expert witnesses is careful, informed, and comprehensive questioning. These professionals must ask effective questions about the people whom they assess, and they must continually question the conclusions they draw about that assessment. They must question their own assumptions, biases, and perspectives, not just once during initial training, but throughout their careers. They must also question claims about scientific discoveries, evidence, and conclusions, no matter how prestigious or popular the source. In clinical and forensic work, uncritical acceptance of scientific claims may be as damaging as reflexive rejection. Therapy and expert testimony may not only suffer, but also inflict harm, when the vigorous authoritative promotion of claims fails to meet vigorous critical examination. This chapter reviews some relatively recent claims about false memories and suggests types of questions that clinicians and expert witnesses may find useful in evaluating these and other claims.

*Note:* This chapter is an adapted version of "Memory, Abuse, and Science: Questioning Claims About the False Memory Syndrome Epidemic," by Kenneth S. Pope, 1996, *American Psychologist, 54,* pp. 957–974. Copyright 1996 by the American Psychological Association.

Complex factors may shape the process by which announced discoveries and conclusions encounter or elude careful scrutiny. Such factors include prevailing scientific paradigms, historical contexts, and the bandwagon effect. They can influence the degree to which people are inclined, willing, and free to question certain claims. These factors are themselves a legitimate and important focus of scientific questioning.

A relatively recent set of claims holds that many therapists—for reasons as diverse as well-meaning naiveté, greed, incompetence, and zealotry—suggest a history of childhood sexual abuse to clients who have no actual abuse history. According to the claims, clients who uncritically accept these suggestions and come to believe illusory memories of abuse with great conviction suffer from an iatrogenic disorder termed *false memory syndrome* (FMS). This psychopathology, which according to Kihlstrom (1996) resembles a personality disorder, has allegedly manifested sufficient numbers of cases to reach epidemic proportions. In the short span of time since the 1992 founding of the False Memory Syndrome Foundation (FMSF), claims about FMS—a condition that the Foundation identified and named—and related phenomena have had a profound impact on issues germane to ethical and competent psychological science and practice. FMSF noted its own "success" as reflected in the "institutionalization of this information in psychology text books, in reference works, in novels, in television dramas, and in hundreds of scholarly papers" (P. Freyd, 1996). The American Psychological Association approved FMSF as a provider of continuing education programs for psychologists ("American Psychological Association Approves," 1995). The FMS concept is addressed in appellate decisions (e.g., *State v. Warnberg*,[1] 1994).

---

[1]Legal determinations that allegations of sexual abuse are false because the witness suffers from FMS generally require expert testimony. The appellate ruling in *State v. Warnberg* (1994), for example, described a set of facts in which sexual assault occurred when Warnberg pulled the car to the side of the road to allow the complainant to be sick, at which time she claimed he approached her from behind, undid her bra, and fondled her breasts while she was vomiting. . . . Warnberg sought to introduce evidence of a sexual assault against the complainant 13 years

Herman (1994) and Landsberg (1996a, 1996b) are among those who have noted the popular media's frequently uncritical acceptance of these claims.

Although it is unusual that a lay advocacy group could produce adequate scientific evidence to support its discoveries and claims, FMSF highlights the contributions of the FMSF Scientific and Professional Advisory Board. They emphasize not only that "board members make substantial donations to the Foundation both in time and money" but also that "[i]t is the presence of the Advisory Board that has given our efforts credibility" ("FMSF Advisory Board Meeting," 1993, p. 3). The FMSF Scientific and Professional Advisory Board includes distinguished and prominent members in the fields of psychology, psychiatry, sociology, and cognitive science[2] (FMSF, 1996a). Their contributions of

---

prior to the alleged assault. He argued that that evidence was relevant to his contention that the complainant's accusation was the result of a psychologically displaced or repressed memory or "false memory syndrome". The trial court rejected Warnberg's proposed evidence on the ground that it could not determine from Warnberg's offer of proof that such a syndrome existed. Warnberg argues that the trial court should have granted his motion for a continuance to allow him to produce an expert who could testify to the validity of the false memory syndrome. A concept such as false memory syndrome . . . requires an expert witness to testify to its existence.

[2]As with virtually any organization's board, the board of the False Memory Syndrome Foundation continues to change in composition over time as some members depart and others join. The following individuals were identified as FMSF Scientific and Professional Advisory Board members in the February 1996 *FMSF Newsletter* (1996a): Aaron T. Beck, MD, DMS, University of Pennsylvania, Philadelphia, PA; Terence W. Campbell, PhD, clinical and forensic psychology, Sterling Heights, MI; Rosalind Cartwright, Rush Presbyterian St. Luke's Medical Center, Chicago, IL; Jean Chapman, PhD, University of Wisconsin, Madison, WI; Loren Chapman, PhD, University of Wisconsin, Madison, WI; Frederick C. Crews, PhD, University of California, Berkeley, CA; Robyn M. Dawes, PhD, Carnegie Mellon University, Pittsburgh, PA; David F. Dinges, PhD, University of Pennsylvania, The Institute of Pennsylvania Hospital, Philadelphia, PA; Henry C. Ellis, PhD, University of New Mexico, Albuquerque, NM; Fred Frankel, MBChB, DPM, Beth Israel Hospital, Harvard Medical School, Cambridge, MA; George K. Ganaway, MD, Emory University of Medicine, Atlanta, GA; Martin Gardner, Author, Hendersonville, NC; Rochel Gelman, PhD, University of California, Los Angeles, CA; Henry Gleitman, PhD, University of Pennsylvania, Philadelphia, PA; Lila Gleitman, PhD, University of Pennsylvania, Philadelphia, PA; Richard Green, MD, JD,

time, money, reputations, and credibility to the goals and work of FMSF may represent a significant, if not crucial, factor in the Foundation's success. The Scientific and Professional Advisory Board's implicit endorsement of the FMS diagnosis may help explain why such FMSF claims are so vividly reflected in the professional literature, expert testimony, and the popular media. If widely accepted, claims about an FMS epidemic traced to therapeutic malpractice may influence diagnosis and treatment for many people, the access or lack of access that individuals have to various services, and the clinical, forensic, and public response to those who report memories of childhood abuse.

This chapter's purpose is twofold. First, it suggests questions that maybe useful for evaluating the evidence that purportedly established the validity of claims about FMS and their policy implications. Second, it proposes that scholarly examination of

---

Charing Cross Hospital, London; David A. Halperin, MD, Mount Sinai School of Medicine, New York, NY; Ernest Hilgard, PhD, Stanford University, Palo Alto, CA; John Hochman, MD, UCLA Medical School, Los Angeles, CA; David S. Holmes, PhD, University of Kansas, Lawrence, KS; Philip S. Holzman, PhD, Harvard University, Cambridge, MA; Robert A. Karlin, PhD, Rutgers University, New Brunswick, NJ; John Kihlstrom, PhD, Yale University, New Haven, CT; Harold Lief, MD, University of Pennsylvania, Philadelphia, PA; Elizabeth Loftus, PhD, University of Washington, Seattle, WA; Paul McHugh, MD, Johns Hopkins University, Baltimore, MD; Harold Merskey, DM, University of Western Ontario, London, Canada; Ulric Neisser, PhD, Emory University, Atlanta, GA; Richard Ofshe, PhD, University of California, Berkeley, CA; Emily K. Orne, B.A., University of Pennsylvania, The Institute of Pennsylvania Hospital, Philadelphia, PA; Martin Orne, MD, PhD, University of Pennsylvania, The Institute of Pennsylvania Hospital, Philadelphia, PA; Loren Pankratz, PhD, Oregon Health Sciences University, Portland, OR; Campbell Perry, PhD, Concordia University, Montreal, Canada; Michael A. Persinger, PhD, Laurentian University, Ontario, Canada; August T. Piper, Jr., MD; Seattle WA; Harrison Pope, Jr., MD, Harvard Medical School, Cambridge, MA; James Randi, Author and Magician, Plantation, FL; Henry L. Roediger, III, PhD, Rice University, Houston, TX; Carolyn Saari, PhD, Loyola University, Chicago, IL; Theodore Sarbin, PhD, University of California, Santa Cruz, CA; Thomas A. Sebeok, PhD, Indiana University, Bloomington, IN; Michael A. Simpson, MRCS, LRCP, MRC, DOM, Center for Psychosocial & Traumatic Stress, Pretoria, South Africa; Margaret Singer, PhD, University of California, Berkeley, CA; Ralph Slovenko, JD, PhD, Wayne State University Law School, Detroit, MI; Donald Spence, PhD, Robert Wood Johnson Medical Center, Piscataway, NJ; Jeffrey Victor, PhD, Jamestown Community College, Jamestown, NY; Hollida Wakefield, MA, Institute of Psychological Therapies, Northfield, MN.

some methods used to promote these claims (e.g., diagnosis and characterization of those who disagree) might reveal factors influencing the degree to which these claims are critically examined. Are the methods used to promote these claims creating a context in which such claims are unlikely to be examined critically, freely, and comprehensively?

## False Memory Syndrome: Claims of a Scientifically Validated Syndrome and Epidemic

Memory's imperfection (see chapter 2) provides a context for the FMSF claims about the supposed syndrome it appeared to discover and helped to institutionalize. According to proponents of this reputed new syndrome, sufficient cases have been diagnosed to constitute an epidemic. These claims of a mental health epidemic provide an opportunity to consider questions that can be useful in evaluating purported scientific discoveries, evidence, and conclusions.

The definition of the false memory syndrome found in the literature published by the False Memory Syndrome Foundation was written by John Kihlstrom, who has served as an FMSF Scientific and Professional Advisory Board member. The current FMSF brochure repeats this description of

> the False Memory Syndrome—a condition in which a person's identity and interpersonal relationships are centered around a memory of traumatic experience which is objectively false but in which the person strongly believes. Note that the syndrome is not characterized by false memories as such. We all have memories that are inaccurate. Rather, the syndrome may be diagnosed when the memory is so deeply engrained that it orients the individual's entire personality and lifestyle, in turn disrupting all sorts of other adaptive behaviors. The analogy to personality disorder is intentional. False Memory Syndrome is especially destructive because the person assiduously avoids confrontation with any evidence that might challenge the memory. Thus it takes on a life of its own, encapsulated, and resistant to correction. The person may

become so focused on the memory that he or she may be effectively distracted from coping with the real problems in his or
her life. (Kihlstrom, 1996; also cited in FMSF's [1995] Amicus
Curiae Brief)

Ceci, Bronfenbrenner, Eckman, and Shepard were among 17
researchers[3] who coauthored a statement objecting to the term
*false memory syndrome* as "a non-psychological term originated by
a private foundation whose stated purpose is to support accused
parents." They urged, "For the sake of intellectual honesty, let's
leave the term 'false memory syndrome' to the popular press"
(Carstensen et al., 1993, p. 23).

## Methodology for Determining That Memories Are Objectively False

Several questions may be useful in assessing the scientific validity of these diagnostic features. First, how did the researchers,
clinicians, or others who validated this syndrome determine in
each case that the memory was "objectively false"? Those claiming that scientific research has validated FMS and identified an
epidemic have a responsibility to disclose the methods for determining that each case involved a memory that was objectively
false. The peer-reviewed scientific literature still lacks adequate
information about this methodology.

It continues to be unclear if the protocol of any research pur-
porting to validate the FMS diagnosis in large numbers of persons used any criterion other than the decision-rule that all
recovered memories of abuse are inherently false. Statements by

---

[3]The authors were listed as Laura L. Carstensen, John Gabrieli, and Roger
Shepard of Stanford University; Robert W. Levenson and Mary Ann Mason of
University of California-Berkeley; Gail Goodman of University of California-
Davis; Richard Bootzin of University of Arizona; Stephen J. Ceci and Urie
Bronfenbrenner of Cornell University; Barry A. Edelstein of West Virginia
University; Michael Schober of New School for Social Research; Maggie Bruck
of McGill University; Terence Keane and Rose Zimering of National Center for
the Study of PTSD (Boston VA Medical Center); Thomas F. Oltmanns of
University of Virginia; Ian Gotlib of Northwestern University; and Paul
Eckman of University of California-San Francisco.

some FMSF proponents have seemed to characterize recovered memories of trauma as objectively false per se. FMSF Scientific and Professional Advisory Board member Harrison Pope and his colleague James Hudson (1995a; see also 1995b) emphasized that "[t]raumatic experiences are memorable" (p. 715); asserted that there has never been a confirmed case of "noncontrived amnesia among neurologically intact individuals over the age of 6 who experienced events sufficiently traumatic that no one would be expected to simply forget them" (p. 716);[4] and asserted that trauma survivors in scientifically valid studies "unanimously remembered the events" (p. 715). Founding FMSF Scientific and Professional Advisory Board members Hollida Wakefield and Ralph Underwager[5] (1994) wrote, "People who undergo severe trauma remember it" (p. 182). Scientific and Professional Advisory Board member Martin Gardner (1993) asserted that "[b]etter-trained, older psychiatrists do not believe that child hood memories of trauma can be repressed for any length of time, except in rare cases of actual brain damage. . . . And there is abundant evidence that totally false memories are easily aroused in the mind of a suggestible patient" (p. 374). FMSF (1992b) itself published the claim: "Psychiatrists advising the Foundation members seem to be unanimous in the belief that memories of such atrocities cannot be repressed. Horrible incidents of child hood are remembered. . . ." (p. 2).[6]

---

[4]Pope and Hudson are not claiming that child sexual abuse per se is never forgotten. They assert that children may actually undergo what a majority of adults would identify as sexual abuse, "but the experience may not seem particularly traumatic or strikingly memorable to the child" (p. 716). Their general argument rests on such premises as "the absence of proof is equivalent to proof of absence." They assert that questioning such premises does not reflect sound reasoning: "[I]t might be argued that absence of proof is not proof of absence; the lack of evidence for repression does not refute its existence. But this argument is flawed" (p. 718).

[5]Underwager is no longer listed as a member of the FMSF Scientific and Professional Advisory Board.

[6]Such statements seem to present a view of memory and painful events that would exclude such concepts as repression, but statements by FMS proponents sometimes appear to support the concept of memory recovery following repression. For example, in one study of women's reported history of child-

It is important to examine these claims that human memory systems process significantly traumatic experiences differently from other stimuli (e.g., that sufficiently traumatic experiences are always available to awareness, are never subject to such varying constructs as forgetting [see Feldman-Summers & Pope, 1994], amnesia, dissociation, or repression, and thus can never be subject to recovered memory), in light of the evidence put forward to establish their validity.

---

hood sex abuse, Loftus and her colleagues found that what they term "repression" and "robust repression" did occur, although the extent was difficult to estimate: "There is a reason to believe that the 19% figure we obtained in the current study may actually be an overestimate of the extent to which repression occurs" (Loftus et al., 1994, p. 81; but see also Loftus, Garry, & Feldman, 1994) and "One could argue that this means that robust repression was not especially prevalent in our sample" (p. 80). Six years earlier, she discussed "motivated forgetting" and presented a documented study of a college professor who became unable to remember a series of traumas, but after a long period of time was able to recover memories of the traumas. "Eventually, R. J. was able to remember all of her traumatic experiences. . . . Even though the return of her memories made her wiser, she was also much sadder. More than most of us ever will, R. J. understood the true meaning in Christina Rosetti's words in "Remember": 'Better by far you should forget and smile than that you should remember and be sad' " (Loftus, 1988, p. 73). Discussing an example of response to a single trauma (i.e., unlike R. J.'s response to a series of traumas), Loftus asserted: "After such an enormously stressful experience, many individuals wish to forget . . . and often their wish is granted" (p. 73). Earlier, Loftus had discussed ways that, according to her, scientists could know that repression of painful events actually occurred:

> Memories that may cause us great unhappiness if they were brought to mind often appear to be "forgotten." However, are they really lost from memory, or are they simply temporarily repressed as originally suggested by Freud (1922)? Repression is the phenomenon that prevents someone from remembering an event that can cause him or her pain and suffering. One way that we know that these memories are repressed and not completely lost is that the methods of free association and hypnosis and other special techniques used by psychotherapists can be used to bring repressed material to mind and can help a person remember things that he has failed to remember earlier. (Loftus & Loftus, 1976, p. 82)

In the same work, she claimed that experimental evidence demonstrated the workings of repression: "This experiment indicates that when the reason for the repression is removed, when material to be remembered is no longer associated with negative effects, a person no longer experiences retrieval failure" (p. 83; the experiment was an analog experiment reported by Zeller [1950]). See also chapter 2.

Other questions emerge when examining claims about the diagnosis of FMS and the supposed epidemic. If there are validation studies for FMS and the epidemic that do not reflexively judge all reports of recovered memories of abuse to be objectively false, what was the research methodology for determining whether the reports were objectively true or false? Does the methodology yield an acceptable rate of false positives and false negatives? Assuming more than one person made each judgment, what was the interrater reliability? How was the methodology itself validated?

Until the methodology and raw data used in identifying and validating the syndrome and verifying sufficient cases to constitute an epidemic are adequately disclosed, it may be helpful to consider the methods and evidence that proponents have set forth to determine whether memories of abuse are objectively false. One proposed set of criteria for distinguishing between objectively true and false memories of abuse focuses on the reactions of the person who experienced the memories. FMSF (1994) published an article entitled "How Does a Person Know That Memories of Abuse Were False?" based on a study of an unspecified number of people who experienced such memories, later decided the memories were false, and subsequently retracted their claims of having experienced abuse. Indicants of false memories included failure to find corroborating evidence, memories described by retractors "as not 'feeling' like other memories" (p. 3), and "the change in their life since they came to this realization" (p. 4) (i.e., "Many describe a sense of peace and comfort with their decision that their memories were false and a sense of well-being that they missed while entrenched in the memory recovery process" [p. 4]).

A second set of criteria for distinguishing true and false memories of abuse emerged from a study of what was described as "a representative sample of families who had contacted the FMS Foundation" (de Rivera, 1994, p. 149).[7] Seven criteria were set

---

[7]The sample was composed of 9 families. The methodology for selecting the sample was: "In order to select a representative sample of families who had contacted the FMS Foundation, the investigator chose a telephone area code and contacted all families within that code who met [certain] criteria" (de Rivera, 1994, p. 149).

forth as appearing to identify false memories. Among these indicants were: "There are no such memories prior to therapy"; "The accused has no history of any pedophiliac tendencies and there is no evidence of any sexual interest in children"; and "The accused and the family are willing to openly discuss the allegations and explore them for logical coherence" (p. 154).

A third set of indicants was set forth by Pamela Freyd, who is currently FMSF executive director, in an article, "How Do We Know We Are Not Representing Pedophiles?" (1992b). Two methods were presented as ways to show that the memories forming the basis of accusations against members are false:

> There are two ways that we will address this concern. The first has to do with who we are. If I had taken a camera to any of the three meetings held here in Philadelphia, I would have been hard put to know whom to photograph. We are a good looking bunch of people: graying hair, well-dressed, healthy, smiling. The similarity of the stories is astounding, so script-like and formulaic that doubts dissolve after chats with a few families. Just about every person who has attended is someone you would likely find interesting and want to count as a friend. . . .
>
> The second way that we will address this concern involves lie detector tests. . . . If all members of the FMS Foundation either have had or express a willingness to be polygraphed, we will have a powerful statement that we are not in the business of representing pedophiles. (p. 1)

Such assertions in support of claims about reliably separating true and false reports of child abuse may or may not be persuasive to the media, clinicians assessing child abuse accusations, the courts, or others, depending on a variety of circumstances. However persuasive they may seem, such claims are best examined in light of such questions as, Is there adequate scientific research to support the claims? Similar claims, such as clinicians' assertion that they can, based upon certain profiles or criteria, reliably and validly determine whether an individual is capable of engaging in sex with a child, benefit from a careful examination of the scientific evidence demonstrating such clinical abilities. In "Legal Aspects of False Memory Syndrome," FMSF (1992b) informed its members that some "psychiatrists will opine that, in their opinion, a particular individual is not a pedophile and perhaps would not or could not have performed the acts complained of" (p. 2). Regardless of whether courts may admit such statements as evidence that a recovered memory of childhood sexual abuse is "objectively false," psychologists have an obligation to examine the scientific basis supporting such assessments.

Claims about valid, reliable identification of false memories of child abuse or of false accusations based on these false memories deserve and require careful evaluation in light of evidence and logic. For example, if self-reports of abuse memories are to be doubted in the absence of external "proof," why are self-reports about retracted memories presented as presumed valid in the absence of external verification? What scientific evidence supports claims that such factors as good looks, dress, health, and smiling serve as valid and reliable indicants of whether or not an individual has engaged in child abuse?

## Methodology for Assessing an "Entire Personality and Lifestyle"

Having determined that the memory was objectively false, how did those who validated the false memory syndrome assess whether that false memory actually "orients the individual's entire personality and lifestyle"? Assessing whether there are aspects of the individual's personality or lifestyle that remain consistent and unchanged (i.e., not oriented to the objectively false "memory") would present a considerable challenge even to the most skilled and experienced clinicians. Disclosing the methodology for making this determination would allow careful examination of the assumptions, evidence, and reasoning that support the research and encourage replication and additional research into FMS.

## Claims of FMS's Similarity to Personality Disorders

It is not clear how similar this new disorder is to the recognized personality disorders to which it is explicitly analogized, or whether this analogy simply makes explicit the notion that the same sort of severe pathology presumed present in the classic personality disorders is present in the alleged FMS. The *DSM–IV*, for example, states that "[a] Personality Disorder is an enduring pattern of inner experience and behavior that deviates markedly from the expectations of the individual's culture, is pervasive and inflexible, has an onset in adolescence or early adulthood, is stable over time, and leads to distress or impairment" (American Psychiatric Association, 1994, p. 629). Does defining FMS to resemble recognized personality disorders imply that its onset does not occur beyond early adulthood? Does it suggest that, whereas the syndrome becomes manifest in adulthood, its foundation—like the foundation of recognized personality disorders—rests on earlier weaknesses or dysfunction in the individual? Wakefield and Underwager (1994), for example, noted that "Gardner sees the women who make false allegations based on recovered memories as very angry, hostile, and sometimes paranoid. He believes that all will have demonstrated some type of psychopathology in earlier parts of their lives" (p. 333). The *Philadelphia Inquirer* quoted Wakefield's description of those who recover memories: "The adult children who 'remember' sexual abuse decades after they say it happened are . . . 'not just anybody. They are women who already have problems, such as personality disorder, and they're likely to be unusually suggestible. . . .' " (Sifford, 1991, p. 12).

## Thousands of Empirically Documented Cases

Within about a year of the founding of FMSF, which identified and named a new syndrome, proponents began to claim that the syndrome was widespread. FMSF Scientific and Professional Advisory Board member Martin Gardner (1993) wrote that among the purposes of the FMS Foundation was "to seek reasons for the FMS epidemic" (p. 375). In the process of researching the problem, FMSF made the following statement:

> FMSF is first a research organization that is documenting the extent of this phenomenon. There is a standard procedure that is followed for phone interviews. We currently have in our files hundreds and hundreds of "Maybe's." Maybe's are

names that are given to us as families that are affected by FMS
but for whom we do not have the standard documentation
information. Unless we have complete and standard documentation, we do not add these people to the count of affected
families. (FMSF, 1993, p. 7)

Two of the founding Scientific and Professional Advisory Board
members cited as validating evidence for FMS "the empirical
data the FMS Foundation has from 12,000 families" (Wakefield &
Underwager, 1994, p. 98).

The FMSF's research evidence allegedly "points with high certainty towards a false memory syndrome that meets the requirements for a syndrome contained in the *DSM–III–R* and the
*DSM–IV*. The thousands of instances that contain those common
elements are likely to be more support for this syndrome than for
any other that has been accepted as a legitimate classification category" (p. 99). Expert witnesses, therapists, policy makers,
reporters, the courts, graduate courses, and continuing education programs could thus cite a growing literature accepting and
helping institutionalize the notion that FMS was not only a scientifically validated disorder caused by psychotherapy, but that
the number of documented cases was exceptionally large. For
instance, Goldstein and Farmer (1993) asserted, "Now we know
that False Memory Syndrome is an iatrogenic disease created by
therapy gone haywire. We know that false memory syndrome
has reached epidemic proportions" (p. 9). By 1996, FMSF distrib-
uted an information sheet and order form (for its video, "False
Memory Syndrome") in which it claimed that "False Memory
Syndrome [is] a devastating phenomenon that has affected tens
of thousands of individuals and families worldwide" (1996b).

It would be helpful, if not critical, for FMSF and its Scientific
and Professional Advisory Board to describe the research protocols or other formal procedures by which FMS has been adequately validated as a syndrome and by which it was
determined that it has affected tens of thousands of individuals
and families. Clearly stating such operationalized procedures
as how reported memories of abuse are found to be "objectively false" in any study that documents the widespread
nature of FMS allows the independent analysis, verification,

and replication that is the hallmark of psychological scientific empiricism. It is possible that the impressive names, prestige, offices, and affiliations of the Scientific and Professional Advisory Board may have, however unintentionally, led fellow scientists, the courts, the popular media, and others to accept without customary skepticism, care, and examination of alternative hypotheses the methodology and arrays of primary data relevant to the notion of FMS and other FMSF assertions as scientifically validated.

It is worth emphasizing that some therapists engage in incompetent, unethical, or well-meaning but misguided behaviors, sometimes with disastrous consequences for patients (see, e.g., Pope, 1990, 1994; Pope, Simpson, & Weiner, 1978). In some instances, these behaviors include using unvalidated, misleading, or bizarre methods for assessing whether a patient was sexually abused as a child (Pope & Vasquez, 1991). However, such facts alone are an insufficient basis for claims that there "is an iatrogenic disease created by therapy" and that this "false memory syndrome has reached epidemic proportions." The scientific evidence that supposedly validates claims about this so-called syndrome, its causes, and its epidemic proportions needs to be made available and carefully examined.

## Informed Consent Issues in Research Validating FMS

Research involving human subjects usually involves the informed consent of the participants. For those independently evaluating or attempting to replicate studies seeming to validate the existence and widespread occurrence of FMS, it would be useful if the procedures for obtaining informed consent—if consent was obtained—from people who were diagnosed as suffering from FMS were disclosed. It appears possible, based on a reading of materials generated by the FMSF, that some might not consider interviewing or clinically assessing the people supposedly afflicted by FMS to be an essential component of a study of the validity and occurrence of the syndrome. If, for this reason, the informed consent of or even direct contact with people diagnosed with FMS has been considered unnecessary in documenting specific cases or the extent of the phenomenon, it would be useful for FMSF and its Scientific and Professional Advisory Board to report any available scientific data about the ability to diagnose FMS without meeting the person alleged to have the disorder. If the person reporting the so-called memory does not participate in the research, how do researchers conclude that the memory is objectively false (rather than simply subjectively judged to be false by those who have been accused)? How do researchers determine that the center of a person's identity and interpersonal relationships is a particular false memory without even meeting the person? How do they examine all aspects of personality without interviewing, evaluating, or even knowing the person?

## Independent Examination of the Primary Data and Methodology

Independent examination of the primary data and methodology used to establish the validity and reliability of a new psycholog ical diagnosis, prior to its application to large numbers of people, is an essential scientific responsibility. Psychological diagnoses lacking validity may gain popularity and undermine clinical and forensic work if distorting influences like confirmation bias, illusory correlation, and false consensus have not been eliminated from the validation studies and subsequent use. However, once set forth as a scientifically valid, established, and institutionalized category, a readily diagnosed formal psychological syndrome gains immense power to influence others. As Rosenhan wrote,

> Such labels, conferred by mental health professionals, are as influential on the patient as they are on his [sic] relatives and friends, and it should not surprise anyone that the diagnosis acts on all of them as a self-fulfilling prophesy. Eventually, the patient himself [sic] accepts the diagnosis, with all of its surplus meanings and expectations, and behaves accordingly. (1973, p. 254; see also Brown, 1995b; Langer & Abelson, 1974; Mednick, 1989; Murphy, 1976; Pope, Butcher, & Seelen, 1993; Reiser & Levenson, 1984)

## The Cause of FMS: Trauma Memories
## Implanted in Therapy

To explain why people who had never been abused would accuse parents or others of sexually abusing them, FMS proponents have tended to assert that therapists implanted the memories. For example, FMSF (1995) claimed "that certain psychotherapeutic techniques, theories and practices have led many people to falsely believe they were sexually abused as children" (p. 1). Seeking research evidence that specific therapist behaviors cause harm poses a dilemma: Investigators cannot randomly assign patients to conditions hypothesized to cause injury. Typically, studies attempt to correct for the absence of random assignment by selecting appropriate comparison groups, by matching patients on relevant variables, and by using measures that are likely to create maximum sensitivity and specificity to the phenomenon at issue. For example, research assessing whether therapists' sexual behaviors were associated with specific patient symptoms might compare a group of patients who had engaged in sex with a therapist with matched (in regard to demographics, etc.) groups of patients who had not engaged in sex with a therapist and of patients who had engaged in sex with a physician who was not a therapist (for reviews of such research, see Pope, 1994; Pope, Sonne, & Holroyd, 1993). In this instance, researchers have tended instead to attempt to demonstrate that false memories of events described as traumatic can be implanted in other contexts, with generalizations from these findings to what must occur in psychotherapy.

Loftus's widely cited experiment in which older family members apparently implanted memories in 14-year-old Chris, 8-year-old Brittany, and three other subjects has been claimed as the "proof" (Loftus & Ketcham, 1994, p. 99) that implanting traumatic memories is possible. When challenged with the assertion, "But it's just not possible to implant in someone's mind a complete memory with details and relevant emotions for a traumatic event that didn't happen," Loftus responded: "But that's exactly what we did in the shopping mall experiment" (Loftus & Ketcham, 1994, p. 212). Proponents described this experiment as demonstrating the creation of an extensive false memory. Lynn and Nash (1994) reported that "Loftus and Coan were able to implant an extensive autobiographical memory"

(p. 198). Lindsay and Read (1994) claimed that "Loftus and Coan . . . demonstrated that people can be led to create detailed and extended 'recollections' of childhood that never occurred" (p. 289). The popular press echoed a similar theme, arguing, for example, that the most practical significance about the lost-in-the-shopping-mall experiment is that "[i]t buttresses an alternative explanation for the source of recovered memories that True Believers purport to have repressed. Namely that the memories have been implanted by some type of suggestion; they are false" (Boss, 1994, p. 12).

Among the kinds of questions that might be useful in evaluating claims about implanting "a complete memory with details and relevant emotions for a traumatic event that didn't happen" based on this research are the following:

1. Does the trauma specified in the lost-in-the-mall experiment seem comparable to the trauma forming the basis of FMS? Loftus (1993) described the implanted traumatic event in the shopping-mall experiment as follows: "Chris was convinced by his older brother Jim, that he had been lost in a shopping mall when he was five years old" (p. 532). Does this seem, for example, a reasonable analogy for a 5-year-old girl being repeatedly raped by her father? Pezdek (1995; see also Pezdek et al., 1996) has suggested that this may not be the case. In attempting to arrive at a more analogous situation—that of a suggested false memory of a rectal enema—her experimental attempts at implantation of a suggestion had a 0% success rate.

2. What is the impact of the potentially confounding variables in claiming the shopping mall experiment to be a convincing analogue of therapy (Loftus, 1993; Loftus & Ketcham, 1994)? For example, is it possible that the findings are an artifact of this particular design; e.g., that the older family member claims to have been present when the event occurred and to have witnessed it, a claim the therapist can never make? To date, replications and extensions of this study have tended to use a similar methodology, that is, either the older family member makes the suggestions in his or her role as the experimenter's confederate, or the experimenter presents the suggestion as being the report of an older family member, thus creating a surrogate confederate.

3. Has this line of research assumed that verbal reports provided to researchers are the equivalent of actual memories? Spanos (1994)

suggested that changes in report in suggestibility research may represent compliance with social demand conditions of the research design rather than actual changes in what is recalled. In what ways were the measures to demonstrate actual changes or creations of memory representations validated and confounding variables (e.g., demand characteristics) excluded? Given that being lost while out shopping is apparently a common childhood experience, how is the determination made that the lost-in-the-mall memory is not substantially correct? What supports the claim that "Chris had remembered a traumatic episode that never occurred" (Garry & Loftus, 1994, p. 83). That is, is there any possibility that Chris' family had forgotten an actual event of this type?

4. If the experiment is assumed for heuristic reasons to demonstrate that an older family member can extensively rewrite a younger relative's memory in regard to a trauma at which the older relative was present, why have FMS proponents presented this research as applying to the dynamics of therapy (e.g., Loftus, 1993; Loftus & Ketcham, 1994) but not to the dynamics of families, particularly those in which parents or other relatives may be exerting pressure on an adult to retract reports of delayed recall? Is it possible that older family members can rewrite younger relatives' memories in regard to traumatic events at which they were present? Might this occur in the context of sexual abuse when the repeated suggestion is made by a perpetrator that "nothing happened" and that any subsequent awareness of the abuse constitutes a false memory?

This line of research has been extended by others, and similar research has been carried out in varied designs (e.g., "false memories" of words that did not appear in a list of words, suggestions of earaches and trips to the hospital at night, suggestions of rectal enemas).[8] One crucial question is, Does this research adequately justify the claims that are being made in

---

[8]For discussions of this and related lines of research from diverse perspectives, see Bowman and Mertz (1996); Braude (1995, pp. 253–268); Brewin, Andrews, and Gotlib (1993); D. Brown (1995a, 1995b); Freyd and Gleaves (1996); Hyman et al. (1995); Koss et al. (1995); Loftus and Pickrell (1995); Pezdek et al. (1996); Roediger and McDermott (1995); Westen (1996); Whitfield (1995); and Zaragoza and Koshmider (1989).

legal cases and elsewhere? An FMSF (1995) amicus brief (which includes a list of the 47 prominent members of FMSF Scientific and Professional Advisory Board as an appendix) presented a typical claim: "Memories of truly traumatic events are easily altered and false recollections, though felt to be actual memories of real events, can easily be induced by suggestion" (p. 20).

Loftus (1992) published claims that are even more sweeping:

> If handled skillfully, the power of misinformation is so enormous and sufficiently controllable that a colleague and I recently postulated a not-too-distant "brave new world" in which misinformation researchers would be able to proclaim: "Give us a dozen healthy memories . . . and our own specified world to handle them in. And we'll guarantee to take any one at random and train it to become any type of memory that we might select . . . regardless of its origin or the brain that holds it.' " The implications for the legal field, for advertising, and for clinical settings are far reaching. (p. 123)

These expansive claims echo those made by Watson (1939) over a half century ago, when a line of behavioral research led to claims that the power of learning theory was so enormous and sufficiently controllable that psychologists with sufficient resources could take individuals at random and produce any kind of people and behavior they might select. If there was a lesson to be learned from the Watsonian claim, it was modesty. Not only did human beings fail to fall helplessly under the power of conditioning, but docile animals often refused to act in accordance with the proclaimed principles of the new science (e.g., Breland & Breland, 1961). It was the rush to uncritically embrace claims that went far beyond the data—the failure to question carefully—that caused the Watsonian fall.

## Therapists as Perpetrators of FMS

An additional assertion with regard to FMS has been claims that significant numbers of therapists engage in behaviors likely to iatrogenically inflict the false memory syndrome. Lindsay and Poole (1995), for example, stated, "In our view there are solid grounds to fear that tens of thousands of people have developed illusory memories or false beliefs about CSA [child sexual abuse] through suggestive memory recovery techniques and ancillary practices in psychotherapy, self-help, or group therapy" (p. 464). In a study to examine clinical practices, Poole et al. (1995) reported data from a study of both United States and British clinicians and suggested that their findings indicated that

> 25% of the members of those organizations who conduct psychotherapy with adult female clients believe that recovering memories is an important part of therapy, think they can identify clients with hidden memories during the initial session and use two or more techniques to help such clients recover suspected memories of CSA. (1995, p. 434; initial findings from the Poole et al. study were previously presented and discussed in an article by Lindsay & Read, 1994)

Lindsay and Read (1994) "refer to such approaches collectively as 'memory recovery therapies' " (p. 282), "are sharply critical of the memory recovery techniques" (p. 298), and fear "that these powerful techniques are being used in ways that are damaging the lives of many clients and their families" (p. 282). They compare memory recovery therapy "to a powerful medicine that may be helpful to victims of a disease, but that can cause great harm when given to people who do not have the disease" (p. 282). They claimed that the self-report of a constellation of beliefs (i.e., recovering memories is an important part of psychotherapy and therapists thinking they can identify clients with hidden memories) and practices (i.e., use any two of a list of techniques in the last 2 years) constitutes a "grave risk" (p. 327).

Others besides the study's authors have cited the results as providing evidence that so-called "memory recovery therapies" are commonly practiced by psychotherapists, and that many therapists are at risk of harming clients by engaging in such behaviors. For example, an FMSF (1995) amicus curiae brief claimed that "recent surveys of therapists' understanding and practices have shown a number of widely held misconceptions, which if communicated to patients, may increase a client's responsiveness to suggestion—and in turn, [lead] to the development of false memories" (p. 5).

FMSF Scientific and Professional Advisory Board member Dawes (1995) characterized the techniques included in the study as "coercive techniques" (p. 12). Loftus (1995) claimed "that these activities can and do sometimes lead to false memories seems now to be beyond dispute" (p. 24). In addition, Loftus et al. (1995) used the Poole et al. data to estimate that as many as 25% of clinicians "may be using techniques that are risky if not dangerous" (1995, p. 304). Because they use some techniques included in the Poole et al. list, specific therapists have been publicly labeled as "dangerous." For example, the *Jerusalem Post* reported opposition to Utrecht University psychology professor Onno van der Hart's plan to lecture in Israel on his treatment of adults who suffered childhood abuse:

> Members of the US False Memory Syndrome Foundation and psychologists in various parts of the world charged that van der Hart and his colleagues were "very dangerous." His critics charged that van der Hart's techniques represented a "harmful and unscientific method of pseudotherapy that must be seen as a threat to psychology in Israel. This 'therapy' makes the patient dependent on the therapist by inventing multiple personalities, false memories and accusations, which have already destroyed tens of thousands of families in the US." (Siegel-Itzkovich, 1996, p. 7)

The Poole et al. study has also been used as the basis for various estimates of the frequency with which illusory memories of abuse may occur. Relying on the Poole et al. claims, Pendergrast (1995) estimated that "25% of doctoral level therapists constitute True Believers" (p. 491; a discussion of True Believers appears later in this chapter) and that "over one million cases of 'recovered memories' each year" (p. 491)—allegedly illusory ones—occur in psychotherapy in the United States. Using similar calculations, FMSF Scientific and Professional Advisory Board member Crews (1995) claimed that "it is hard to form even a rough idea of the number of persuaded clients . . . a conservative guess would be one million persons since 1988 alone" (p. 160). Dawes (1995) estimated a "lower bound of 1,475,833 [cases of recovered memory] for the last two years proving that 'Wakefield and Underwager are absolutely correct in their assessment that recovered memory therapy is widespread' " (p. 12).

Olio (1995a, 1995b, in press) suggested, however, that such conclusions might not be valid. She formulated questions about the research design, statistical tests, and inferences that might be useful in evaluating this study, among which are the following four:

**1. Did the survey construction lead to confounded results?** Olio noted that the critics of recovered memories have repeatedly emphasized the thesis that memory may be particularly susceptible to distorting or confabulating influences when responding to questions (especially related to the past) or giving self-reports. Ironically, this study relies on similar data-gathering procedures in which people are asked numerous questions based on their memory of past complex events. Poole herself acknowledged that the data "do not necessarily index what clinicians do in their offices because they are retrospective self-report measures" (Poole, 1996, p. 1).

The study failed to use free recall questions. For example, rather than asking, "Do you use any memory-recovery techniques, and if so, what are they?" Poole et al. used a potentially suggestive technique of the type the authors criticize therapists for using. Participants were first told that other "therapists use special techniques to help clients remember childhood sexual abuse" (p. 430) and then were provided a list of techniques to check. Olio suggested that in light of current theory on memory, recall, and the impact that questioning may exert on responses, the use of these techniques may have unintentionally shaped the findings to confirm the beliefs of FMS proponents.

**2. Do the measures have face validity?**   According to Olio, the Poole et al. study's conclusions are based on the unproven assumption that clinicians with certain (self-reported) beliefs practice differently from clinicians with other beliefs, and that these differences in practice create greater risk for the production of illusory memories. She questioned this assumption that beliefs are reliable predictors of behaviors. The complex chain of assumptions (i.e., reported belief to actual belief to behavior to consequences for patients) may be questionable at best. For example, Polusny and Follette (1996) found that despite therapists' beliefs about the prevalence of repressed memories, the majority of therapists holding these beliefs reported that they had not seen any cases of adult clients who entered therapy with no memory of CSA and subsequently recalled abuse during therapy.

Poole et al., according to Olio, apparently drew inferences about implanting or creating illusory memories of childhood abuse in clients who report no memories of childhood abuse at the beginning of psychotherapy and who do not in fact have an actual history of childhood abuse. Unfortunately, key questions in the survey do not inquire specifically about the use of various therapy techniques with this particular population. The questions used were:

> Survey I: "Some therapists use special techniques to help clients remember childhood sexual abuse. Check any technique that you have used with abuse victims in the past 2 years."
>
> Survey II: "Check on the left ["tick" for the British survey] any technique that you have used in the past two years to help clients remember childhood sexual abuse." (p. 430.)

The question on Survey I specifically asks about techniques used with "abuse victims" and does not inquire how many (if any) of these were clients who denied abuse, but whom the clinician suspected might have abuse histories. Similarly, the inquiry regarding techniques used to "help clients remember childhood abuse" in Survey II does not differentiate between techniques used with clients who report a history of abuse (both those with continuous or accessible memory and those who recovered memories of abuse prior to psychotherapy) and techniques used with clients who deny such a history.

Olio suggested that other inconsistencies between the actual survey questions used and the reported conclusions may be important. For example, Poole et al. claimed that "25% . . . believe that recovering memories is an important part of therapy" (p. 434), whereas the actual survey question asked respondents to rate "how important is it that a *client who was sexually abused acknowledges or remembers* the abuse in order for the therapy to be effective" (p. 430; emphasis added). Poole et al. suggested that their survey "indicates that . . . some clinicians believe they can identify clients who were sexually abused as children even when those clients deny abuse histories" (p. 434). However, the survey question (in Survey II) asked about instances in which the client did not explicitly report any abuse, not about instances in which the client denies abuse histories. Finally, Poole et al.'s claim that 25% "think they can identify clients with hidden memories during the initial session" (p. 434) is based on questions that asked (retrospectively) "of adult female clients whom you *suspected* were sexually abused as children what percentage initially denied any memory of childhood abuse" (p. 430; Survey I; emphasis added) and asked if participants "had ever *suspected* that a client had been abused although the client did not explicitly report any abuse" (p. 430, Survey II; emphasis added). It seems that a clinician's acknowledgment that he or she sometimes had suspected an abuse history significantly differs from a belief that he or she could identify those with hidden abuse memories (see subsequent section "Not Suspecting Child Abuse").

**3. Are the techniques risky?**   Poole et al.'s characterization of potentially risky behaviors practiced by 25% of clinicians relied on a "constellation" of three self-report items (discussed previously): two items relating to beliefs and one to practice. Olio observed, however, that there are no validation studies for this constellation of reported beliefs and practice, and therefore there is no way to determine what is actually being measured by these items, no way to determine what outcome(s) result from this constellation, and no way to know how the results might differ from other psychotherapy practices. According to Olio, the study apparently assumed that some techniques are risky per se, rather than recognizing that virtually all psychotherapy techniques have the potential for damage, depending on the manner, context, and timing in which they are used.

Olio noted that Poole et al. did not offer any criteria or research to define what might constitute a risky frequency of use for the listed techniques. Despite expressing concerns regarding approaches to therapy "that combine several techniques . . . in a prolonged search for suspected hidden memories" (Lindsay, 1995a, 281–282) in the Poole et al. data, the criteria for questionable practice are satisfied with the single use of any two techniques (even on a single occasion) during the last 2 years. Therefore, a therapist who allows one client to keep a journal and bring in family photos as a way of decreasing the anxiety and pain of the remembering process would be counted among those engaging in coercive, risky practices that can create false memories and would be classified as a potentially dangerous recovered memory therapist.

Olio argued that in essence Poole et al. have created an unvalidated checklist (for risky practices), not dissimilar to the unvalidated checklists of symptoms that Lindsay and Read (1994), among others, correctly criticized some clinicians for using to identify histories of childhood abuse. Responding to Olio's critique, Lindsay (1995b) conceded that he did "agree that there are far too little data to make firm statements about the prevalence of 'risky' memory work, and that even the above 3 criteria are somewhat lax" (p. 1).[9]

**4. Do Poole et al. incorrectly infer causality?**    Olio noted that Poole et al. claimed, "our survey . . . indicates these interventions can have serious implications for clients (e.g., lead some clients to terminate relations with their fathers)" (p. 434). This conclusion is based on responses to the question, "Of the adult female clients who initially denied any memory of sexual abuse, what percentage came to remember childhood sexual abuse during the course of therapy?" (p. 431). Poole et al. reported that in "Survey I, we asked respondents to report the percentage of clients, among those who through therapy remembered abuse, who confronted their abuser . . . and who cut off relations with the abuser" (p. 432).

Thus, all abuse reported by therapists as having been recalled during the course of therapy (p. 431) was claimed by the authors to represent cases of abuse remembered "through" therapy (p. 432). Olio observed that this is a form of the logical fallacy *post*

---

[9]The three criteria were based on self-report items in the Poole et al. (1995) survey. These survey items attempted to assess belief about the importance of recovering memories in therapy, the forming of suspicion under certain circumstances that a client was sexually abused as a child, and the use of various techniques in therapy. The wording and meaning of these questions was discussed in the sections "Did the Survey Construction Lead to Confounded Results?, " "Do the Measures Have Face Validity?," and "Are the Techniques Risky?"

*hoc, ergo propter hoc* ("after this, therefore on account of this").
Poole et al. committed this fallacy, according to Olio, with their
claim that because therapists reported having used certain techniques and reported that some clients recovered memories during this time span, the techniques must have caused the
memories. Further, Poole et al. used this logic to claim that the
use of those particular techniques had serious implications; that
is, it was the use of those techniques that led clients to terminate
relations with their fathers. In both instances, presumed correlation is confused with causation.

Olio noted that such assumed correlations may be misleading.
She used the example of a hypothetical survey in which respondents were asked if their patients got older during the course of
therapy. Even if 100% of the therapists reported that their clients
became older during therapy, it does not provide evidence that the
aging process was attributable to or even differentially associated
with therapy. Olio emphasized the importance of placing such data
within a $2 \times 2$ (whether patients recovered memories by whether the
therapist used specified interventions) or similar model, and of
assessing whether randomization and other procedures were adequately considered. Such a statistical model would assess the relationships among (a) patients recovering memories during therapy
as reported by therapists using specified interventions, (b) patients
not recovering memories during therapy as reported by therapists
using specified interventions, (c) patients recovering memories during therapy as reported by therapists not using specified interventions, and (d) patients not recovering memories during therapy as
reported by therapists not using specified interventions.

## Redefining Malpractice and the Standard of Care

FMSF and its proponents have published claims not only about
scientific findings, but also about the nature of malpractice and the
standard of care. Pending systematic surveys and other research
addressing the issue, it is impossible to know the degree to which
such published statements by a prominent organization or professionals may have a chilling effect upon the professional services

provided by therapists who disagree with these claims. What impact will clinicians' knowledge that prominent expert witnesses may testify that certain services constitute malpractice have on the availability of those kinds of services? As with claims of scientific findings, it is important to respond with neither reflexive acceptance or rejection, but rather careful questioning.

## Should Therapists Be Required to Seek External Validation?

One set of claims asserts that without seeking external validation through family members or others, the therapist violates the legal standard of care by providing treatment when recovered memories of abuse are at issue. FMSF has highlighted in its publications such statements about the standard of care by its Scientific and Professional Advisory Board members as "To treat for repressed memories without any effort at external validation is malpractice pure and simple" (McHugh, 1993b, p. 1; for an alternate view, see American Psychological Association Task Force, 1996, p. 74). FMSF (1992a) has also published a statement, adapted from Scientific and Professional Advisory Board members, of the 13 steps a therapist needs to take in regard to gathering external validating information when adult patients allege childhood sex abuse. The therapist of a person who has sought treatment for recovered memories of incest not only must contact the parents and seek other sources of validation, but also must provide comprehensive information about the patient to clinicians working on behalf of the parents; to refuse to provide such information raises the question of an absence of "good faith" (McHugh, 1993a, p. 3).

Questions that might be useful in evaluating this claim include: Do FMSF proponents imply that therapists can accept without external validation reports based on memories that have been continuously accessible rather than recovered; that is, is there no legal mandate to seek external validation when an adult's memories of child sex abuse have been continuous? If so, what research findings support this distinction? Do FMSF proponents imply that therapists are legally required to seek external validation only when a patient reports child sex abuse; that is, is there no legal mandate to seek external validation for all patient reports of violence, abuse, crimes, or other such interactions? If so, what research findings support this distinction?

## Behavioral and Pharmacological Therapies and Directing Feelings

Recent claims in this area address the kinds and content of therapy. Loftus (1995b), in *The Skeptical Inquirer*, for example, supported the development, evaluation, and use of "behavioral and pharmacological therapies that minimize the possibility of false memories and false diagnoses" and urged therapists to avoid "dwelling on the misery of childhood" (p. 28). Maintaining that patients are best served when therapists adhere to the following principles, Loftus wrote:

> Borrowing from John Gottman's (1994) excellent advice on how to make your marriage succeed, patients might be reminded that negative events in their lives do not completely cancel out all the positives (p. 182). Encourage the patient to think about the positive aspects of life—even to look through picture albums from vacations and birthdays. Think of patients as the architects of their thoughts, and guide them to build a few happy rooms. The glass that's half empty is also half full. . . . Campbell (1994) offers similar advice. Therapists, he believes, should encourage their clients to recall some positive things about their families. A competent therapist will help others support and assist the client, and help the client direct feelings of gratitude toward those significant others. (Loftus, 1995b, p. 28)

Among the questions useful in carefully evaluating these claims are:

1. Is there research demonstrating that behavioral and pharmacological therapies produce fewer false memories and false diagnoses than other forms of therapy?

2. What evidence supports the claim that to be competent, a therapist must render help to third parties in their efforts to support and assist a therapy client?

3. What evidence supports the claim that to be competent, a therapist must help clients to direct feelings of gratitude to third parties?

## Not Suspecting Child Abuse

Claims that such factors as clothing, attractive appearance, smiling behavior, and chatting provide a reliable basis for concluding that a person has never engaged in child abuse stand in contrast to claims that presenting symptoms must never lead anyone to suspect that a person may have been sexually abused. For example, Kihlstrom (1995b; see also Olio, 1995c) wrote that "it is not permissible to infer, or frankly even to suspect, a history of abuse in people who present symptoms of abuse." He similarly asserted that "You can never, never, never, never, never, infer a history of sexual abuse from the patient's presenting symptoms. Nevernevernevernevernevernevernevernevernevernevernevernevernevernevernevernevernevernevernevernevernevernevernevernevernevernevernevernevernevernevernevernevernevernevernev-ernever." These claims taken together seem to suggest that although presenting "symptoms of abuse" never justify suspicion that a person was involved in child abuse, presenting factors such as clothing and appearance can reliably demonstrate that a person was not involved in child abuse.

In evaluating the effects of prohibiting suspicion of child abuse based on presenting symptoms, one question may be useful to ask: How will it affect mandated reporting of suspected child abuse? Reviews of state laws suggest that almost 50% use a form of the verb "suspect" (e.g., "suspect that a child has been abused") in legislation requiring therapists to report suspected child abuse (Kalichman, 1993). Other states use similar concepts but different wording.

A separate question for evaluating this prohibition is, to what degree, if at all, might therapists refrain from pursuing diagnostic leads based on presenting symptoms because of the threat of malpractice suits? Decisions to report suspected child abuse may be covered by at least a qualified immunity, but assessment and treatment actions generally are not. Without research data concerning the potential influence of this prohibition, it is impossible to know if or how it will affect clinicians' responses to presenting symptoms.

A third question useful for assessing this claim is, to what degree do various arrays of presenting symptoms lead at least some therapists to suspect child abuse as one possible event that may be associated with the symptoms and warrant consideration in the assessment process? Approaches to research gathering relevant information to address this third question might take a variety of forms, such as presenting symptom arrays to clinicians and asking if they might lead to a suspicion of abuse. For example, a cluster of presenting symptoms for a young girl might include panic and avoidant behavior in the presence of her father; nightmares occurring every few hours that, according to the patient, involve a shadowy figure grabbing at her genitals; and refusal to allow a physical examination although she had previously allowed them during medical office visits. Clinicians might also be asked if the notion that chart notes or other evidence revealing that such presenting symptoms led them to suspect child abuse as a diagnostic possibility might subject them to a malpractice suit affected their responses to these symptoms.

## Unacceptable Books and Ideas

In some instances, published works condemned by FMSF proponents become targets of legal action. Lawsuits in two California cities blamed a book for leading people to believe false memories of childhood sex abuse ("Author Target of False-Memories Lawsuit," 1994, p. B3; Butler, 1994; Pope, 1995). A licensing complaint was filed against a therapist asserting "that an article she had written . . . for a journal titled *Medical Aspects of Human Sexuality* could suggest false incest diagnoses" (Butler, 1995, p. 28).

Therapists may themselves face formal complaints for using books containing unacceptable ideas. The *Philadelphia Inquirer*, for example, quoted a past president [Paul Fink] of the American Psychiatric Association's statement about therapists giving *The Courage To Heal: A Guide for Women Survivors of Child Sexual Abuse* (1988/1994) and similar books to their patients: "There's a name for this—bibliotherapy. . . . To give a book that espouses a narrow thesis of mental functioning is malpractice. . . ." (Sifford, 1992, p. D-6).

Careful evaluation of such legal restrictions on the flow of ideas may include consideration of such questions as:

1. At what point does a thesis of mental functioning become defined as sufficiently narrow that any book espousing it must be banned from therapy? For example, B. F. Skinner relegated so-called mental functioning to an unobservable epiphenomenon, irrelevant as a variable in the scientific study of human behavior.

Would this thesis of mental functioning be considered sufficiently narrow that a behavior therapist giving one of Skinner's books to a client would be considered malpractice?

2. Is it essential to the malpractice claim that the harmful ideas appear in the form of a published book? For example, if instead of giving the book to a patient so that the patient can study and form an opinion about the thesis him- or herself, the therapist were to say to a patient, "There is a book by Bass and Davis that espouses this view of mental functioning" or otherwise discuss the ideas within the book, is that, too, malpractice?

3. If it is malpractice for therapists to give such books to their patients, would it also constitute malpractice for supervisors to give such books to their therapy trainees, hospitals and clinics to make such books available in their libraries, professionals leading workshops to use them as texts, or professors to assign them to their students?

4. How, if at all, does the prospect of encountering expert testimony that giving a particular sort of book to a patient is per se malpractice influence the behavior of therapists and the range of services, ideas, and choices available to those in need?

## Checklists for Assessing Incompetence and Other Forms of Malpractice

Some FMSF proponents have created and endorsed checklists by which patients can supposedly determine whether a therapist is incompetent, is causing harm, or is engaging in other forms of malpractice. For example, an FMSF Scientific and Professional Advisory Board member noted that "whether or not a therapist has a doctoral degree, is irrelevant to his psychotherapeutic competence" (Campbell, 1994, p. 49) and published a 40-item checklist by which patients can supposedly assess a therapist's competence (p. 251). With minor revision, this instrument has been published by others (e.g., Wakefield & Underwager, 1994). The number of "yes" responses supposedly indicates the likelihood that the therapist is "incompetent" and that the therapist is causing "much more harm than good." The book, however, provides no references to published research establishing the validity, reliability, sensitivity, or specificity of this instrument. If there is a scientific basis for this instrument, it would be useful for the FMSF Scientific and Professional Advisory Board members endorsing it to provide those research data so that these claims can be carefully evaluated.

## Careful Examination—The Scientific Process

Questioning scientific claims may be difficult if a prestigious group portrays them as the only legitimate scientific view, sufficiently established as to preclude serious consideration of any alternative views. For example, a prominent regional psychological association invited an array of scientists to discuss the debate about memory and abuse from a scientific perspective. Suggestions that a more balanced program might be achieved by supplementing the members of the FMSF Scientific and Professional Advisory Board who had been invited as speakers with scientists who might present alternatives to the FMSF view were rejected by FMSF as unscientific. The *FMSF Newsletter* set forth the rationale for the rejection:

> A memory researcher told us that research academics "don't even know what this memory debate is about. They see the evidence and to them the science of memory is obvious." He is right. The "science" of the "memory" is established. . . . How could a scientific program about memory be "balanced?" The notion makes no more sense than trying to balance a program in astronomy by including astrologers. ("A Social Political Movement," 1996)

As noted previously in this volume, the factors that can discourage careful questioning of scientific claims or consideration of alternate views are many. Scientists must be aware of these factors and must carefully and responsibly question claims and consider other explanatory models, regardless of the prestige of those who might assert that a particular thesis about memory and abuse is beyond question.

Responsible scientific questioning of specific claims bears at least one similarity to conducting well-designed experimental research. Experimental research must attend not only to variables of primary interest, but also to potentially confounding factors. Similarly, careful examination of reported scientific findings and principles must attend not only to central claims, but also to potentially confounding factors that may influence the degree to which people are inclined, willing, or free to question or reject certain claims. This section examines such potentially confounding factors and their implications.

## Picketing

Picketing therapists is a highly visible tactic. If therapists who disagree with certain claims, voice their disagreement, and behave in ways that are inconsistent with those claims fear that their patients may be forced to cross a picket line in order to obtain their services, it may affect the degree to which people feel free to carefully question and rationally consider the claims.

As early as 1992, in an *FMSF Newsletter* article titled "What Can Families Do?" the tactic of picketing was discussed (FMSF, 1992c, p. 4). FMSF members picketing therapists has emerged as a topic at professional conferences and in the literature of this area, sometimes including discussion of the experience of a therapist targeted for picketing (e.g., Brown, 1995a; Calof, 1996; see also Butler, 1995). Among questions that might be useful in evaluating the potential consequences and implications of this tactic are the following:

1. What is the impact on patients who are forced to cross a picket line to obtain treatment from a provider of a particular form of legal health care service? Will patients choose to cross picket lines, forego treatment altogether, or pursue treatment from someone acceptable to FMS proponents who establish picket lines?

2. Some patients or potential patients may perceive and value a right of privacy, and believe it important that no one else know that they seek mental health services. Those wishing to seek treatment for concerns such as sexual abuse from family members, domestic violence, or torture may fear that, should the fact that they are seeking professional help become known, their own lives or the lives of their families might be endangered or that

other negative consequences might occur (see, e.g., Calof, 1996; J. Freyd, 1996; Herman, 1992; Koss et al., 1994; Pope & Garcia-Peltoniemi, 1991; Salter, 1995). How does forcing patients to cross picket lines affect such privacy concerns?

3. How do patients (or therapists) evaluate or anticipate what may happen to them should they cross through the picket line (e.g., do they believe it possible or likely that they will be followed, their license plate number taken down, their picture taken, and so on)? How do clients form opinions about what the pickets, FMSF, or others may view as justifiable steps to take when targeted services continue despite picketing? Butler (1995) quoted the FMSF executive director: " 'If somebody came into your house and shot your child, it would probably be justifiable homicide if you did something, and that's how these parents feel,' says Freyd. 'When you get between parents and children, you can expect things to happen' " (p. 75).

## Describing and Diagnosing Individuals Who Disagree

Diagnosing and otherwise categorizing those who disagree may influence the degree to which people are inclined, willing, and free to question scientific claims. When such diagnoses and categorizations are set forth, it is important to examine the scientific evidence on which they rest, their social or policy consequences, and their potential effects on scientific deliberations. Two founding members[10] of the FSMS Scientific and Professional Advisory Board published an article examining why UCLA professor Roland Summit and others persist in believing in child abuse phenomena that, according to some claims, are unscientific and absurd. They concluded that the cause of such beliefs among professionals lay not in the evidence for the hypotheses, nor in social or contextual variables, nor in differing perspectives, but rather in the relational dysfunctions or psychopathology of those who believe these ideas. Underwager and Wakefield (1991) wrote, "The answer to the question why do some professionals

---

[10]Underwager is no longer listed as a member of this board.

believe and not others is in the internal variables of the personalities of the believers. It ranges from factors that may make a person difficult to relate to but remaining functional to serious psychopathology" (p. 190).

**Paranoid.** Those disagreeing may be characterized more specifically as manifesting paranoid beliefs or responses. FMSF Scientific and Professional Advisory Board member Richard Ofshe wrote, "These responses signal the collective paranoia of a social movement turning inward" (Ofshe & Watters, 1993, p. 16). Another FMSF Scientific and Professional Advisory Board member explained, in an American Psychological Association divisional presidential address, that the belief of "abuse-believers" frequently "takes on a paranoid cast. . . ." (Spence, 1993, p. 7; see also Wakefield & Underwager, 1994, pp. 41–43).

**Cult and Sect.** *The Washington Post* quoted the FMSF executive director as characterizing those who work to open up the topic of sex abuse to public awareness as cultlike. " 'I can understand,' says Freyd, 'people who are trying to open up the area of sexual abuse being infuriated by us. They feel we aren't helping their work. But they are a little like a cult.' " (Sherrill, 1995, p. F1). Pendergrast (1995) recommended different terminology: "Some have called the Survivor Movement not only a religion, but a cult. . . . It is all too easy to label any fervent group a 'cult,' with all its negative connotations. I prefer the word 'sect' " (p. 478). This characterization addresses the motivation of certain therapists who disagree:

> Most of the therapists appear to be True Believers on a mission. That fits Hassan's general observations: "They believe that what they are doing is truly beneficial to you. However, they want something more valuable than your money. They want your mind! Of course, they'll take your money, too, eventually." Similarly, trauma therapy guarantees a protracted period of recovery and, hence, a steady income. (Pendergrast, 1995, p. 479)

**True Believers.** One of the most commonly used labels to describe individuals who disagree with FMSF is True Believer. Loftus used the concept of True Believer to support her claim that resistance to her work is based not on evidence, reason, and good faith, but rather on prejudice and fear (e.g., "I know the prejudices and fears that lie behind the resistance to my life's work" [Loftus & Ketcham, 1994, p. 4]). She split the profession into two groups. Identifying herself as a skeptic, she and her colleague wrote,

> On one side are the "True Believers," who insist that the mind is capable of repressing memories and who accept without reservation or question the authenticity of recovered memories. On the other side are the "Skeptics," who argue that the notion of repression is purely hypothetical and essentially untestable, based as it is on unsubstantiated speculation and anecdotes that are impossible to confirm or deny. (Loftus & Ketcham, 1994, p. 31)

Loftus makes clear her source by quoting from Hoffer's (1989) well-known text, *The True Believer*. If the skeptic demands proof, how does the True Believer decide what to believe in? Hoffer observed that True Believers shut themselves off from facts, ignoring a doctrine's validity while valuing its ability to insulate them from reality (p. 80). Hoffer described the True Believer's passionate hatred and fanaticism, noting "the acrid secretion of the frustrated mind, though composed chiefly of fear and ill will, acts yet as a marvelous slime to cement the embittered and disaffected into one compact whole" (p. 124). Among the most prominent professionals who are True Believers, according to the false memory literature, are psychologists Judith Alpert, Laura Brown, and Christine Courtois, three members of the APA Working Group on recovered memories. Pendergrast (1995) wrote, "[T]he American Psychological Association has created a six-person committee to study the repressed-memory issue. Three of the members are experimental researchers who are skeptical of massive repression, including Elizabeth Loftus. The other three are True Believer therapists. . . ." (pp. 503–504; see also Wakefield & Underwager, 1994, p. 349). The term *True Believers* characterizing those who disagree now appears in the peer-reviewed scientific literature, for example, an article by a member of the FMSF Scientific and Professional Advisory Board (Crews, 1996, p. 66).

**Use of Holocaust Imagery.**   Those who disagree with FMSF have also been compared to fascists. In her book, *Diagnosis for Disaster: The Devastating Truth About False Memory Syndrome*, Wassil-Grimm (1995, p. 91), for example, uses the imagery of the Holocaust, explicitly referring to Hitler and the Jews: "Hitler had the Jews; McCarthy had the communists; radical feminists have perpetrators" (p. 91). The *Oregonian* quoted the FMSF executive director as describing the behavior of professor Jennifer Freyd as "Gestapolike" (Mitchell, 1993, p. L6), a term she had previously used in a journal article (Doe,[11] 1991, p. 155) later reprinted as a book chapter (Doe, 1994, p. 29). Another use of imagery related to the Holocaust, this time to compare an FMSF Scientific and Professional Advisory Board member to those who risked their lives to save Jews from the Nazis, appeared in the *Boston Globe*: " 'I feel like Oskar Schindler,' Loftus muses, referring to the German financier who rescued doomed Jews from the Nazis. 'There is this desperate drive to work as fast as I can' " (Kahn, 1994, p. 80).

It is important to examine the use of imagery related to the Holocaust to compare explicitly or implicitly one who disagrees to Hitler, the Gestapo, and Nazis or to portray an FMSF proponent as engaged in a desperate rescue. Among questions to be addressed in careful examination of this use are the following: Do such statements reflect on the motivation, character, and decency of those who disagree with FMSF claims? Do such statements promote a climate of hate and hostility toward those who fail to accept FMSF claims? Do such statements have a chilling effect on some who otherwise might voice questions about FMSF claims? How might such statements affect the scientific and popular (e.g., media) evaluation of FMSF claims about the difficult and complex issues of remembering child sex abuse?

## Obtaining and Revealing Disclosures to Therapists

According to the Portland *Oregonian*, FMSF director Pamela Freyd recommended tactics to learn about someone else's therapy:

---

[11]In late February 1992, when she wrote that she was "going to serve as Executive Director of the FMS Foundation," Pamela Freyd confirmed in the *FMS Newsletter* that "You already know me as Jane Doe" (p. 1).

"Follow your child to the office, hire a private detective, pry the information from other relatives your child may talk to, pose as a patient yourself" (Mitchell, 1993, p. L1; see also FMSF, 1992c; "What Can Families Do?" p. 4; Loftus, 1993, pp. 529–530). Finding out and revealing what people have said to their therapists has placed communications to therapists about alleged child abuse in a new context. The *Myth of Repressed Memories* (Loftus & Ketcham, 1994) reprinted quotes from a *Playboy* article (Nathan, 1992) that were apparently verbatim statements by women who were meeting with therapists as part of a 4-day "retreat for survivors of sexual abuse, physical abuse, emotional abuse and neglect" (p. 202). The *Playboy* article's author was an investigative journalist who had attended the retreat for survivors and therapists. Among the questions that may be useful in evaluating the potential impact of such efforts to reveal disclosures about alleged abuse to therapists are the following:

1. Does knowing about such published accounts affect the decisions of those who view themselves as having experienced sexual abuse, physical abuse, emotional abuse, and neglect about whether to seek services in group settings?

2. Do the accounts of people's disclosures to therapists accord them basic respect and dignity? For example, *The Myth of Repressed Memory* used such characterizations as the following to describe women talking with therapists about abuse: "Soon it was time to plunge into the gory details. A veritable competition . . . began as one woman after another related her grisly stories, progressively upping the ante of horror" (p. 203). FMSF has helped popularize what appears to be ridicule of those who claim to be abuse survivors through publication of such articles as "Whining About Abuse is an Epidemic" (Nethaway, 1993, p. 6). Research could be useful in exploring whether the manner in which disclosures to therapists about alleged abuse are characterized in books, newsletters, and other works by FMSF proponents has any influence on the willingness of those who view themselves (accurately or inaccurately) as survivors of various forms of abuse to seek professional help.

3. Do those who make such disclosures to therapists have concerns about the uses to which their statements may be put? Would they fear that their statements might be used in legal

actions to deprive them of their civil rights, that is, that their statements would be construed as evidence of FMS, rendering them unable to make their own decisions? In "Legal Aspects of False Memory Syndrome," for example, FMSF (1992b) informed parents that they "may take the legal position that the accusing child is incompetent and seek guardianship proceedings" (p. 3).

4. Do these data-gathering activities and publications impose specific informed consent duties on therapists? Do patients have a right to know that other patients, clerical or support staff, shelter volunteers, or others present may actually be detectives, reporters, and so on, and that what they say in the presence of these other people may be published or put to use in other ways? Are patients who believe that they are talking to therapists or other helpers aware that in certain circumstances they may find their words quoted, even with a pseudonym. Pseudonyms may not prevent recognition of a specific individual (see, e.g., Pope, 1995). Is it possible that the information gathered may be used in a way patients would not have chosen or given consent for? If informed consent and informed refusal are fundamental rights of those seeking health care services, and if the consent process involves telling potential patients about factors that might reasonably affect their decision to consent to or refuse treatment (Caudill & Pope, 1995; Pope & Vasquez, 1991), it is difficult to imagine any legitimate justification for withholding information about such possibilities from those who will be most affected. This is an important question of professional responsibility and public policy, and deserves careful and comprehensive discussion.

# Conclusion

Claims about a new diagnostic category (FMS) reaching epidemic proportions, the ease with which extensive autobiographical memories about trauma can be implanted, and the large number of therapists engaging in behaviors likely to cause false memories of trauma in their patients deserve careful consideration.

It is important to examine carefully the evidence and logic of the claims and to ask "What if these claims are valid?" The profound implications for individual lives, public policy, the standard of care, clinical work, and education and training have been compellingly set forth in books by Crews (1995), Dawes (1994), Goldstein and Farmer (1993, 1994), Loftus and Ketcham (1994), Ofshe and Watters (1994), Underwager and Wakefield (1994), and Wassil-Grimm (1995).

An open, fair, and independent analysis must also allow for the possibility that the evidence and logic do not convincingly establish the validity of some, or perhaps any, such claims. Therapists and expert witnesses must be prepared to examine the profound implications for individual lives, public policy, the standard of care, clinical work, and education and training if these widely accepted and institutionalized claims are invalid. What if, for example, tens of thousands of individuals have been wrongly diagnosed with a label lacking adequate scientific validation?

It is equally important to examine the process by which these claims are evaluated and institutionalized, including tactics used to promote them. Therapists and expert witnesses must be as attentive to factors that, however unintentionally, may confound the process of consideration and discussion as they are to factors that may confound an individual experiment. If disagreement with certain claims is determined to reflect impaired functioning or serious psychopathology, the scientific process may be subverted. If those who question, doubt, or disagree are authoritatively characterized by professionals as hate-filled True Believers, paranoid cultists, or Hitler-like zealots, the process of free and independent analysis of FMSF claims may be affected. If patients seeking currently legal health care services from those who question or disagree with FMSF are forced to cross picket lines to obtain those services, if the privacy of their therapy is invaded, or if they are diagnosed without their participation as suffering from a false memory syndrome, then their freedom of choice may be affected.

Claims grounded most firmly in the scientific tradition are those emerging from hypotheses that are falsifiable. Therapists and expert witnesses bear an essential responsibility to examine primary data, research methodology, assumptions, and inferences. Science, therapy, and forensic practice work best when claims and hypotheses can be continually questioned. That which tends to disallow doubt and discredit anyone who disagrees is unlikely to promote clinical and forensic practices based on scientific principles. Each scientific claim should prevail or fall on its research validation and logic.

The kind of questions suggested in this chapter and, more important, the constant process of questioning can be helpful, if not essential, for therapists and expert witnesses. They help therapists and expert witnesses to encounter the full range of research, therapy, assumptions, and approaches with an active inquisitiveness and useful skepticism rather than reflexive acceptance or rejection. Such questioning is part of the essential preparation for practice (and part of practice itself) when reports of delayed memories of abuse are at issue, but sound preparation can also enable us to engage in this questioning more effectively. It is to the topic of preparation for safe and competent practice that we turn in chapter 4.

# 4

# Practicing Safely and Competently

It is relatively simple for a mental health professional to read books about treating adult survivors, to take workshops about using particular techniques, to seek specialized supervision, or to engage in other usual activities that mental health professionals pursue in order to become prepared to work in a given field of endeavor. But none of these activities is a guarantee of safe and competent practice. The client's experience of intrusive seeming recall of apparent abuse, as well as of whatever factors lead to such seeming recall, may represent a crisis. Therapists and expert witnesses must prepare themselves to practice safely and competently when they encounter reports of such recall. The conflicts described in chapter 1 underscore the need for extensive preparation. This chapter highlights a few major aspects of the continuing process of preparing for safe and competent practice, and focuses on the therapist's self-awareness regarding those cognitive, affective, and contextual factors that might undermine competent practice.

## Avoiding Cognitive Distortions

One aspect of preparing for safe and competent practice is developing a heightened awareness of one's own cognitive style, processes, and routines as they affect practice in this area. Our personal experience as clinicians and expert witnesses sometimes leads us to learn lessons that are—or at least seem—absolutely accurate for our own experience, but are utterly unsupported by the available scientific data. Such experience may represent a skewed, incomplete, or particularized version of reality. It may— or may not—be useful and accurate within carefully delimited boundaries, but may not be generalized past those limits.

Work in this area involves awareness not only of theory and research in the relevant areas, but also of how the individual's background and characteristics, and thoughts and feelings, influence the work. Unfortunately, research and training have not tended to adequately address the background experience and emotional reactions of the clinicians responding to reports of delayed memories of abuse.

## Inadequacies of Training and Experience

One very common source of cognitive distortions regarding childhood sexual abuse is the lack of training and experiences that most clinicians bring to this work. This is true as regards both formal training and experiential exposure to the topic. A national survey of clinicians concluded that from "any standpoint, these participants found that graduate training related to childhood and adult abuse was woefully lacking" (Pope & Feldman-Summers, 1992, p. 357). Participants rated their graduate training in every area of abuse but one (nonsexual violence against adults is the exception) as "very poor."

The therapist's personal history of abuse is rarely mentioned in graduate training programs, supervision, research, or articles in scientific and professional journals. Yet, as Table 4-1 illustrates, about a third of the male psychologists and over two thirds of the female psychologists in a national survey reported having experienced some form of abuse (either physical or sexual or both) during childhood, adolescence, or adulthood. Even factoring in the possibility that therapists with such a history overresponded to the survey instrument and other cautions and qualifications discussed in the research report, the numbers are potentially quite striking. Put another way, significant proportions of psychologists report having no adequate training in this area, although many may have lived through an experience of abuse, which, if overgeneralized and sub-

## Table 4-1

*Percent of Male and Female Participants Reporting Abuse*

| Type of Abuse | Men | Women |
|---|---|---|
| *Abuse During Childhood or Adolescence* | | |
| Sexual abuse by relative | 5.84 | 21.05 |
| Sexual abuse by teacher | 0.73 | 1.96 |
| Sexual abuse by physician | 0.0 | 1.96 |
| Sexual abuse by therapist | 0.0 | 0.0 |
| Sexual abuse by nonrelative (other than those previously listed) | 9.49 | 16.34 |
| Nonsexual physical abuse | 13.14 | 9.15 |
| At least one of the above | 26.28 | 39.22 |
| *Abuse During Adulthood* | | |
| Sexual harassment | 1.46 | 37.91 |
| Attempted rape | 0.73 | 13.07 |
| Acquaintance rape | 0.0 | 6.54 |
| Stranger rape | 0.73 | 1.31 |
| Nonsexual physical abuse by a spouse or partner | 6.57 | 12.42 |
| Nonsexual physical abuse by an acquaintance | 0.0 | 2.61 |
| Nonsexual physical abuse by a stranger | 4.38 | 7.19 |
| Sexual involvement with a therapist | 2.19 | 4.58 |
| Sexual involvement with a physician | 0.0 | 1.96 |
| At least one of the above | 13.87 | 56.86 |

*Note*: From Pope and Feldman-Summers, *Professional Psychology: Research and Practice*, 23, p. 355. © 1992 by the American Psychological Association. Used with permission.

stituted for formal training, may lead to problems of cognitive distortion. These data are likely to hold true for other mental health professions. It is not just the lack of information and training that influences our understanding and response to claims of recovered memories, but also the tacit message and modeling when the topic of abuse goes unmentioned or is handled very poorly in training programs.

Even if therapists tend to rate their training in the area of abuse as inadequate, research suggests that most therapists will encounter at least one client who reports the delayed recovery of memories of childhood sexual abuse; such recall occurs either prior to entering treatment or during the course of psychotherapy. A recent national study of psychologists found that over two thirds of the participants reported assessing or treating one or more clients who had recovered such memories (Pope & Tabachnick, 1995). If training and personal experience have not adequately prepared the therapist for this possibility, the client is obviously at risk for services that are based on something other than expertise or even competence.

## Therapists' Personal Experiences of Delayed Recall as a Factor

One of the most intriguing factors that may be influencing attempts to explore and understand recovered memories are clinicians' own experiences of recovering memories of abuse. Research suggests that perhaps about 40% of therapists who report being abused also report a period when they could not recall some or all of the abuse (Feldman-Summers & Pope, 1994). These self-reports suggested that (a) not only sexual, but also nonsexual, abuse was forgotten for periods of time (consistent with Elliott and Briere's [1995] findings that delayed recall has been reported for all varieties of trauma); (b) being in therapy was the most frequently reported factor related to recall (see Table 4-2); and (c) reports of forgetting were unrelated to psychologists' gender or age, but were related to severity of the abuse (a finding generally consistent with those reported by Briere & Conte, 1993; Herman & Schatzow, 1987; and Loftus et al., 1994).

About half of those who reported recalling abuse that had been previously forgotten also reported some form of external corroboration that the abuse had occurred, as shown in Table 4-3. Statistically, psychologists who reported that therapy was a factor in their recalling the abuse were neither more nor less likely to report finding corroboration than were psychologists whose recall was triggered by factors exclusive of psychotherapy.

As clinicians, we are dedicated in each hour of psychotherapy to the well-being of the individuals with whom we are sitting. But our

## Table 4-2

*Events, Experiences, or Circumstances That Triggered Recovery of Memories of Abuse*

|  | Number | Percentage |
|---|---|---|
| A book, article, lecture, movie, or t.v. show reminded me | 8 | 25.0 |
| Someone who knew about the abuse reminded me | 6 | 18.8 |
| In therapy, the memory began to return | 18 | 56.2 |
| In a self-help group or peer group (i.e., not a therapy group), the memory began to return | 2 | 6.2 |
| Some other event seemed to trigger or elicit the memory | 9 | 28.1 |
| Nothing seemed related to my remembering the abuse | 3 | 9.4 |

*Note*: From Feldman-Summers and Pope, *Journal of Consulting and Clinical Psychology, 62*, p. 638. © 1994 by the American Psychological Association. Used with permission.

consultation rooms do not exist in isolation. We bring to our work the sometimes silent factors of personal, social, and political beliefs, pressures, and inhibitions. On the matter of recovered memories of childhood sexual abuse, the social and political context has sometimes had a chilling and, sometimes, an overstimulating, effect on many practitioners and their clients, and may exert powerful pulls towards premature closure, avoidance, minimization, or intrusive advocacy. It is the inescapable responsibility of all clinicians to maintain awareness of how such contextual factors affect them and their ability to render adequate services to those in need.

## Examples of Common Cognitive Distortions

Errors of judgment, of both omission and commission, are sufficiently frequent as regards reports of delayed memories of abuse

## Table 4-3

*Sources That Support, Corroborate, or Confirm the Memory of the Abuse*

|  | Number | Percentage |
| --- | --- | --- |
| The abuser(s) acknowledged some or all of the remembered abuse | 5 | 15.6 |
| Someone who knew about the abuse told me | 7 | 21.9 |
| Journals or diaries kept by the abuser(s) described or referred to the abuse | 0 | 0 |
| My own journals or diaries (that I had forgotten about) described the abuse | 2 | 6.2 |
| Someone else reported abuse by the same perpetrator | 5 | 15.6 |
| Medical records referred to or described the abuse | 2 | 6.2 |
| Court or other legal records referred to or described the abuse | 0 | 0 |
| No support, corroboration, or confirmation has been found | 16 | 50.0 |

*Note*: From Feldman-Summers and Pope, *Journal of Consulting and Clinical Psychology, 62*, p. 638. © 1994 by the American Psychological Association. Used with permission.

that it is possible to uncover and describe certain common themes in the cognitive errors made by therapists. Consider the following hypothetical claims that clinical and forensic practitioners might make on the basis of their own professional and personal experience:

- Within 5 minutes they know whether a new client has been sexually abused as a child.
- All children who have engaged in sex with adults have been willing in some way.
- They can tell by a person's body language whether the person has fully recovered from the effects of child sex abuse.
- They know on the basis of interview and observation when another person enters and leaves a hypnotic or quasi-hypnotic state.
- They can identify sexually abused children who are in denial by the strength of their unwillingness to acknowledge the abuse.

- They are certain on the basis of an interview that a father will never again engage in incest.
- Because a memory of abuse seems contradicted by certain facts, the memory was a fiction designed to cover up some more horrible form of abuse.
- Because the district attorney found insufficient evidence to prosecute an accusation, the allegation was false.
- A client's report about recovered memories of abuse must be true because the report and the situation fit those of several prior clients whose allegations were shown to be valid.
- A client has changed her story about recovering memories of abuse several times, and therefore no version of the story is valid.

Challenged about such conclusions, clinicians in case conferences or expert witnesses during cross-examination may attempt to draw upon their professional authority and refer to their "clinical wisdom." But a clinical approach that ignores the range of research seems to have little, if anything, to differentiate it from superstition. As Jerome Singer (1980) wrote,

> The practice of psychotherapy by psychologists, psychiatrists, social workers, psychiatric nurses, or other mental health workers is an outgrowth of basic knowledge in psychology, behavioral and social sciences more broadly and, to a somewhat lesser degree, the biological sciences. The ethical practice of psychotherapy must reflect the current status of knowledge in those fields. The practitioner who has not examined recent developments in the research literature or who has not kept abreast of evaluation studies of various forms of treatment may well be violating a central ethic of the profession. . . .
> I'm arguing that psychotherapy is best understood as an application of available scientific knowledge. Psychotherapists must share a value presumption that knowledge about human behavior is susceptible to systematic inquiry through a variety of scientific procedures and that modifications both of theory and practice must reflect the most recent findings of empirical research. (p. 372)

Conversely, what some might call a "science" that does not take sufficient account of clinical reality seems at best an incomplete and potentially misleading science–perhaps a false one or a pseudoscience. Beginning over a decade ago, psychologists Lynne Bravo Rosewater and Mary Anne Dutton demonstrated how a clinically incomplete actuarial procedure led to misdiagnosis of a particular vulnerable population—battered women. According to L. S. Brown (1994),

> [Rosewater and Dutton's] work has involved collecting data on large numbers of battered women and identifying common patterns of response on the testing. In effect, they have noted that the standard mainstream texts and computerized scoring systems for the MMPI do not take into account the possibility that the person taking the test is a woman who currently is, or recently has been, beaten by her spouse or partner. . . . As Rosewater first pointed out, without the context, specifically the identification of the presence of violence, battered women look like schizophrenics or borderline personalities on the MMPI. With the context of violence explicitly framing the interpretation of the test findings, however, it is possible to note that the sort of distress indicated on the testing is a reasonable response to events in the test-taker's life. That is to say, when a woman's partner is beating her, it makes sense that she is depressed, confused, scattered, and feeling overwhelmed. It is not necessarily the case that this state of response to life-threatening violence is either usual for the woman in question or a sign of psychopathology. (p. 187)

Each of the following examples demonstrates the possible presence of a cognitive distortion in the clinicians. Sound preparation for work in this area includes learning about cognitive maneuvers that tend to lead to distortions and continuing careful monitoring to search for such maneuvers in our practice. The following sections present a few representative samples of these maneuvers.

## Premature Cognitive Commitment

Some clinicians and expert witnesses may believe that virtually all clients of a particular type—such as those with anorexia nervosa or vaginismus—have experienced some form of childhood abuse. Others may believe that virtually no client of a particular type—such as a client who wishes to sue, who is angry, or whose parents seem loving or attractive—has actually experienced child sex abuse.

The risk is that such clinicians, upon seeing some indication of the type, will then instantly but incorrectly conclude that this client must (or must not) have a history of abuse. Any questioning virtually ends right there: The diagnosis is made. Psychologist Ellen Langer (1989) describes this process of "forming a mindset when we first encounter something and then clinging to it when we reencounter that same thing. Because such mindsets form before we do much reflection, we call them *premature cognitive commitments*" (p. 22; emphasis added).

## Confirmation Bias

In this scenario, the clinician may, for whatever reason, form an early opinion about whether the client has or lacks a history of abuse. That opinion then shapes subsequent questioning so that only confirming data are sought or acknowledged. As Evans (1989) noted,

> Confirmation bias is perhaps the best known and most widely accepted notion of inferential error to have come out of the literature on human reasoning. The claim . . . is that human beings have a fundamental tendency to seek information consistent with their current beliefs, theories or hypotheses and to avoid the collection of potentially falsifying evidence. (p. 41).

The clinician who believes that all reports of delayed memories of abuse are true may tend to look only for evidence that the alleged abuse actually occurred, that the alleged perpetrator is a "bad" person, or that the client is an honest and reliable person. The clinician who believes that actual memories of abuse are never unavailable for years only to return later, may tend to look only for evidence that the client who reports recovered memories is unstable, unreliable, highly suggestible, or "bad" or has been victimized by some person or group that implanted false memories.

## Hindsight Bias

Clinicians whose work is biased in such ways may gain confidence in their ability to identify true or false reports of abuse through retrospective memory processes. Consider, for example, a clinician in a case conference reviewing the records of a person newly admitted to the inpatient unit—a woman who had a documented history of incest when she was 5 years old (including a confession by her father, a sworn statement by her mother who had witnessed some of the acts, laboratory tests, and a criminal conviction). Because the clinician already knows that the woman had experienced incest, prior test and historical data may be interpreted retrospectively in light of this information, perhaps in a biased and unjustifiable manner (e.g., that prior psychological test results or symptom patterns clearly showed that she had experienced incest). Arkes, Saville, Wortmann, and Harkness (1981) conducted research indicating that if professionals were given a symptom pattern, various alternative diagnoses, and the supposedly correct diagnosis, the professionals tended to overestimate significantly the probability that they would have chosen the correct diagnosis had they only known the symptom patterns and the diagnostic alternatives. This phenomenon is known as *hindsight bias*:

> Those who know an event has occurred may claim that had they been asked to predict the event in advance, they would have been very likely to do so. In fact, people with hindsight knowledge do assign higher probability estimates to an event than those who must predict the event without the advantage of that knowledge. . . . (Arkes et al., 1981, p. 252)

A fascinating example of how an erroneous "known fact" can—through hindsight—influence interpretation of a broad array of other information is Freud's application of the principles of psychoanalysis to understanding the life of Leonardo da Vinci (Coles, 1973; see also Fischoff, 1982; Pope, 1994). The key to Freud's analysis was da Vinci's account of how, as an infant, he was touched on the lips by a vulture that swooped down out of the sky.

Freud's astonishing breadth of knowledge led him to recognize that, in Egyptian, the hieroglyph for "vulture" is the same as that for "mother." From this fundamental observation, Freud conducted an incisive and insightful psychoanalysis of da Vinci, about whose younger years there was virtually no other illuminating information. The analysis seemed to spring from and cohere through da Vinci's recollection of an event that seemed to represent themes concerning an intimate relationship with his mother.

It was only later discovered that the translation Freud had been using contained an error. The Italian word for "kite" had been mistakenly translated into the German word for "vulture"; it was a kite, rather than a vulture, that had caressed da Vinci's lips as he lay in his cradle.

## Relying on Representativeness

Clinicians may try to avoid the essential responsibility of evaluating each report of recovered memory carefully and fairly on an individual basis by relying on their view of what is representative, sometimes using the most unsupported stereotypes. Tversky and Kahneman (1982) described this process that tends to lead to serious errors:

> [C]onsider an individual who has been described by a former neighbor as follows: "Steve is very shy and withdrawn, invariably helpful, but with little interest in people, or in the world of reality. A meek and tidy soul, he has a need for order and structure, and a passion for detail." How do people assess the probability that Steve is engaged in a particular occupation from a list of possibilities (for example, farmer, salesman, airline pilot, librarian, or physician)? How do people order these occupations from most to least likely? In the representativeness heuristic, the probability that Steve is a librarian, for example, is assessed by the degree to which he is representative of, or similar to, the stereotype of a librarian. Indeed, research with problems of this type has shown that people order the occupations by probability and by similarity in exactly the same way (Kahneman & Tversky, 1973, p. 4). This approach to judgement of probability leads to serious errors, because similarity, or

representativeness, is not influenced by several factors that
should affect judgements of probability. (p. 4)

Such issues as relying on representativeness can also be important not only in assessing clients, but also in evaluating scientific
claims. FMSF's claim that its membership is free of pedophiles,
for example, seems to rely on such representative properties of
looking good, dressing well, smiling, and chatting in an interesting, friendly way (see chapter 3).

## Defensive Questioning

Readers of this book are likely familiar with the medical concept
of *defensive testing*. A patient enters the hospital for a routine
operation. The surgeon orders numerous tests that she is sure the
patient doesn't need. The tests are for the doctor's rather than the
patient's welfare. Some clinicians for whom a traumagenic etiology is the most (or only) salient hypothesis about distress may
ask questions almost entirely about abuse so that the focus of the
session is shifted toward abuse issues, regardless of whether
these questions serve the needs of the clients. The questions
intentionally or unintentionally are to move the focus to an area
where clinicians are comfortable, feel effective, and maintain
interest. Similarly, therapists who find a traumagenic etiological
hypothesis less useful might skew their attention to such matters
as birth order, family norms and rules, familial histories of
depression or alcoholism, or one of any number of other possible
explanatory models.

Other clinicians, mindful of lawsuits filed against therapists
whose clients reported recovering memories, may long for a
clientele who will never report abuse—real or imagined. Some
may, as they have confided to the authors, take steps to discontinue working with abuse victims. In order to further reduce the
likelihood of involvement, they may screen out those who they
believe might be at risk for developing the experience of recovered memories, or those who are reporting the emergence of
such material as their chief complaint.

Premature cognitive commitment, confirmation bias, hindsight bias, reliance on representativeness, and defensive ques-

tioning are but a few examples of factors that may push the unaware therapist off track. One fundamental step that mental health professionals may take is simply to become aware of such factors and constantly to question themselves about the degree to which these phenomena may influence their work. Another fundamental step is to ask themselves the degree to which they possess various kinds of competence.

## Competence

One kind of competence is *intellectual competence*. This concept refers to the development of information—based on empirical research and sound clinical scholarship—about working with specific populations, problems, and methods. It also refers to a therapist's general ability to assess, conceptualize, and plan for appropriate assessment and treatment. Intellectual competence also means knowing what one does not know. For example, a psychotherapist may be extremely experienced and knowledgeable about working with women who have a history of sexual abuse. This does not necessarily mean that the same therapist will be equally skilled and competent in working with men with the same sort of history. Similarly, competence in working with sexually abused clients of one culture may not translate adequately to working with sexually abused clients of another culture

Another kind of competence, one less frequently addressed in the training of therapists and forensic experts, is *emotional competence*. This term refers to psychotherapists' emotional capacities to work effectively with people who may be despairing, terrified, sexually aroused, enraged, violent, frantic, or experiencing other intense feelings or impulses. It refers to therapists' ability to carry on this work without responding to the emotional intensity through sealing themselves off, allowing their own personal issues or biases to distort the therapy, or feeling empty and resentful. Not all therapists can work with all clients or all kinds of problems. To acknowledge limitations and constantly monitor how close one is to them is not a sign of weakness; it is an essential part of clinical work. However, many therapists may feel pressured to see whoever comes to their office, and are rarely trained to consider this factor in making decisions about whom to accept into treatment. The fear of disappointing and perhaps alienating a referral source, the need for a client's fee in order to cover the office rent, or the procedures for assigning patients within a managed care setting are among the factors that may push therapists to work with patients in the absence of competence.

Both forms of competence are essential. For many, it is likely that one type of competence comes easier than the other (and at times most will feel that neither type comes very easily). Questioning one's own competence is an essential ethical and professional responsibility in clinical and forensic work when recovered memories are at issue. The following sections examine more specific components of competence in this area.

## Intellectual Competence: What Should a Therapist Know?

As in so many endeavors, in providing help to people who report recovering memories of abuse, the more you know, the more you realize that you have yet to know. The field of child sexual abuse recovery, and the question of whether memories for trauma can be lost to conscious access and then return later in life draws upon knowledge in a wide range of topic areas. It is unlikely that any one person—no matter how scholarly and committed to the pursuit of knowledge—will be entirely conversant and up to date on all of these foundational sources of data.

The immensity of the underlying knowledge base should not, however, discourage (or excuse) therapists from developing a basic level of intellectual competence, if for no other reason than to be able to know the limits of their knowledge, which in turn informs caution in application of that knowledge base. As Stricker (1992) put it, "[A]lthough it may not be unethical to practice in the absence of knowledge, it is unethical to practice in the face of knowledge. We all must labor with the absence of affirmative data, but there is no excuse for ignoring contradictory data" (p. 564).

We propose that competent practice in this field requires some basic working knowledge of the following topics: (a) developmental theory, (b) models of memory, (c) trance and suggestibility, (d) trauma theory, (e) trauma and dissociation, (f) specific survivor treatment information, (g) models of distress, pathology, assessment, and diagnosis, (h) the checklist as assessment tool, and (i) critical thinking. We also propose that specialty practice with survivors implies that the therapist has gone beyond minimal competence to a more complete mastery of the field. Listing some of these major domains, however, in no way implies that these are the only relevant areas.

## Developmental Theory

Developmental research and theory are fundamental to clinical work. To take an obvious example, the clinical assessment of a 4-year-old is likely to involve different methods than the clinical assessment of a 70-year-old. Knowledge of what is and is not known about how the human infant progresses through babyhood to childhood to adolescence to adulthood and on into old age informs approaches to assessment and therapy. The research and literature provide a scientific framework for attempts to understand the manner in which someone develops intelligence; the enjoyment of play; a sense of self; a moral sense; confidence and security; cognitive–affective processes; behavioral habits and skills; ways to be with others and communicate; the capacity to be alone; abilities to assess, accept, and challenge social and cultural norms; and, to borrow from Freud, the abilities to love and work. Because trauma, if and when it occurs, does not happen to a generic organism, but rather to a specific individual at a given point in development, a therapist's capacity to comprehend the possible effects of trauma and to interpret materials produced by a client require familiarity with basic concepts of developmental psychology and psychopathology.

For example, some clients have produced material in therapy that the client believes to reflect memories from the first few months of life. Even when this material is very emotionally compelling, there is good evidence, summarized in chapter 2, to demonstrate that to date we have not identified any neurocognitive capacities that appear sufficiently developed by this age to allow for storage and retention of a memory under most circumstances. This does not mean that nothing occurring during that time is meaningful; clients may know of events that occurred during the period of infantile amnesia through the accounts of third parties and feel distressed by learning that certain things happened to them. Additionally, learning does occur even in the absence of formal capacity to recall. To take a more extreme example, if an infant were tortured and raped every day for a year during age 2, this assault might constitute an extremely meaningful aspect of the person's subsequent development and experience, even if the individual were unable to remember any aspect of it as an adult.

The nature and persistence of symptoms may reflect ages and developmental stages at which a trauma occurred. Incest at age 4 may influence development, experience, and functioning in ways that differ significantly from incest at age 14. Sexual abuse in childhood is not a unitary phenomenon. Therapists adequately knowledgeable about developmental research and theory can hypothesize in an informed way about what capacities might have been available to a child, given the points in development at which the abuse occurred. Therapist and client will be better able to work together to understand the relevant issues for assessment and therapy.

## Models of Memory

The study of human memory, while long a focus of inquiry, has itself gone through considerable development and change in the past two decades. One of the most useful models for understanding human memory has changed from a primarily associationist paradigm to a more mixed paradigm that takes into account both the constructive and active aspects of memory, as well as the prior associationist models (see chapter 2). The study of memory has moved toward a greater focus on questions of reconstruction and suggestibility. Studies of how the brain stores and retrieves different types of information become more sophisticated as the technology for brain imaging becomes more precise. Memory for traumatic experience has been, at the time of this writing, one of the less well-studied aspects of memory until the recent controversy over recovered memories of childhood trauma began to spark increased interest in this topic.

Research and theory in the field of memory is another domain of information fundamental to therapists working with trauma

survivors or with people who experience what are believe
intrusive recollections of prior trauma. Simplistic models
memory works—such as memory understood as an infalliDle
camera or videorecorder—have been invalidated by empirical
research. The complexity of memory and the degree to which it
is still not understood lend increased significance to two fundamental premises of this book: first, that the work of the clinician
and the expert witness involves constant questioning, and second, in light of the current state of scientific data and knowledge,
each report of recovered memory of abuse must be carefully and
fairly evaluated on an individual basis.

## Trance and Suggestibility

The effects of trance states (including, but not limited to, formal
hypnosis) on accuracy of memories, both under hypnosis and
afterward, is another fundamental part of a therapist's domain of
knowledge in this area. Guidelines for practice of hypnosis in
regard to delayed recall of trauma have been published by the
Hammond, Garver, & Mutter (1995). Even if the therapist does not
use formal hypnotic strategies in treatment, this is a necessary
foundational topic, because such knowledge may be important in
answering clients' questions (about, for example, whether it would
be helpful to use hypnosis to search for memories assumed to be
buried in the unconscious) or responding to cross-examination.
Therapists should also be familiar with scholarship regarding suggestibility as a factor in psychotherapy, and the manner in which
high levels of client suggestibility can lead to confabulations even
absent any procedure such as hypnosis (D. Brown, 1995a, 1995b).
Highly suggestible persons can enter trance states without formal
trance induction procedures. Therapists can, however, screen for
the presence of high suggestibility in their clients using one of several standard measures of suggestibility (D. Brown, 1995a, 1995b),
so as to increase their use of safeguards against suggestibility with
that subset of clients who meet the criteria for high suggestibility.
Conversely, people who lack this trait appear somewhat resistant
to suggestion even when in deep trance.

The legal implications of using hypnosis may be quite complex. After the California Supreme Court held hypnosis to be

inherently unreliable and not to be used to support a criminal prosecution (*People v. Shirley*, 1982), the legislature enacted a statute that provides that the testimony of a witness in a criminal proceeding is not inadmissible, even if the witness has formerly been hypnotized to recall events, if each of several requirements—e.g., testimony is limited to matters recalled prior to hypnosis, the witness gave informed consent to the hypnosis—is met (Caudill & Pope, 1995, p. 464).

Any therapist considering the use of hypnosis must address such questions as (a) Am I competent in the clinical uses of hypnosis as demonstrated by my education, training, and experience? (b) Have I adequately considered alternative approaches that do not involve hypnosis? (c) Have I consulted with a qualified attorney to ensure that I understand the ways that using hypnosis may affect the client's legal rights (e.g., admissibility of claims, testimony, or other evidence based on hypnotically refreshed recollection)? (d) Am I adequately aware of the research and theory about the use of hypnosis for this population in this situation? and (e) Have I accorded the client full informed consent or informed refusal? Similar questions and cautions should be raised when considering such techniques as eye movement desensitization reprocessing (EMDR) because this procedure can potentially weaken and blur a memory trace for a traumatic event (Shapiro, 1995).

## Trauma Theory

A fourth fundamental domain for therapists and expert witnesses when delayed memories of childhood sexual abuse are at issue is research and theory about trauma. Because it is an interpersonal trauma and often a repetitive event, models of traumatic stress that allow for an understanding of this sort of traumatic stressor can be especially helpful in understanding and making sense of posttraumatic response patterns. Some factors may mitigate the affects of trauma, sometimes as the trauma is occurring. Consequently, paradigms for resilience are a complementary domain of knowledge that should be included in any study of traumatic stress. Work pioneered by Garmezy and his colleagues (Luth & Zigler, 1991; Masten, Best, & Garmezy, 1991) on resilient children and other work on resilience among trauma survivors (Anderson, 1995; Liem, James, & O'Toole, 1994; Morrow & Smith, 1995) are a particularly valuable resource for the clinician, especially in being able to respect and respond to the wide variations in presentation emerging from diverse client reports of childhood sexual abuse histories.

Trauma is a complex psychobiosocial event. By this we mean to emphasize that it happens to the entire organism and has impacts at the cognitive–affective, physical, interpersonal, and sometimes spiritual levels. Increasingly, research has been able to identify trends that tend to characterize single-event trauma and repetitive trauma, interpersonal traumas and those resulting from natural disasters such as earthquakes and floods, trauma experienced alone and trauma experienced in a group, and childhood versus adulthood trauma. The interpersonal aspect of sexual abuse trauma, especially as it pertains to issues of betrayal (Freyd, 1994, 1996) and challenges to beliefs about justice and safety (Janoff-Bulman, 1992), is particularly important in understanding the diversity of posttraumatic impacts that childhood sexual abuse can cause. Herman's (1992) model of *complex post-traumatic stress disorder* (PTSD) may be quite helpful because it offers a concise construct with which to understand this range of posttraumatic responses.

Much recent research has illuminated the impact of trauma on biological processes, such as the impact of traumatic stressors on brain neurochemistry (van der Kolk, 1992; van der Kolk & Saporta, 1991; see discussion in chapter 2, this volume) and a variety of illnesses such as chronic pelvic pain (Walker, Katon, Harrop-Griffith et al., 1988) and irritable bowel syndrome (Walker, Katon, Roy-Byrne, Jemelka, & Russo, 1993). Data emerging as this chapter was written suggest that trauma may create permanent changes to the hippocampus, a structure in the brain that is implicated in the storage and retrieval of affect-based memories and the integration of cognitive and affective aspects of a memory (Bremner et al., 1995). Specifically, MRI studies found shrinkage of the hippocampus in 17 women with documented histories of severe childhood sexual abuse. The same researchers have reported that similar changes to hippocampal volume have also been observed in combat veterans with PTSD.

## Trauma and Dissociation

The link between trauma and dissociation was hypothesized in the work of Pierre Janet. Various research studies report findings that demonstrate this link (Marmar et al., 1994; Putnam, 1994). Learning about theory and research on dissociation is part of the essential preparation of clinicians and expert witnesses in this area. Ian Hacking (1995) has traced some evolutionary lines of the term and concept of dissociation, beginning with Janet, noting that Janet formulated a theory of multiplicity, and its dynamics, a model suggested by his choice of French words such as *dissociation* and *désagrégation*. The word *dissociation* entered English in 1890, thanks to William James. Morton Prince, the great American pioneer of multiple personality, also used the word in print in 1890 after his visit to France, and his works helped make the term well known among those who speak and read English.

Dissociation appears to affect a broad range of cognitive and affective functions, including the manner in which data are stored and retrieved in memory (APA, 1994; Spiegel, 1994; Steinberg, 1995; Yates & Nasby, 1993). Dissociative phenomena may most likely accompany the responses of those traumatized as young children, when the natural capacity for dissociation seems relatively heightened, although peri-traumatic dissociation has now been empirically documented to occur in adults exposed to combat (Bremner et al., 1995; Marmar et al., 1994) and natural disaster (Spiegel, 1994) forms of trauma as well. Dissociative disorders are hypothesized to result primarily from exposure to traumatic stressors (Kluft, 1990; Putnam, 1989; Ross, 1990) and have been documented in one prospective study as occurring at a higher than population rate in a group of sexually abused girls (Putnam & Trickett, 1993). Consequently, therapists who work with this population should have basic familiarity with the features of the more common disorders, differential diagnosis, and treatment planning concerns when dissociation is at issue.

As previously mentioned, the study of resilience complements the study of trauma because most trauma survivors seem to possess psychobiosocial factors that may help the person survive and cope with trauma. Research and theory about resilience can form a central resource when clients have been abused, particularly when they are in crisis, experience helplessness and hopelessness, and are overwhelmed by flashbacks, intrusive thoughts, unbidden images, and similar cognitions. Attention to potential resilience can help to engage the clients' strengths in treatment, and lend hope to both parties in the therapy relationship. People who are identified as successful or resilient survivors of childhood sexual abuse have identified a number of factors that have been helpful in achieving a positive outcome, even when the type of sexual abuse they have experienced was severe and/or frequent (Anderson, 1995; Morrow & Smith, 1995). These findings parallel more general research on children's resilience, which is an important component of conceptualizing the adult survivor as a person with potential for healing and change. Understanding resilience can also help the survivor to identify and credit his or her internal and personal resources.

## Specific Information About Treatment of Sexual Abuse Survivors

The past decade has seen an outpouring of published materials on the treatment of adult survivors of childhood sexual abuse, including a number of books and journal articles that have either directly or tangentially addressed the topic of recovered memories (Alpert, 1995; Briere, 1996, in press; Courtois, 1988; Frank, 1996; Harvey, 1996; Harvey & Herman, 1994; Olio, 1992, 1995a; Olio & Cornell, 1993; Salter, 1995; Sgroi, 1989; Whitfield, 1995). Much of this material uses a stage-oriented treatment model for working with adult survivors of childhood sexual abuse. This model first focuses on helping the individual with containment, stability, and safety. The second phase of treatment focuses on the metabolization and integration of memory—both never-forgotten memories and delayed recall—and on helping the client to reassess the original coping responses to the event of being sexually abused. The final stage of treatment in this model addresses existential issues in which the person attempts to revise his or her life narrative in the face of acknowledging both the reality of the trauma and the ultimate lack of blame for its occurrence.

Although it will likely be useful for clinicians or expert witnesses to read as much of this literature as possible, in our opinion it is essential to evaluate the degree to which such material is supported by or consistent with empirical research and rigorous scholarship. The process of careful, continuing questioning of assumptions, theory, research, and practice (see chapter 3) can never be turned off, set aside, or dismissed, regardless of the prestige of the author, the material's acceptance by various professional associations or foundations, accordance with clinical policies established by agencies, or the practitioner's own inclination.

## Models of Distress, Pathology, Assessment, and Diagnosis

Sophisticated models of distress, pathology, assessment, and diagnosis—and the degree to which they are informed by or are isolated from current empirical research and scientific scholarship—are another fundamental resource when delayed memories of abuse are at issue. Unfortunately, some popular press and self-help books seem unaware of this resource. They may, for example, state or imply that childhood sexual abuse is the paramount or sole cause of many symptoms and syndromes. The current state of knowledge regarding sexual abuse in childhood is that it can be *a* (not *the*) risk factor for a range of possible disorders, such as PTSD, dissociative identity disorder, borderline personality disorder, and various depressive disorders. However, and most importantly, we wish to stress that *there is no one symptom, syndrome, or diagnosis that inevitably results from sexual abuse in childhood. Nor is there any single psychological symptom that is pathognomonic of a history of child sexual abuse.* For instance, the presence of flashbacks or flashback-like episodes, or of intrusive thoughts of sexual abuse, experiences or nightmares containing images of sexual abuse, are not by and of themselves indicative of sexual abuse having taken place. This variability in presentation underscores the importance of a basic knowledge of the domain of psychopathology, so that careful differential diagnosis informs any treatment.

## The Checklist as Assessment Tool: Possible Pitfalls

One of the more problematic manifestations in the recent literature on childhood sexual abuse has been a proliferation of checklists that purport to be able to diagnose the hidden presence of
sexual abuse, or the presence of false memories or some other
factor relevant to the possibility that a person is experiencing
delayed recall. Clinicians have at times come to rely upon such
documents, particularly when they are not trained in formal psychometric assessment techniques, as valuable data about their
clients; at times, this leads to errors in both assessment and treatment. Such checklists have also faced vigorous criticism from
some scientists who see them as sweeping with an overly broad
brush. As a consequence of both their popularity and the history
of critique, we have chosen to address at length the topic of
checklists as an assessment tool.

Including more than one symptom—sometimes in the form of
an unvalidated checklist—as a way to determine whether an
adult client experienced child sex abuse may, to some, give the
appearance (but only the appearance) of a more sophisticated,
rigorous, and valid approach. Numerous checklists (e.g., Blume,
1990; Gardner, 1993; Wakefield & Underwager, 1994; see also
chapter 3) have been developed in an effort to determine which
individuals may have experienced or perpetrated sexual abuse.
One significant problem with many of these checklists is that
they rely on a *post hoc, ergo propter hoc*—"after this, therefore on
account of this"—fallacy, the sort of hindsight reasoning
described previously as a common cognitive error. There is an
unvalidated assumption of simple causality (i.e., each effect is
produced by one and only one cause).

As an extreme hypothetical example that illustrates the problems inherent in this methodology, consider researchers who
select a sample of 100 prisoners whose records indicate that they,
as children, had experienced sex abuse. In what they believe is an
excess of caution and methodological rigor, the researchers also
select four control groups, each of which includes only people
who deny any history of child abuse: (a) 100 college professors,
(b) 100 college students, (c) 100 members of the local police force,
and (d) 100 members of the city's clergy. The researchers in this

fictional vignette then publish a popular book describing their new child abuse checklist that their research has shown to produce no false positives and no false negatives. According to their faulty reasoning, anyone who checks all four items is inevitably someone who experienced child sex abuse. The four items are (a) "I believe the criminal justice system is unfair," (b) "I believe prison discipline is too strict," (c) "I have been a defendant in a criminal trial," and (d) "I have sometimes longed for parole."

This hypothetical example shows vividly what may not be so obvious in some popular checklists that purportedly identify people who have experienced or perpetrated child sex abuse: (a) that the phenomenon that the checklist seeks to identify may not inevitably be followed by (or otherwise associated with) the items on the checklist, and (b) the items on the checklist may not inevitably follow (or be otherwise associated with) the phenomenon. Even when the phenomenon is always associated with the checklist items, the checklist may lack usefulness and essential aspects of validity. For example, the item "wearing baggy clothes," which appears on one popular sexual abuse checklist (Blume, 1990), may in no way represent a consequence of child sexual abuse, and might even simply constitute a fashion choice.

As another fictional vignette using exaggerated concepts to clarify the principle, consider a checklist designed to identify a history of childhood sex abuse among adults by relying on three aspects of the person's experience within the current week. The researchers have demonstrated that all people in their sample with a history of child sex abuse exhibit these three characteristics in adulthood. The three items on their checklist are (a) "Within the past week I have felt strong emotions," (b) "Within the past week I have been uncertain at times," and (c) "Within the past week I have been uncomfortable with my body size at least some of the time." Although it may be true that all people with a history of childhood sex abuse in the typical sample would show these three characteristics, it is likely also true that all people without a history of childhood sex abuse in the typical sample might show these three characteristics. Purely for the purpose of this hypothetical example (and without any presumption that the figure is actually true), assume that as many as 20% of all people in a particular population have a history of childhood sexual abuse. Even though all people in this population show the three criteria, if all we know about a person selected at random from this population is that he or she showed all three criteria, then on an actuarial basis, the person who shows all three criteria has an 80% likelihood—all other things being equal—of having no history of childhood sexual abuse.

Are checklists ever useful? Part of the answer might rest on whether the items in the checklist are sufficiently valid and reliable in helping to differentiate the phenomenon at issue from other phenomena. Another part of the answer might rest on the intended and actual use of the checklist. A checklist of sufficiently valid and reliable items might be similar to the list of warning signs developed by the American Cancer Society. This cancer checklist offers a number of symptoms that *might* reflect the presence of cancer and, as such, warrant further thoughtful exploration and evaluation by a physician. But as anyone knows who has experienced one of these symptoms and been worried and obsessed for weeks, finally had the problem checked out, and discovered that whatever it is is benign and nothing to worry about, the raised index of suspicion caused by the presence of even a valid and meaningful symptom is not prima facie evidence that anything is wrong. This checklist can never be used in and of itself to show that a person does or does not have cancer. Although there may be many false positives and false negatives, the cancer checklist may play a role in helping a person to monitor whether there might be some increased likelihood of the *possible* presence of cancer. The checklist is not constructed or intended to be used to reach a conclusion about whether cancer is present, but rather to suggest a reasonable action to investigate further (e.g., a call to the physician).

An important point made here is that some checklists may in fact be well-developed, reliable, and valid instruments. Some items on some such documents may have a great deal of specificity and sensitivity in differentiating abused from nonabused populations. For example, Briere's Trauma Symptom Inventory (Briere, 1995), which was empirically validated, focuses on distinguishing between abused and nonabused clinical populations. The Dissociative Experiences Scale (DES), also a checklist, has been empirically demonstrated to distinguish with a high degree of specificity those individuals in a nonclinical population with a history of abuse from those without such a history (Bernstein & Putnam, 1986). However, most of the available checklist-style assessment instruments lack that degree of power, and consequently can be used only extremely cautiously, if at all, as an aide to the overall process of assessment.

## Critical Thinking as an Aspect of Competence

The subtle issues inherent in a scientific evaluation of specific checklists underscores a major theme of this book: the need for clinicians and expert witnesses to question continually their assumptions, theory, research, and instruments and to engage in critical thinking that takes them past stereotypes. Therapist Anna Salter provides an example of one form of such questioning applied to research findings. She wrote:

> In a survey of families who contacted them for information (Remembering "Repressed" Abuse, 1992), the False Memory Syndrome Foundation of Philadelphia found that four fifths of the parents were still married and four fifths of those happily so. Most of the parents were well educated. Two thirds of the fathers and half of the mothers had obtained a college or graduate school degree. Median family income was between $60,000 and $69,000. The parents reported that they routinely ate together, vacationed together, and were actively involved with their children growing up. The results were used to support the parents' contentions that their adult children's accusation of child sexual abuse were false. "These appear to be families that have realized the American dream," Hollida Wakefield is reported to have said (Remembering "Repressed" Abuse, 1992, p 7).
>
> Setting aside for a moment the issue of whether the parents were exaggerating the degree of early harmony, what evidence is there that child molesters can be recognized by their level of education, their vacation plans, or their dining arrangements? On the contrary, sex offenders appear to come from every occupational and socioeconomic group. (Salter, 1995, p. 27)

Salter's comments underscore the necessity that therapists challenge their knowledge base for possible stereotypes or misinformation. As noted previously in this volume, Brewin, Andrews and Gotlib (1993) found that parents tend to misremember the childhood of their now adult offspring by distorting to create a more positive image of what has happened, whereas the offspring themselves tend to have more accurate recollections. Kihlstrom and Harackiewicz (1982) discovered similar tendencies toward distortion in the direction of positive or neutral renderings among people who had experienced trauma. These findings seem to refute "common sense" and stereotypes about how people will describe and recall events, which illustrates the necessity for therapists and expert witnesses wishing to practice competently to examine critically both their own assumptions and the data underlying the assumptions.

Another strategy practitioners can use to self-assess competence and the thoroughness of grounding in a particular knowledge base is to anticipate that the therapist might be cross-examined on his or her knowledge base. Trying to imagine the range of questions that a skilled attorney would ask can be helpful in identifying weaknesses, fallacies, and incomplete analyses and thus point out directions for further study. The following example is taken from a discussion of 80 cross-examination questions in the area of clinical and forensic assessment. Readers might imagine how they might respond were they asked such questions on the witness stand. Consider the following:

> **Are you able to distinguish retrospective accuracy from predictive accuracy?** [Alternative or follow-up questions could involve distinguishing sensitivity from specificity, or Type I error from Type II error.]
>
> This is a simple yes-or-no question. If the expert indicates understanding of these concepts, the attorney may want to ask a few follow-up questions to ensure that the answer is accurate.
>
> If the expert replies "no," then the attorney may consider a subsequent question, such as "So would it be fair to say that you did not take these two concepts into account in your assessment?" If the witness has indicated inability to distinguish between the two concepts, he or she is in a particularly

poor position to subsequently assert that the concepts were taken into account in the assessment.

+

The two concepts are simple, but . . . crucial. . . . Assume that an industrial firm announces that they have developed a way to use the MMPI to identify employees who have shoplifted. According to their claims (which one should greet with skepticism), the MMPI, as they score and interpret it, is now a test of shoplifting. *Predictive accuracy* begins with the test score. This hypothetical new MMPI score (or profile) will either be positive (suggesting that the employee who took the test is a shoplifter) or negative (suggesting that the individual is not a nonshoplifter). The predictive accuracy of this new test is the probability, given a positive score, that the employee actually *is* a shoplifter, and the probability, if the employee has a negative score, that the individual *is not* a shoplifter. Thus the predictive accuracy, as the name implies, refers to the degree (expressed as a probability) that a test is accurate in classifying individuals or in predicting whether or not they have a specific condition, characteristic, etc.

*Retrospective accuracy*, on the other hand, begins not with the test but with the specific condition, characteristic, etc. In the example above, the retrospective accuracy of this hypothetical MMPI shoplifting test denotes the degree (expressed as a probability) that an employee who is a shoplifter will be correctly identified (i.e., caught) by the test.

Confusing the "directionality" of the inference (e.g., the likelihood that those who score "positive" on a hypothetical predictor variable will fall into a specific group versus the likelihood that those in a specific group will score "positive" on the predictor variable) is, in a more general sense, a cause of numerous errors in assessment and in testimony on assessment, assessment instruments, and assessment techniques.

+

The confusion of predictive and retrospective accuracy may be related to the logical fallacy known as *affirming the consequent*. In this fallacy, the fact that x implies y is erroneously used as a basis for inferring that y implies x. Logically, the fact that all

versions of the MMPI are standardized psychological tests does *not* imply that all standardized psychological tests are versions of the MMPI.
(Pope, Butcher, & Seelen, 1993, pp. 151–153)

Only when mental health professionals are adequately aware of current models of distress, pathology, assessment, and diagnosis— as well as of their psychometric properties and their consistency with empirical research and scientific scholarship—are they adequately knowledgeable to conduct clinical and forensic evaluations when delayed memories of childhood sexual abuse are at issue. For most practicing therapists, although there is a reduced likelihood of being put to the sort of examination encountered in a legal cross-examination, the creation of an imaginary questioner of this sort can help prompt seeking out additional information and guard against intellectual complacency in this rapidly evolving field.

## Emotional Competence

Even when a therapist has obtained basic grounding in these domains of knowledge and become intellectually competent, however, she or he has not finished the process of developing the competence necessary for safe and effective practice with the client who reports memories of sexual abuse. Emotional competence is just as crucial. And unlike intellectual competence, which can often be measured as knowledge is acquired and which grows over time and with experience, emotional competence is vulnerable to shifts in the therapist's life and may sometimes decrease over time if a therapist becomes worn down by what she or he hears in the consulting room. Clinical work may involve intense emotional reactions such as anger or fear, for which many therapists may lack adequate training (Pope, Sonne, & Holroyd, 1994; Pope & Tabachnick, 1993). Working with trauma survivors may require therapists to confront stories of true horror, which would be taxing to almost any person's ability to realize, accept, or comprehend. Not everyone can hear these stories; not everyone who sometimes can listen is always capable of doing so. Not every therapist who can listen can also or always work effectively in the face of such suffering. Even those of us who have vast experience in this work find ourselves at times at an emotional loss (Pearlman & Saakvitne, 1995).

Emotional competence requires therapists to monitor their evolving capacity to perform the tasks of their profession, their need for personal support, breaks for rest and replenishment, and professional resources. There are a large number of factors for a therapist to take into account in assessing emotional competence for working with trauma survivors in general and with people recalling intrusive images of childhood sexual abuse in specific.

Factors to consider include the therapist's own history of trauma and victimization. Adult survivors appear to be well represented among the therapist population (Pope & Feldman-Summers, 1992). There is no research supporting the notion that all those who have a history of abuse are more competent or less competent when recovered memories of abuse are at issue, or that those who have no history of abuse are more or less competent. Each instance must be assessed on an individual basis, with the full range of available information and without prejudice. The therapist who does have a history of abuse must take responsibility to ensure that she or he is not becoming retraumatized in a manner that might lead to impairment. The therapist with no such history must take care to avoid the possibility of failures of empathy based on the lack of experiential comprehension of the realities of sexual abuse. Siegel (1990) discusses the risks of unjustified assumptions that one event or experience can be automatically generalized to other clients, situations, and forms of abuse. She asserts that each experience of violation or oppression is unique; to assume that one can make absolute inferential leaps from different experiences can ignore or silence the uniqueness of the client's life history.

Part of the therapist's monitoring involves assessing the need for personal therapy, the adequacy of that therapy in addressing that need, and the ways that personal therapy influences the therapist's own approach to clinical work. A national survey of therapists found that 84% had themselves been in personal therapy; less than 1% of the participants reported that it was not helpful, and 22% had found it had what they considered harmful aspects (regardless of the positive aspects). The research findings suggest that many therapists experience at least at one or more times intense emotional distress. For example, 61% reported experiencing clinical depression, 29% reported suicidal feelings, 4% reported attempting suicide, and about 4% reported having been hospitalized (Pope & Tabachnick, 1994). Table 4-4 presents some features of therapists' own experience of therapy. Clinicians and expert witnesses may consider their own experiences in light of these research findings.

That which the therapist brings to the work is not the only factor impacting on emotional competence. What the work involves is also important. Clinical and forensic work may, to say the least, present emotional challenges. Table 4-5 presents research findings about experiencing and expressing intense emotion in therapy. Again, readers may consider their own experiences in light of these findings. Pearlman and Saakvitne's (1995) volume on the impact of trauma on the therapist may be especially helpful.

As additional steps in monitoring and enhancing emotional competence, therapists and expert witnesses can secure professional consultation. This may take a number of forms, including peer group or pair consultation, seeking advice from an expert on a regular basis, and involvement in professional organizations of other similarly practicing therapists. Therapists must assess whether they can or want to work with certain kinds of people and problems, and be willing to make referrals to colleagues when a client presents with something that is outside the range of the therapist's emotional comfort. The therapist who works well with a survivor who is suicidal and self-mutilating may do very poorly working with a survivor who is depressed and lethargic. Someone who feels quite comfortable working with people sexually abused by men may find it hard to cope with the reality of sexual abuse involving a female perpetrator. No therapist can be or should attempt to be all things to all clients. One essential aspect of considering consultation is to address issues of privacy, confidentiality, and privilege. An attorney can advise the therapist whether various kinds of consultation are or are not privileged, and under what conditions the privilege will continue or disolve.

## Table 4-4

*Therapists' Experiences in Their Own Therapy*

| Item | 0 | 1 | 2 | 3 | 4 |
|---|---|---|---|---|---|
| In your own personal therapy, how often (if at all) did your therapist (N = 400): | | | | | |
| cradle or hold you in a nonsexual way | 73.2 | 2.7 | 8.0 | 8.8 | 6.0 |
| touch you in a sexual way | 93.7 | 2.5 | 1.8 | 0.3 | 1.0 |
| talk about sexual issues in a way that you believe to be inappropriate | 91.2 | 2.7 | 3.2 | 0.5 | 1.3 |
| seem to be sexually attracted to you | 84.5 | 6.2 | 3.5 | 3.0 | 1.5 |
| disclose that he or she was sexually attracted to you | 92.2 | 3.7 | 1.0 | 1.3 | 0.8 |
| seem to be sexually aroused in your presence | 91.2 | 3.7 | 2.2 | 0.8 | 1.3 |
| express anger at you | 60.7 | 14.3 | 16.8 | 5.7 | 1.8 |
| express disappointment in you | 67.0 | 11.3 | 14.8 | 4.7 | 1.3 |
| give you encouragement and support | 2.5 | 0.8 | 6.2 | 21.8 | 67.5 |
| tell you that he or she cared about you | 33.7 | 6.7 | 19.5 | 21.8 | 16.3 |
| make what you consider to be a clinical or therapeutic error | 19.8 | 18.0 | 36.2 | 19.0 | 5.5 |
| pressure you to talk about something you didn't want to talk about | 57.5 | 7.5 | 21.3 | 8.8 | 4.0 |

**Table 4-4**   (Continued)

*Therapists' Experiences in Their Own Therapy*

| Item | 0 | 1 | 2 | 3 | 4 |
|---|---|---|---|---|---|
| use humor in an appropriate way | 76.7 | 8.8 | 10.0 | 2.2 | 1.5 |
| use humor in an inappropriate way | 5.2 | 2.5 | 12.5 | 35.0 | 43.5 |
| act in a rude or insensitive manner toward you | 68.7 | 13.0 | 12.0 | 4.0 | 1.5 |
| violate your rights to confidentiality | 89.7 | 4.5 | 2.7 | 1.3 | 1.8 |
| violate your rights to informed consent | 93.2 | 3.2 | 1.3 | 0.3 | 0.3 |
| use psychotropic medication as part of your treatment | 84.7 | 7.0 | 3.0 | 3.0 | 1.5 |
| use hospitalization as part of your treatment | 96.2 | 1.8 | 0.5 | 0.5 | 1.0 |
| In your own personal therapy, how often (if at all) did you ($N = 400$): | | | | | |
| feel sexually attracted to your therapist | 63.0 | 8.0 | 14.0 | 7.5 | 6.5 |
| tell your therapist that you were sexually attracted to him or her | 81.5 | 6.2 | 5.5 | 3.0 | 2.7 |
| have sexual fantasies about your therapist | 65.5 | 8.0 | 12.8 | 7.0 | 5.2 |
| feel angry at your therapist | 13.5 | 9.5 | 32.7 | 28.5 | 15.0 |
| feel that your therapist did not care about you | 49.5 | 13.0 | 19.0 | 12.3 | 5.5 |
| feel suicidal | 70.0 | 8.5 | 9.5 | 8.3 | 3.0 |
| make a suicide attempt | 95.5 | 2.5 | 1.0 | 0.0 | 0.0 |
| feel what you would characterize as clinical depression | 38.5 | 15.8 | 16.0 | 16.5 | 12.5 |

*Note:* Codes: 0 = never, 1 = once, 2 = rarely (2–4 times), 3 = sometimes (5–10 times), 4 = often (over 10 times). From Pope & Tabachnick, *Professional Psychology: Research and Practice, 25,* p. 252. © 1994 by the American Psychological Association. Used with permission.

**Table 4-5**

*Experiencing and Expressing Intense Emotion in Therapy*

| Behavior | Study 1 | Study 2 | Study 3 |
|---|---|---|---|
| Disclosing details of current personal stresses to a client | | 38.9% | |
| Crying in the presence of a client | 56.5% | | |
| Telling a client that you are angry at him or her | 89.7% | | 77.9% |
| Raising your voice at a client because you are angry at him or her | | | 57.2% |
| Having fantasies that reflect your anger at a client | | | 50.9% |
| Feeling hatred toward a client | | | 31.2% |
| Telling clients of your disappointment in them | 51.9% | | |
| Feeling afraid that a client may commit suicide | | | 97.2% |
| Feeling afraid that a client may need clinical resources that are unavailable | | | 86.0% |
| Feeling afraid because a client's condition gets suddenly or seriously worse | | | 90.9% |
| Feeling afraid that your colleagues may be critical of your work with a client | | | 88.1% |
| Feeling afraid that a client may file a formal complaint against you | | | 66.0% |
| Using self-disclosure as a therapy technique | 93.3% | | |
| Lying on top of or underneath a client | | | 0.4% |
| Cradling or otherwise holding a client in your lap | | | |
| Telling a sexual fantasy to a client | | | 6.0% |
| Engaging in sexual fantasy about a client | 71.8% | | |
| Feeling sexually attracted to a client | 89.5% | | 87.3% |
| A client tells you that he or she is sexually attracted to you | | | 73.3% |
| Feeling sexually aroused while in the presence of a client | | | 57.8% |

**Table 4-5**    *(Continued)*

| Behavior | Study 1 | Study 2 | Study 3 |
|---|---|---|---|
| A client seems to become sexually aroused in your presence | | | 18.2% |
| A client seems to have an orgasm in your presence | | | 3.2% |

*Notes:* Study 1: A national survey of 1,000 psychologists with a 46% return rate (Pope, Tabachnick, & Keith-Spiegel, 1987). Study 2: A national survey of 4,800 psychologists, psychiatrists, and social workers with a 49% return rate (Borys & Pope, 1989). Study 3: A national survey of 600 psychologists with a 48% return rate (Pope & Tabachnick, 1993). Blank cells indicate a behavior not addressed in a given study. All Sources © American Psychological Association. Adapted with permission.

Therapists and expert witnesses can also remain alert to specific challenges to emotional competence. Developmental milestones in the life of the therapist, including relationship changes, childbirth, loss, illness, or aging, as well as a therapist's own experience of psychological distress, can all temporarily impair emotional competence. Should this occur, therapists can protect clients through increased supervision of their work, transfer of clients (if necessary or desirable), or temporary withdrawal from working with the topic of sexual abuse trauma. Therapists need to remember that they may be terrified, numbed, and overwhelmed by what they hear (McCann & Pearlman, 1990; Pearlman & Saakvitne, 1995). Self-care, in the form of time off, vigorous physical activity, humor, petting the dog or cat, and time with significant others may play important roles in maintaining emotional competence.

## Competence in Doing

Intellectual and emotional competence, while necessary, are not sufficient. There is a competence to do certain work that evolves only through carefully supervised experience and formally monitored practice in "real-life" situations. The gifted scientist may have memorized her speech and practiced it countless times in front of the mirror and before her friends. Yet once she walks to the lectern and sees hundreds of people looking at her, she may become literally speechless. The dedicated medical student may have mastered the medical literature and intellectual knowledge about surgery and mentally rehearsed his first incision almost constantly, but may literally faint at the first sight of blood. Intellectual and emotional competence unfortunately are not the same as competence in doing. If they were, renowned art historians would themselves be capable of painting masterpieces, those learned in music theory could sing like Shirley Bassey, Frank Sinatra, K. D. Lang, or Willie Nelson, and knowledgeable proprietors of health food stores would all look healthy. Competence in doing requires skill or ability and the opportunity to do, as well as feedback from an informed source on what we have done.

Having attended to these fundamental steps in laying a groundwork for safe and competent practice, the therapist and expert witness are in a better position to consider clinical issues more specific to delayed recall of childhood sexual abuse, which are the focus of chapter 5.

# Clinical Work With People Who Report Recovered Memories

T his chapter outlines some special concerns in providing assessment and therapeutic services to those who report recovering memories. Although the material that follows may remind readers of a few basic principles of clinical work when child sexual abuse is at issue, the purpose is to focus on special considerations for reports of recovered memories of abuse. Our review of clinical issues in this material focuses largely on matters related specifically to memory recall, rather than to other aspects of treatment of adult survivors. However, the question of recall and integration of memories takes place most effectively within an overall framework of a stage-based treatment, in which there is an initial emphasis on safety and containment, followed by integration of memory, affect, and meaning. This stage-based model (described briefly in the previous chapter) that is emerging as the dominant paradigm in the field of abuse-survivor treatment, has been quite well described by other authors,[1] and so will not be discussed in detail here except as it relates to our case example material.

---

[1]Readers are referred to texts by Briere (1996), Courtois (1988), Herman (1992), and Salter (1995) and recent articles by Harvey and Herman (1994), Harvey (1996), and Roth and Liebowitz (1988) for a review of overall treatment considerations for adult survivors of childhood sexual abuse.

The sort of concerns likely to appear in work with a client who reports the recovery of what are believed to be memories of childhood sexual abuse emerge most vividly from actual examples of clinical work. We include case materials from our clinical work and that of colleagues with whom with have consulted. In these cases from the authors' own work, all details have been changed to protect the identities of clients and colleagues, and in most cases the example represents an amalgam of several persons rather than one specific client. Informed consent was obtained from the clients to use this material in disguised form.

## Assessment and Therapy as a Complex Process

This book's approach avoids an assembly-line method pushing a client through an unvarying set of steps. What is essential is that each client be assessed and helped as a unique person. The therapist must simultaneously seek ways to empower the client towards healing and choose treatment strategies that reduce the risk of harming the client in the process. Various clients may share important similarities, but each differs from all others in important ways. Each experience of sexual abuse is unique in its nature, intensity, frequency, duration, and the developmental stages and tasks it affects. It follows a course against a history and background unique to that individual, and may have happened in concert with other experiences that were painful or empowering for this person. Each client alleging delayed recall of childhood sexual abuse will present with different symptoms, problems, and focuses of concern. Each must be carefully evaluated, without bias, on an individual basis. All work with such clients is founded upon the development of the competencies described in the previous chapter.

Therapists can find ways to support the client without jumping to create premature closure or certainty. Both client and therapist need room for ambivalence and confusion. Both must tolerate doubt, ambiguity, and uncertainty. One of the most memorable statements heard by one of the authors during graduate training was that "good therapists have high tolerance for ambiguity." Such an aphorism is never more true nor more timely than when therapist and client are faced with the profoundly ambiguous material that emerges during a process of delayed recall in which the thing being explored is often fragmentary, vague, and dissociated, and may emerge in a form that might never allow for the development of clear recollection. At times, the therapist, patient, or both must summon courage to endure and explore accounts of actual sexual abuse or the tormenting illusions of cognitions that seem to portray actual events but may not. The urge to rescue a client who is in misery over the barrage of intrusive imagery by reassuring that client of the absolute accuracy of what is being remembered or by using techniques that appear to move towards quicker and more absolute certainty can be strong. There can also be a strong urge in the other direction: to attempt to rush to the judgment that the events that seem to be recalled never occurred. Ross (1992) notes the example of the problems that emerged in the poet Anne Sexton's therapy when assumptions were made by her treating therapist that her frequent reports of continuously recalled sexual abuse in childhood (see Middlebrook, 1991) must have been false.

However uncomfortable it may make us as clinicians or expert witnesses, we do not have the answers, let alone all the answers, let alone all the right answers. Keeping an open mind, avoiding premature cognitive commitment and prejudice, and repeatedly rethinking even that which we *know* to be true are crucial to responsible practice, and to the healing and empowerment of the client. Our clients' well-being is far more important than proving our theories about the nature of human distress. There is no escape into the pseudosafety of unscientific proclamations and illusory certainty, as much as therapists and clients might be temporarily comforted by authoritative pronouncements. Unfortunate developments have emerged from the sense of urgency coloring therapists' responses to the needs of adult survivors. For instance, in the past decade some practitioners and authors have carelessly transferred emerging information about risk factors or a client's hints toward a possible history of childhood sexual abuse into invariant and overly broad generalizations in which sexual abuse comes to be identified as the *primum causum* of all distress—a cognitive error addressed previously in this book. A polar opposite response in which abuse is dismissed as being of no importance is similarly problematic; both hypotheses ignore the complexity of the differential contributions of childhood abuse experiences to the development of distress in adulthood, and both risk a failure of empathy with the client.

Unquestioned "rules" about the treatment of this population not only fail to help, but also can harm, because they can obscure the individuality of the client behind the supposed power of the rule. Rather than relying on such substitutes for critical thinking or for respecting the uniqueness of each client and situation, therapists must acknowledge that they confront enormously complex situations, which often evolve in a quick and unpredictable manner, for which relevant information may be incomplete or distorted.

The absence of such rules does not free therapists to rely solely on intuition, impulse, and improvisation or to avoid accountability. The very lack of such sets of one-size-fits-all prescriptions underscores even more clearly therapists' responsibility to know the evolving research and theory about memory, suggestibility, and abuse (see chapters 2 and 3) and to ensure adequate preparation to work in this area (see chapter 4). The therapist must constantly ask her- or himself which interventions are most likely to help, heal, and empower the client, and which are most likely to give the client a sense of renewed competence and autonomy even in the face of intrusive recollections and overpowering feelings. Therapists must be alert to possibly replicating abusive dynamics by imposing invariant prescriptions that state explicitly or imply that clients' failure to follow through on the therapists' commands will lead to a failure of therapy.

Clinical work in this area proceeds not from rule to rule, but rather from concern to concern, from question to question, and from hypothesis to hypothesis. In each phase of the work, therapists must address certain concerns. The answers to these concerns are not ready-made but must emerge from therapists' efforts to explore the concerns, and to aid the client in becoming an active participant in making sense of what is being recalled, and in deciding how, when, and at what speed to take the next steps in therapy and in life.

The balance of this chapter sets forth some of the major concerns in an order in which they might occur in some courses of therapy. We emphasize that this order is for purposes of dicussion here and not a lock-step pattern to be followed by the therapist. Once these concerns emerge, they rarely disappear forever, but rather persist or recur from time to time during the course of treatment. In most instances the concerns will likely emerge in some variation of the order below; circumstance can push virtually any of these concerns to demand initial or immediate attention at virtually any time.

## Assessing and Addressing Crises or Urgent Situations

People seeking treatment because of the onset of intrusive recollections often feel in crisis. They may present to treatment with florid symptoms of distress and profound difficulties in functioning in their daily lives. Or, individuals who have been in treatment for a period of time and then find themselves in the midst of delayed recall may transform quickly from a relatively stable client to one who is making daily crisis phone calls. However a clinician may encounter the client with delayed recollections, it is imperative to engage in careful screening, at the initial contact and throughout the course of treatment, for possible risks to the safety of the client and others.

With a new client, some of this assessment should ideally be conducted in the initial telephone contact, prior to agreeing to make an appointment. We make this recommendation because, as discussed in chapter 4, not all clinicians will have the time, willingness, and resources to work with a client who presents with intense instability, or suicidial or homicidal feelings. Consequently, it is very useful, and sometimes essential, to have this information prior to agreeing to work with a client. Although ethical clinicians will make a referral if they realize early in treatment that a given client's needs are beyond their technical or emotional skills or availability, changing therapists may add yet another burden to a client who is already feeling overwhelmed by daily life. Therapists should also make clients aware immediately of any limitations on their availability; a therapist who travels frequently or will not return phone calls after office hours may not meet the needs of a client who requires more easily accessible support.

Therapists working with clients who report delayed recall of trauma should be familiar with standard assessment protocols for suicide and homicide risk (Pope & Vasquez, 1991). Homicidality is not a frequent complaint of this population, but suicidality and, in some instances, chronically elevated levels of suicidal ideation, are quite common (Briere, 1996, in press; Courtois, 1986; Harvey & Herman, 1994). The absence of a client-intiated report of suicidality should not lull the clinician into believing that such cognitions are necessarily absent; the clinician needs to take responsibility to monitor this potential risk throughout the treatment process.

For example, in the case of a woman treated by one of the authors, the client, a long-time recovering alcoholic who had terminated therapy 6 months earlier because her condition had stabilized, called with a casual demeanor to request a followup therapy session because, she said, "a few little things are bothering me." In the session, the client seemed vague about what was going on, and was somewhat bland in her affect. The therapist finally asked the client if she was feeling "slippery" (at risk to drink). This question elicited a tearful report of new intrusive recall, which was a catalyst for suicidal ideation and behaviors that placed the client at risk for relapse. The client stated that she had felt ashamed of having "failed" her therapy by the emergence of new materials, and had not wanted to tell the therapist the truth about how bad she felt.

It is also helpful to assess the client's sense of the capacity to maintain and contain him or herself in between sessions. Therapists need to directly assess with clients their self-perceived sense of risk, and develop strategies with the client to reduce risk. Such questioning is best done well before the last 2 minutes of the therapy hour, so that ample time can be available to develop such coping plans, work on internal images of a safe place where the client can retreat from intolerable material, arrange for brief daily telephone check-ins, schedule an additional session if this is deemed necessary by both parties, or take other steps.

Restating the therapist's between-session availability and the means to contact the therapist in an emergency and giving gentle encouragement to use that option can also be helpful. Many people who are in a crisis of delayed recall tend to be somewhat counterdependent, used to "toughing it out" on their own. It can also be helpful to explore with clients possible upcoming sources of distress. For instance, a client who is remembering sexual abuse by her stepfather and is due to go home for the holidays in 3 months must be worked with to plan well in advance for safety and self-care in a context that has been recently rendered difficult.

As therapists, it is sometimes difficult for us to recall that our clients were adults who lived their lives adequately, if with difficulty, before they met us. Balancing availability with support for the client's actual or emerging autonomy and adulthood can be especially challenging when working with someone who is experiencing flashbacks, nightmares, panic attacks, intense affects, and other manifestations of delayed recall of trauma. It can be helpful for therapist and client to take time during sessions to explore what sort of therapist availability is likely to be most helpful to the client while still maintaining the latter's sense of autonomous capacity to cope. Two of many possible strategies for empowering clients at this point in the process include agreeing upon criteria for what constitutes a crisis worth calling about or developing a list of strategies for self-care that the client commits to attempt prior to making a call to the therapist. Such strategies are also an immensely important part of developing the therapeutic relationship and of working through the noxious long-term effects of the traumatic experience.

Reassuring a highly anxious client is a common task for a therapist who is working with recovery of abuse memories. Clients who, in the dissociative states of flashbacks or in intrusive words and images, are reliving or recalling episodes of painful violation by caregivers may also reexperience feelings related to *betrayal trauma* (J. Freyd, 1994, 1996)—an awareness of the terror that they will be abandoned if they tell the truth about abuse by a caregiver. This dynamic is likely to powerfully reassert itself in the therapy relationship, often with intensity and immediacy. Providing clients with concrete reassurances that they will not be abandoned—e.g., through the provision of emergency contact numbers and clear therapy contracts that specify clients' rights to care—can be among several helpful interventions that can be made early on and that will make clear that such care is noncontingent and does not require a client to produce or retract memories, stick with or change an initial story of sexual abuse, or comply with therapist demands for any particular course of action. Additionally, when clinically appropriate, therapists can discuss with clients why it is that they may be experiencing such terror and such a need for this virtual stranger, their new therapist. Providing the client with a cognitive framework for understanding this affective experience of intense connection engages adult coping skills that may, in turn, empower the client to feel less frightened and more capable of engaging self-soothing mechanisms already in their own repertoire.

For instance, a woman in her early forties sought help from one of the authors because, after serving on the jury of a burglary case, she had begun to experience frightening intrusive images of her uncle sticking his penis in her mouth and physical sensations that left her gagging as if from a large object in her throat. Early on, the therapist discussed with the client what she might do to care for herself at such times. In addition to clarifying how to contact the therapist between sessions, the therapist also discussed with this client what she had done in the past to soothe herself, validating for the client that such images would be frightening to most people and might temporarily lead someone to forget their usual self-care strategies. The client, who had been feeling quite overwhelmed and disconnected from her prior coping skills, remembered that there were a number of things that she could do when the images haunted her, and began to make plans to do some of those things, especially those that increased her sense of physical safety and strength, such as working out and returning to a self-defense class she had previously taken. This, combined with assurances about the therapist's availability, was helpful to the client in becoming less panicked about her symptoms and more willing to take the time necessary to make sense of what was happening, rather than rush towards an immediate certain answer.

Many possible conclusions emerge from this sort of precrisis problem-solving. What is essential in the process, as we have emphasized before, is to develop an agreement reflecting this particular client's unique situation, skills, strengths, and needs. One client may benefit from a daily brief telephone check-in during a period of crisis; another may find this overly intrusive and prefer to initiate contact on her or his own. There is no set formula other than that the therapist carefully evaluate and constantly question the nature, effects, adequacy, and implications of such arrangements.

It is also important to determine if the client is currently safe. A person who is currently in an abusive relationship or living on the street is in need of support to get safe before any other treatment goes forward. Lack of safety in the here-and-now may be a trigger for delayed recall of traumatic events. It can also seriously aggravate the problems faced by the client whose coping skills are temporarily impaired by traumatic memories or frightening confabulations. Walker (1994) discusses the creation of a safety plan with clients who are currently in abusive relationships. It is also possible for a perpetrator of sexual abuse to still be present and posing a threat to a client, particularly if long-hidden abuses are beginning to come to light. Some people who were sexually abused as children have difficulty knowing how to assess when an interpersonal situation is safe and when it is not (Kluft, 1990), and may be living in circumstances that are not conducive to their well-being. Therapists need to explore with clients what steps need to be taken to reduce risks to physical safety, so as to avert possible crises that are in fact preventable.

Just as it may be useful to assure the client that he or she is not alone, the therapist also must recognize that other resources may be available and that he or she need not attempt to provide clinical services alone during a crisis. Working with others may be useful for both therapist and client to strengthen and enrich the set of resources available to an endangered client; seeking outside help may also prevent the client from feeling that the primary therapist is the only professional to whom he or she can turn. The following brief case study illustrates the potential value of professionals collaborating when a client is in crisis:

> In an instance in which a woman required daily sessions during a critical time in her life, colleagues accepted [the therapist's] request that they serve pro bono as an interdisciplinary team, offering detailed daily consultation to him and providing periodic psychological assessment and clinical interviews

for the woman. Her meetings with diverse professionals let her know that many people cared about her. These colleagues mobilized to help a battered woman, a victim of multiple sexual assault, now penniless and homeless, living in her car and hiding from a stalker. She and [the therapist] began meeting daily (later gradually reduced to weekly) for crisis intervention. They agreed that the first priority was her safety. [The therapist] gave her the number of an old college friend in another state. The friend immediately wired her $500 for food and housing and an airline ticket with an open date for use any time she felt in danger from the stalker. The friend asked her not to repay this loan directly to him but rather to give the money to someone else for whom it would make a difference as it did for her now. Within a year, the woman had taken legal action against the stalker and recovered enough to support herself. ("Biography," 1995, p. 242)

In all instances, it is the clinician's responsibility to assess whether the client is at critical or lethal risk and, if so, to work toward ensuring a safe working environment with adequate resources for the client's clinical needs.

## What Brought the Client to Seek Help?

A second early assessment focus involves the question of why this person is seeking therapy now, and why from you. Whose desires are motivating this treatment? Is it the client who is seeking relief from distress from intrusive materials? Is this person court-ordered into treatment, or seeking therapy so as to avoid prosecution or harsher sentencing? In some cases, a client may recover what she or he believes to be memories of sexual abuse and then encourage sisters and brothers to seek treatment and memory. The clinician who works with one of the sisters or brothers must be cautious and not assume—even if it has been clearly established that the initial client was abused—that because abuse happened to one sibling, it necessarily happened to others. Is the client seeking therapy because the clinician has a stated philosophy or approach to treatment that appears congenial to the client? For example, a person may seek a Christian counselor so that therapy will support rather than challenge important and deeply held religious beliefs, or may desire a therapist of the same ethnic or cultural group for a sense of shared community.

Alternatively, a client may seek therapy with no stated concerns regarding childhood sexual abuse or delayed recall of trauma and develop these concerns during the course of treatment. Some authors have described this as a *disguised presentation* of a sexual abuse history (Courtois, 1988). However, the therapist must never reflexively assume that an individual who presents with any of an array of symptoms for which sexual abuse is a risk factor has in fact been abused, or that a specific array of characteristics necessarily represents a disguised presentation. Or, a client may have been exposed to material that has led her or him to an a priori assumption that the client has unfound memories of abuse, and seeks therapy with the stated goal of uncovering such memories. Clinicians must respond to such persons with a careful mixture of respect for their desires and reality testing about the value of embarking on such a course of therapeutic archeology or the lack thereof. The therapist should also remain aware that such people, because of their prior beliefs, may be especially suggestible regarding the presence or absence of an abuse history.

An example of the latter can be found in a case where one of the authors served as the therapist's clinical consultant. The client was a man in his thirties who had a long history of difficulties in functioning. He also appeared to have poor reality testing and too often confused fantasy with reality. He seemed to his therapist to be easily swayed by the comments of others. He had entered therapy with the assertion that, having seen a segment of a TV talk show on male survivors, he was convinced that he, too, must have been sexually abused and wished to uncover these memories in therapy. In this case, the therapist, not wishing to be disrespectful of the client, was nonetheless concerned about the client's possible suggestibility. It seemed as if there were both the potential for the creation of pseudomemories and the risk of ignoring something that might be real. The therapist thus focused on strategies that would help the client with reality testing, and frequently reminded the client that more important than digging for theoretically lost memories was believing and trusting in himself and deciding for himself what paths to pursue during therapy. The therapist also referred the client for an extensive psychometric evaluation because of concerns about possible thought disorder; this evaluation yielded information suggesting the usefulness of psychotropic medications. Because the therapist had not ignored the client's stated request to search for memories, but rather had agreed to a treatment plan in which this desire was blended with careful assessment and reality testing, the client became amenable for the first time ever to trying medication. No memories of abuse ever emerged, although the client continued to think that he might have experienced abuse; but the client became more functional and learned to protect himself better from his suggestibility.

It is also possible that some clients plagued by flashbacks, nightmares, and intrusive images seeming to reflect a history of child sex abuse may seek therapy to gain professional confirmation that recovered memories are per se false. Many clients are greatly troubled when what appear to be memories of abuse begin to emerge. Some may be told by parents that such abuse never occured, could not have occurred, and that continued dwelling on such nonsense indicates that the person suffers from false memory syndrome (see Chapter 3). Some may be sent documents stating that recovered memories are always false. Some may be threatened with the FMSF document informing accused parents that they could seek to have the person claiming to have been sexually abused declared legally "incompetent" by virtue of FMS ("Legal Aspects of False Memory Syndrome," 1992, p. 3). Regardless of what the client has been told about recovered memories being always true or always false, each report of recovered memory of abuse must be carefully and fairly evaluated on an individual basis.

## Asking About Abuse

If the clinician does not hold the assumption that a client will promptly mention a history of abuse if there is one, and if the presence or absence of abuse is considered a standard part of clinical history, then taking an adequate history may involve direct or indirect inquiry. It is this process of clinical inquiry that is in great need of open discussion and extensive research. One question that must be addressed is how, if at all, a clinician can inquire about the possibility of abuse (or other aspects of history) without somehow suggesting or biasing the response. Numerous factors may influence a clinician to distort the assessment process.

In every instance in which therapists first meet a new client, we virtually never know with certainty whether there has been a history of incest or other form of abuse. Although there are instances, as with the client in the opening vignette of chapter 1, in which clients come into treatment to address issues related to sexual abuse, for many people, revelation of this sort of information tends to require time and a certain degree of trust. It also may require getting a good history from the client at intake. Taking an adequate history usually involves, at a minimum, finding out if the client reports a history of abuse. The first step toward practicing safely and competently is, consequently, a commitment to getting good historical information from all clients and avoiding making assumptions about what will be found based on initial impressions. A thorough history queries possible risk factors, including, but not limited to, experiences of various traumatic events.

One option might be simply to talk to the client and ask very general questions that do not address abuse on the assumption that any abuse surely would be mentioned. A number of research studies have unfortunately invalidated this reasonable-sounding assumption; in fact, research suggests that most people do not volunteer abuse histories to the clinician (Briere & Zaidi, 1989; Bryer et al., 1987; Jacobson, Koehler, & Jones-Brown, 1987; Jacobson & Richardson, 1987; Lanktree, Briere, & Zaidi, 1991. For instance, Briere and Zaidi (1989) randomly selected and reviewed 50 charts of nonpsychotic female patients assessed at a psychiatric emergency room (ER). They compared these charts with another 50 charts of similar female patients. They had asked ER clinicians for the latter group of patients to include specific questions about possible child abuse in their structured interviews. Only 6 of the 50 charts of the first group (i.e., the "don't ask" group) reported child abuse; 35 of the 50 charts of the second group reported child abuse. It is important to note that at this stage the dependent variable is *reports* of child abuse, which may or may not be accurate. (There are those who believe that even inquiring along the lines of "Do you have any history of child sex abuse?" within a structured interview asking similar questions about developmental milestones and common childhood diseases may be sufficiently suggestive to elicit a false report that otherwise would not have emerged; however, no research data exist to support this assertion). Jacobson and her colleagues' studies had similar findings. When hospitalized inpatients were not directly asked, information about childhood or adult physical or sexual abuse was rarely volunteered; however, when direct questions were asked, more than three quarters of the 100 patients queried reported at least one of these types of abuse in their histories (Jacobson et al., 1987; Jacobson & Richardson, 1987).

Clinicians wishing to avoid suggestion while obtaining adequate information regarding a sexual abuse history may consider using more general terminology, adapting strategies developed by researchers in the field of acquaintance rape, who asked their research participants about specific experiences by behaviorally describing them rather than asking if the participant had ever been raped (Gidycz & Koss, 1988). For example, clients can be asked if they had any experiences in childhood that they found sexually inappropriate, uncomfortable, or frightening.

One of the authors was the consultant to a treating therapist in a case in which the client misunderstood what the therapist meant by *sexual abuse*. The misunderstanding might have been less likely to occur had the therapist asked if the client had experienced sexual events that seemed inappropriate, uncomfortable, or frightening. The client was asked on intake if she had been sexually abused and responded in the negative. Later in treatment, it emerged that she had been coercively manually manipulated for many years by her much-older brother. She explained to her therapist that she had not thought that this constituted sexual abuse because there had been no penetration and the perpetrator had been her brother; in the patient's mind, sexual abuse equalled rape by a father or father figure. The client had a great deal of distress and shame about what had happened to her, and the therapist, by asking the question in a manner that miscommunicated the universe of possibilities, had spent months not knowing that this was an aspect of the client's concerns.

## Assessing Influences: The Client's Context

Another component of the early assessment process in therapy is that of the client's context and those factors that are influences on the client's belief systems. Research by Pedzek and her colleagues (Pedzek, 1995; Pedzek et al., 1996) suggests that attempts to implant pseudomemories in adults via the suggestions of older relatives may be entirely unsuccessful when the material being suggested is unfamiliar. Consequently, it can be valuable to know how familiar certain things are to the client, to get a feel for his or her epistemic milieu. Not all clients will have an epistemology based on scientific principles as the clinician understands them; therapists must respect their clients' belief systems, but also exercise caution when they cannot be empirically supported. If the client's theology includes a belief in the reality of Satan (a feature of many mainstream religions), such a person might consequently find suggestions of Satanic abuse well within the realm of familiarity. When someone is acquainted with many people who have been sexually abused, then sexual abuse is a familiar and plausible reality. Such people may find it easier to believe suggestions that they themselves have been sexually abused. They may even approach therapy wondering what is wrong that they have not had memories like those of their friends. In contrast, the person who believes, "in my culture there is no sexual abuse," is likely to be highly resistant to any suggestions that sexual abuse has happened to him or her because this notion seems alien. People who believe that only men sexually abuse children may be unlikely to believe that they were sexually abused by a female perpetrator.

In addition to considering such broad factors, it can be helpful for the clinician to know other possible sources of suggestions or confusion in a client's life. Does this person frequently watch TV shows or movies featuring sexual abuse, delayed recall, and so on? Has the client read popular press books, autobiographies of survivors, or novels like *A Thousand Acres* or *The Pawnbroker* that depict delayed recall of horrifying events? Does the client watch pornography in which simulated scenes of sexual abuse are enacted? Is the client an active member of self-help support or therapy groups in which others are sharing stories of having been sexually abused? Has a previous therapist been insistent that abuse either did or did not occur?

In a case reported by a colleague of one of the authors, a woman in her late twenties moved to a new city and changed therapists. The client was a devotee of alternative rock music and an avant-garde artist, and had many pierced body parts and tattoos in conspicuous places. When the new therapist obtained the case notes from the previous therapist, the notes were full of assertions and interpretations of the tattoos and piercings as evidence of ritualistic abuse. The client expressed her desire to the new therapist that this line of interpretation not be pursued, insisting that she decorated her skin for aesthetic reasons rather than as a covert communication about abuse. The client had felt under pressure to adopt her previous therapist's formulation and, in the process, had never been able to address her primary concern in therapy, which was grieving the traumatic loss of a sibling in an accident.

The therapist may also find it helpful to collect information on the abuse histories of the client's family members as an aspect of assessing influences on the client's personal narrative. As a number of authors have noted (e.g., Danieli, 1985; Vogel, 1994), it is possible for individuals to internalize and then produce images of trauma experienced by parents or other caregiving figures, and then to phenomenologically perceive it as their own experience. Vogel described the case of a woman whose mother was a concentration camp survivor and who herself had intrusive images and experienced flashback-like material of being stopped or questioned by Nazi guards. In this instance, it was easier for therapist and client to be certain that these were not the client's own memories because the client had been born and raised in the United States well after the war.

It is also theoretically possible for a person to carry images of a parent's sexual victimization. Vogel also described a case of a woman whose clinical presentation might raise questions of a sexual abuse history in many clinicians. However, what became clear during the course of treatment was that the client was reenacting experiences of her mother's sexual abuse, rather than her own direct experience. When a parent's abuse or victimization has been part of the emotional context in which a client was raised, the parent's abuse may come to represent itself symbolically as materials that appear to be memories but are not.

## Potential Conflicts of Interest, Roles, and Goals

Therapists must assess for themselves whether their agreement to work with a given client contains any possible conflicts of interest for either person. Thus, parents might sue a private mental health center after paying for the therapy of their adolescent daughter who, in the course of treatment, began to allege sexual abuse by the same parents. Depending on the specific facts of such a case, the parents might have a cause of action because they had hired the therapist to treat their daughter. In this instance, the therapist's duty to those who were paying conflicted with the best interests of the client herself. Even more neutral-appearing third-party payors can become a source of problems if they create divided loyalty for the therapist. For example, one large managed mental health care firm recently revised its contract to prohibit therapists from providing treatment to clients—even on a private-pay basis—once the managed care firm decided that therapy was no longer "medically necessary" (Homans, 1995).

Other potential dual roles should always be carefully assessed and avoided whenever possible. A therapist using an individual treatment model (i.e., not conducting family therapy) to provide therapy to one sibling should refrain from seeing others under most circumstances so that assumptions about the family experience and childhood of one adult do not usurp either adult's right to a completely open-minded therapist. There may be important exceptions to this norm (for example, a therapist in a reservation or rural area health clinic may be the only person skilled in working with sexual abuse or the only therapist available within a 50-

mile radius). In such circumstances, it becomes imperative for the therapist to seek continuing consultation so as to avoid the risk of contaminating any one client's therapy with materials or suggestions deriving from another client's therapy.

A therapist should also attend to how and whether her or his other affiliations may create a conflict of interest in treating the client with a completely open mind regarding the presence or absence, or accuracy or error, of material presented as a recovered memory of abuse. Therapists who have gone on record to state that they have never in a lengthy career encountered such a phenomenon may, out of an allegiance to their own public image, not have the ability to hear a client who is genuinely experiencing a delayed recall of trauma. Similarly, if a therapist has written that all clients eventually go on to recall forgotten and hidden abuse, it may be difficult to place this a priori assumption aside in favor of the possibility that what is being produced by the client represents a confabulation. Therapists must also explore whether they are consciously or unintentionally entrapping clients into treatment by either confirming or denying the reality of clients' productions.

## Informed Consent and Informed Refusal

Earlier segments of this book have discussed the importance of competence; continually monitoring oneself and questioning assumptions, theory, research, and practice; evaluating any issue of delayed memories of childhood sex abuse on an individual basis without prejudice; and so on. Before moving further on to clinical concerns specific to recovered memories, there is one more general issue of safe and competent practice occurring at the onset of therapy that is of overwhelming importance: informed consent and informed refusal.

Psychotherapy is, among other aspects, a relationship between people in which each is asked to take certain kinds of risks in order to obtain valued ends. For the client, it may be healing and a surcease from distress. For the therapist, it may be the satisfaction of having been an ally in a healing process. However, because of her or his training, the psychotherapist is often privy to information about the nature and risks of therapy and other clinical endeavors, and the client is not. This imbalance of knowledge—and therefore power—is both unnecessary to successful therapy and probably inimical to a good outcome because of the potential for creating an area of greater dependency in the client where this is neither therapeutically indicated nor theoretically necessary.

Although the notion that the imbalance of knowledge is somehow essential to therapy lacks empirical justification, there is a more fundamental rationale for providing informed consent and informed refusal to clients: it is the right of clients to make adequately free and informed decisions to consent or to refuse consent for clinical procedures—both assessment and therapy—that may profoundly affect their psychological well-being and their future. Professional arrogance, negligence, and other factors must never destroy that right. As one landmark court case put it, "[I]t is the prerogative of the patient, not the physician, to determine for himself [sic] the direction in which he believes his interests lie. To enable the patient to chart his course knowledgeably, reasonable familiarity with the therapeutic alternatives and their hazards becomes essential" (*Cobbs v. Grant*, 1972, p. 514). As another court held the same year,

> A reasonable revelation in these aspects is not only a necessity but, as we see it, it is as much a matter of the physician's duty. It is a duty to warn of the dangers lurking in the proposed treatment, and that is surely a facet of due care. It is, too, a duty to impart information which the patient has every right to expect. The patient's reliance upon the physician is a trust of the kind which traditionally has exacted obligations beyond those associated with arms-length transactions. His [sic] dependence upon the physician for information affecting his well-being, in terms of contemplated treatment, is wellnigh abject.

✝

> Duty to disclose is more than a call to speak merely on the patient's request, or merely to answer the patient's questions: it is a duty to volunteer, if necessary, the information the

patient needs for intelligent decision. The patient may be
ignorant, confused, overawed . . . or frightened . . ., or even
ashamed to inquire . . . . Perhaps relatively few patients could
in any event identify the relevant questions in the absence of
prior explanation.
(*Canterbury v. Spence*, 1972, pp. 782–783)

The information that the therapist provides will do the patient
no good whatsoever if it is not understandable. In contrast to
Brown's (1994) concept of empowered consent (defined later), all
too many therapists seem to provide a rote speech of general
principles or a standardized form, neither of which is particular
to the specific patient (i.e., the speech and form are equally relevant—or irrelevant—to cognitive therapy for major depression,
behavior therapy for a minor phobia, pharmacotherapy for
schizophrenia, and group therapy for anorexia). As Pope and
Vasquez (1991) have noted in their discussions of informed consent and informed refusal,

Nothing blocks a patient's access to help with such cruel effi-
ciency as a bungled attempt at informed consent. . . . The
doors to our offices and clinics are open wide. The resources
are all in place. But not even the most persistent patients can
make their way past our intimidating forms (which clerks
may shove at patients when they first arrive), our set speeches
full of noninformative information, and our nervous attempts
to meet externally imposed legalistic requirements. A first
step in remedying the situation is to recognize that informed
consent is not a static ritual but a useful process. (p. 74)

Well-written, understandable, informative forms can play a useful role in the consent process. Putting the most important issues
into written form (or another permanent medium for people
who are print-impaired) helps ensure that none is overlooked,
minimizes the chances of miscommunication, and guards
against memory's distortions. It also gives the patient something
that can be taken home and studied at leisure. A written explanation can help the patient secure consultation or advice from
others about what may be an exceptionally important set of deci-

sions. It is equally important, however, to avoid the potential pitfalls of using forms as a substitute for, rather than a component of, informed consent. As Gutheil and his colleagues wrote,

> The overriding danger of the form is that it tempts the clinician to treat the transaction as a discrete task that is accomplished, and thus terminated, once the patient has signed the form. This unfortunate misuse of the form defeats the very purpose of informed consent, which is to foster and sustain an ongoing dialogue . . . . At any point along the way, the patient should feel free to ask questions about the impact of the treatment, the impact of medication, the effects of the procedure, and so on. (Gutheil, Burstajn, Brodsky, & Alexander, 1991, p. 79)

The notion of *empowered consent* developed by Brown (1994) may be useful in framing what would constitute a genuine and competent informed consent process, and one that would reduce the risk of a therapist's unilateral imposition of risky or unwanted interventions on a client. Empowered consent involves the therapist carefully analyzing the quality of information made available to the client and presenting it in a manner that is educational and accessible to the client. The therapist also works to maximize the client's capacity to freely consent to all aspects of the therapy relationship, rather than to feel or be coerced in any way. In this process, the therapist considers such factors as the client's skills at communicating and possible barriers to effective comprehension of the information being given, the client's state of mind at the time of the consent process, and the availability of other sources of support for the client so that clients do not feel rushed to sign a form in order to get any sort of care at all, which can happen during moments of intense distress and crisis.

A goal of the empowered consent process is that the client gains access to the kind of relevant knowledge that the therapist already has about the therapist's training and background, and about the various risks and benefits of therapy. Empowered consent clarifies that the client is the ultimate arbiter of what is helpful and has the right to refuse any intervention, seek a second opinion, request that the therapist get consultation, or terminate treatment at any time without punitive consequences or having that refusal labeled as a form of pathology. This empowerment of the client as a partner in decision-making in therapy does not abrogate the therapist's responsibility for careful treatment planning; rather, it underscores respect for the autonomy and adulthood of clients and for their right to challenge interventions that feel wrong and may be countertherapeutic. This form of consent demonstrates that therapists seek to avoid unilaterally and dictatorially imposing their own goals on the client. The fact that the therapeutic privilege belongs to the client, not the therapist, must be made clear because many people in therapy mistakenly believe that they are constrained from talking to others about their own treatment. A sample form for empowered informed consent can be found in Appendix D. It addresses such questions as the apparently mundane issue of payment, as well as more complex ones regarding the risks of certain therapeutic interventions, in a manner that supports the client as an autonomous decision-maker.

The net effect of this sort of empowered consent should be a strong communication to clients that this is their therapy and they have rights and privileges that do not disappear no matter how frightened or vulnerable they feel, which include a collaborative participation in plans for what will happen in therapy. A corollary aspect of this communication is that the therapist is committed to the protection of those rights and sees the empowerment of the client as integral rather than incidental to the therapy process itself. In sum, "Informed consent is an attempt to ensure that the trust required of the patient is truly justified, that the power of the therapist is not abused intentionally or inadvertently, and that the caring of the therapist is expressed in ways that the patient clearly understands and desires" (Pope & Vasquez, 1991, p. 75).

## Diagnosis and the Power of Naming as a Treatment Influence

There are many legitimate ways to assess clients or arrive at a diagnosis (not all of which necessarily involve the use of formal diagnostic systems such as *DSM* or *ICD*). Diagnoses should be construed as informed hypotheses; care must be taken not to reify the diagnosis as a form of absolute evidence that something has occurred in a person's life. Discussing a potential diagnosis with clients can empower clients, emphasizing their active role in addressing the situation, fostering a collaborative relationship between clients and clinician, and demystifying the clinical process (Brown, 1994). Ochberg (1988) suggested that an aspect of what he describes as *posttraumatic therapy* be a joint reading by therapist and client of the diagnostic criteria for PTSD from the *DSM*, as a means of helping clients to normalize symptoms.

One important concern with the use of this treatment approach, however, is avoiding premature cognitive commitment, self-fulfilling prophesies, and what Irving Janis termed *group think*. A diagnostic formulation provides a powerful resource. It can help clinician and patient to make sense of what is going on. It can, for example, suggest whether medication may be helpful. It is virtually impossible to create a reasonable treatment plan if no one has even a provisional idea of what needs to be addressed.

On the other hand, therapists must address concerns about the potential for a diagnosis to cause trouble. Both clinicians and patients may tend to deny or ignore behavior or characteristics that are inconsistent with the diagnosis. Patients may come to be perceived and (literally) treated as if they *were* their diagnoses. Even if certain patients do not originally "fit" their diagnoses, they may eventually come to fit them because of self-fulfilling prophesies (see chapter 3). When clients believe themselves to be recovering memories, but remain uncertain of whether a trauma has occurred, assigning a diagnosis of PTSD may serve as a communication of the therapist's certainty about the existence of sexual abuse. This, in turn, might, with suggestible clients, lead to artificially enhanced credibility of supposed memories at a point in treatment at which it would have been more helpful to sustain a certain degree of ambiguity. As Herman (1992) points out, people with a history of childhood sexual abuse often do not fit the classical picture of PTSD, which is a single-event trauma paradigm, and may present with a more extensive symptom picture that she calls *complex PTSD*, and that van der Kolk (van der Kolk & Fisler, 1994) calls *disorder of extreme stress not otherwise specified* (DESNOS). Because sexual abuse in childhood may be a risk factor for, but not a sole cause of, a variety of forms of psychological distress, the invariant linkage of intrusive recall with childhood trauma or a diagnosis of PTSD will likely lead to misdiagnosis and consequent mistreatment (i.e., a treatment plan based on an invalid assessment of the problem to be addressed in treatment).

Certain diagnoses may carry stigma. Hospital staffs may try to minimize their contact with anyone diagnosed as having borderline personality disorder, for example, and in some settings people labeled as having dissociative identity disorder are considered to be confabulating and manipulative. In other settings, the existence of a particular diagnosis is denied because it fails to fit within the epistemological system of the treatment setting. For example, prior to the publication of the *DSM–III*, in which PTSD was officially identified for the first time, it was common for Viet Nam veterans with PTSD being treated in the VA system to be labeled "character disordered" because the prevailing wisdom was that Viet Nam service was not traumatic; in that context, PTSD simply did not exist.

It is important to attend carefully to factors that may lead to misdiagnosis or misuse of a diagnosis. Reiser and Levenson (1984), for example, explored six ways that the borderline personality disorder diagnosis is often misused. These include using a borderline diagnosis to avoid working with a client's sexual issues, to cover the therapist's sloppy diagnostic procedures, to rationalize a lack of success in the treatment, to prevent the use of psychopharmacological or other medical interventions that might help the patient, to express the therapist's countertransference hate, and to rationalize the therapist's acting out. Becker and Lamb (1994) recently documented the ways in which this diagnosis reflects gender biases. They noted that women tended to receive the diagnosis more frequently than men with precisely the same symptoms when therapist response was assessed under controlled experimental conditions. It is important to question not only the potential misuse of a diagnostic concept, but also the potential usefulness. How does a particular diagnosis help clinicians provide effective services? How does it inform and guide interventions? How *specifically* is the treatment plan different for this particular diagnosis than it would be for any of the other diagnostic possibilities for this individual client? In some cases, as Kazdin (1978) noted, "the direct implications of diagnosis for patient care have been minimal. To many investigators, diagnosis merely provides a label; it does not supply clear implications about what will happen in the course of the disorder or treatment" (p. 26).

A diagnosis of PTSD given in the absence of a well-established history of trauma may influence both patient and therapist to assume that a specific trauma must have occurred. This diagnosis might consequently lend premature validation to allegations of childhood sexual abuse, leading both therapist and client to assumptions that something did occur rather than exploring the possibility that what is reported is metaphoric, confabulated, or otherwise not reflective of sex abuse. As the *DSM–IV* notes, a person may have the symptoms of PTSD without having experienced a trauma, suggesting that the symptom pattern may arise from other sources.

Clinicians considering the possibility of a diagnosis of PTSD might consider the most widely used standardized psychological test—the MMPI-2—as a strategy for helping to confirm clinical diagnostic impressions.[1] Additionally, scales designed specifically for the assessment of PTSD, such as the Impact of Events Scale (IES; Horowitz, Wilmer, & Alvarez, 1979) or the Trauma Symptom Inventory (Briere, 1995) may be employed. Meichenbaum (1994) includes an extensive discussion of the use of formal psychometric instruments for the assessment of PTSD in his volume on its treatment, and describes and references several hundred different measures used for the assessment of PTSD in different situations.[2]

The diagnosis of dissociative identity disorder (DID) is one that is frequently associated with a history of childhood sexual

---

[1]For detailed discussion of the use of the instrument to assess PTSD, particularly using the Keene PTSD Scale, see Pope, Butcher, and Seelen (1993).

[2]Readers interested in the formal psychometric assessment of PTSD are encouraged to consult that volume, as well as a forthcoming book by Briere (in press), as extremely useful resources.

abuse (Kluft, 1990; Putnam, 1989; Ross, 1990). However, it is also a diagnosis that is considered in some but not all quarters to be somewhat controversial; some authors (Mersky, 1992; Spanos, 1994) suggest that it is a primarily iatrogenic phenomenon induced by the suggestions or inappropriate interventions of therapists.[3] Nonetheless, in light of complex diagnostic, treatment, and forensic implications of this diagnosis, therapists may wish to seek a consultative interview for their client with another therapist experienced in dissociative disorders to obtain a second opinion. The clinician may consider using a standard screening device, the Dissociative Experiences Scale (DES; Bernstein & Putnam, 1993), when a dissociative disorder is suspected. Recent research in collaboration with the original authors of the DES by Waller indicates that a taxonomic difference between pathological and nonpathological dissociation can be demonstrated by response to specific DES questions (Waller, 1994). High scores on the DES might lead the clinician to consider administering the SCID-D (Steinberg, 1995), a structured diagnostic interview for dissociative disorders that is constructed to carefully confirm or refute the presence of one of several *DSM–IV* dissociative disorders. Childhood sexual abuse is frequently present in confirmed cases of DID, but caution should be taken to avoid any one-to-one or presumptive inference of sexual abuse from DID because it is possible for this disorder to emerge in response to other, nonsexual traumata in some instances. Some emerging data suggest that the copresence of severe physical abuse or neglect with sexual abuse may be the most common picture in the history of individuals with DID.

A case example illustrates how a specific diagnostic hypothesis may influence the process of therapy and allow the client to become more in charge of the process of knowing and recall. A woman in her late thirties sought clinical services from one of the

---

[3]Readers wishing to find a more complete exploration of the iatrogenesis question are referred to articles by Ross, Norton, and Fraser (1989) and Gleaves (1996b), which contain an extensive empirical challenge to that hypothesis; additionally, emerging cross-cultural information regarding the presence of DID and other dissociative disorders in non-North American clinical settings would appear to offer arguments against the iatrogenic model.

authors. She described a history of compulsive sexual relation-ships with older men, disordered eating, and emotional lability. The client reported no history of sexual abuse on intake. A tentative working diagnostic formulation of an anxiety disorder with obsessive–compulsive features was made based upon the available information, and therapy focused on helping the client to gain greater mastery over her compulsive behaviors and reduce ambient anxiety. When, approximately a year into treatment, the client began to report intrusive imagery of sexual abuse by an older family member, the therapist discussed with her the possibility of the client gathering information from other family members. The client was able to obtain corroboration for everything that she had recalled, including the reports of a covictim, a slightly older cousin, who had never forgotten the details of the sexual abuse and had been aware of the client's victimization. The client later asked if sexual abuse had ever been suspected by the therapist and, upon being told that the therapist had given some consideration to it as a possibility, informed the therapist that it was good that it had never been suggested; the client felt that, even with the corroborative information, the memories would have been far harder to trust. The more "neutral" diagno-sis—in this case of an anxiety disorder—gave the client a chance to gain mastery, which in turn provided the sense of internal safety that empowered the client to arrive at and trust her own reality independently of the therapist's suspicions of a possible traumatic etiology of many of the symptoms.

Ambivalence about abuse is also quite common among sur-vivors, even when the abuse has never been forgotten. Therapists must develop strategies to be respectful of the client's potential discomfort with any diagnostic hypothesis (e.g., his-tory of child sex abuse, confabulated child sex abuse, transgener-ational transmission, borderline personality disorder) and avoid pushing the client to accept the therapist's paradigm or hypothe-ses during any stage of assessment or treatment. Notions of "denial" and "resistance" are less than helpful at this juncture. Instead, respect for the client's timing and pacing and readiness to integrate certain experiences into his or her reality are the hall-mark of good treatment. It may be necessary for the client to have time and space to alternatively consider and reject over and over again any notion of having been sexually abused until the client is ready—without coercion—to embrace this as reality, reject it, or continue to live with the ambiguity. Because sexual abuse involves the overpowering of a child's reality, body, and perceptions by a powerful adult, it is important that the therapist not replicate this experience through attempts to force a new version of reality on a client.

## Reducing Power Imbalances in Treatment

Coercion, subtle or overt, is far more likely to occur in therapy when the imbalance of power between therapist and client is magnified in some way. Whereas ultimately the power resting in the hands of the therapist is likely to be greater simply as a function of the roles of therapist and client, a clinician can take steps to minimize the imbalances of power and strengthen the client's capacity to resist suggestion from the therapist or anyone else. When the clinician operates from this perspective, the likelihood of either avoiding dealing with real traumatic memories or creating pseudomemories will be reduced. Such egalitarianism is a hallmark of some therapeutic approaches (e.g., feminist therapy [Brown, 1994] and some approaches to trauma treatment [McCann & Pearlman, 1990; Meichenbaum, 1994; Ochberg, 1988]), but can be integrated into virtually any theoretical perspective with thought and care.

The therapist who asserts or implies that the conduct of treatment is a mysterious process in which the client is to be a passive and compliant recipient is at much greater risk of taking over the client's life history and creating for the client a frightening new personal history than is one who constructs the therapy process as a cooperative venture taking place with two experts. When therapists see their clients as expert in themselves and expert in knowing aspects of their own experience, and see themselves as expert in the processes of creating safety and containment and facilitating change, then they have the parameters of a situation in which the risks of coercion and suggestion are greatly reduced. It can be difficult for some therapists to adopt the mindset necessary to produce this collaborative model. At times, therapist training has focused on "managing the client" and "controlling the session"—notions that fail to allow for the client's authority and power. Sometimes, the demands of third-party payors to "solve the problem" also can lead to an authoritarian treatment strategy in which clients' needs for respect and careful timing and pacing are ignored in deference to maintaining favor with a case manager.

Similarly, it can be difficult for both therapist and client to see the latter as an expert and authority when she or he is feeling emotionally overpowered by intrusive images of childhood abuse or awakens to find her- or himself huddled in a corner, clutching a blanket, and shivering with terror. However, as we discussed previously, as therapists, we can never for a moment forget the adult autonomy of the people with whom we work. Even in their moments of pain and terror, the people with whom we work maintain some knowledge of what is real and true for them; if they are confused, our task as clinicians is to assist them in regaining the power to emerge from that confusion, not to impose artificial certitudes reflecting the needs, convenience, or prejudices of the therapist. We can collaborate with clients in attending to what Spielberger (1995) and his colleagues call *psychological vital signs*: emotional states and personality traits. The idea is never to ignore, obliterate, or override intense feelings such as panic, terror, or despair with the prefabricated "reality" as viewed by the therapist, but rather for therapist and client to work together to respect and understand the client's feelings. Therapists can also support clients in differentiating their needs, feelings, and realities from those of the significant persons in their lives.

Because clients who are experiencing delayed recall may be in a state of crisis and severe distress, they are likely to be more vulnerable than usual to abuses of therapist power, both those that most clinicians would agree are malign, as well as others that are more benign-appearing on the surface but can still serve to strip the client of power and reduce active participation as an adult in the therapy process. Many people who have been in such a crisis state will describe how eager they were to cooperate with whatever their therapist asked, even when required to suspend critical judgment and "go with the program." The desperation experienced by a person who is experiencing painful intrusive recollections cannot be underestimated as a motivating factor for compliance; many clients will do whatever it takes to get better and rely upon the therapist to define what those necessary steps might be. People with a history of sexual abuse may be at particular risk for revictimization (Kluft, 1990). Some of the most striking evidence for this willingness to comply emerges from cases involving abuse in psychotherapy (see Pope, 1994).

For example, in a case evaluated by one of the authors, a man in his twenties entered treatment after beginning to experience intrusive recollections of sexual abuse by his stepfather. The therapist convinced the client that in order to get better, he must experience sexual contact with the therapist so as to reenact the abuse from an adult perspective. This, said the therapist, would allow the feelings of being sodomized and fellated to become associated with his adult body rather than with his childhood recollections. The client had never been consensually sexual with a man, but complied with this directive because, as he later told the evaluator, despite his disgust and distaste for what the therapist was prescribing, he was desperate to get well.[4] The client recalled rationalizing that "a medicine which cures will have to taste very terrible." People who have been sexually abused, in addition, may have been well socialized to comply with the apparently irrational demands of authority figures in exchange for care and nurturance. Thus, apparently absurd requirements of therapy may not be questioned.

This extreme willingness of some clients to do virtually anything an exploitive therapist asks of them may be very difficult for some to accept and empathize with. Why would anyone allow someone else to do something so unwanted by the person? An analogy is sometimes helpful. Those of us who have undergone surgery might have difficulty explaining to someone who has no familiarity with the process why we would ever let a virtual stranger stick a knife into us.

A key concern for any therapist is the willingness of potential clients to enter evaluation or therapy. Do they feel pressure (e.g.,

---

[4]For research, theory, and discussion of therapists' sexualization of therapy, see Pope, 1994; and Pope, Sonne, and Holroyd, 1993.

from family members, employers, law enforcement officers, the courts) to undertake a venture that they fear, don't believe in, don't want to enter, or have no commitment to? If so, how can the therapist act to mitigate that pressure and reassure clients that they continue to have choice even though they are currently feeling out of control?

If the person does seem eager for clinical services, does he or she understand what will be provided? This is a fundamental aspect of the informed consent process discussed above. If the person has no idea or understanding of what the assessment or therapy entails and its potential consequences, it is hard to know just what the eagerness or consent mean. Frequently reassessing the client's consent to treatment and reviewing the treatment plan with the client on a regular basis can aid in reducing the risk that a client is compliantly participating in treatment simply to alleviate distress, but feeling uncertain and uncomfortable all the while with the therapist's interventions. It can be useful to remind the client that there are always alternatives, some of which do not involve participating in therapy. Clinicians can also ask the client to be an active participant in identifying what is important and useful in therapy.

In a case in which one of the authors was a consultant to a therapist, the client, a woman in her middle forties who had avidly researched questions of how to further her treatment, came into a session one day after having read on an Internet bulletin board about a new technique for reducing traumatic imagery. She suggested that this might be a helpful strategy for her use in controlling the intrusive material that had been plaguing her for several years now with little surcease. The therapist and client discussed several alternatives, including the therapist obtaining the new skills necessary to use the technique or making a referral to a therapist with training in it. Ultimately, the client decided that it would make the most sense for her to try this out with a consultant before having the therapist go ahead and invest in the training. The therapist agreed to simultaneously do further reading on the technique to see whether it would mesh well with current approaches to practice. When the technique proved somewhat helpful to the client, the therapist was spurred to learn it and to integrate it into the client's ongoing treatment.

Considering options that do not involve therapy, such as medication, spiritual practice, self-help groups, or changes in diet and exercise, may be threatening or disconcerting for some therapists. When a client suggests that it may be better to switch to another therapist or discontinue therapy altogether, therapists may feel criticized, guilty, ashamed, angry, or sad, or have other uncomfortable feelings. All too often, therapists may reflexively label a client's questions about continuing therapy as resistance. It may be much more helpful to welcome a client's wondering about termination as a reflection of the client's taking increased responsibility for thinking through possibilities, an opportunity for therapist and client to question the treatment plan and the results it has or has not produced, and a reminder of options and resources beyond therapy sessions.[5]

Finally, an extreme eagerness, a willingness to please, and a readiness to do whatever the therapist says are not uncommon in clinical work. Only if therapists recognize, respect, and appreciate these factors are they in a position to understand their implications for assessment and therapy and to ensure that they do not mishandle, exploit, or abuse these factors and the client. Eager, desperate clients are at potential risk to be exploited or harmed when a therapist prescribes certain steps for getting well—be they the excavation of memories of childhood, the complete avoidance of such material, required attendance at daily psychotherapy, sexual contact with a therapist, cutting off all contact with the family, forgiving and reconciling with a perpetrator, or filing a lawsuit against the alleged perpetrator. Therapists working with clients in such a state of crisis must explore how they can communicate reassurance and comfort to the client without implying that it is only through certain invariant courses of action that relief or healing will emerge. Instead, the clinician in such circumstances must continually seek ways to enhance the client's active and autonomous participation in the treatment process, even when this is anxiety-provoking for the therapist. *If, as therapists, we can expect our clients to contain the*

---

[5]See, e.g., Cooper & Cooper's [1991, pp. 173–189] chapter on "How People Change With and Without Therapy."

*distress and ambiguity inherent in a careful examination of intrusive recollections, so, too, can we contain the anxiety inherent in sharing power with our clients.*

## Monitoring the Therapist's Emotional, Cognitive, and Other Responses

There are few greater challenges to a therapist than to sit as witness to stories of the abuse of children. While it may be possible to intellectualize and distance oneself from war, crime victimization, and natural disaster, all therapists have been children themselves, and many have children of their own. The capacity for empathy with, and thus the risk of boundary loss to, the pain, confusion, shame, or terror of the client who was once a sexually abused child may be significantly heightened. It is telling that, in their volume on vicarious traumatization, Pearlman & Saakvitne (1995) chose as the prototypical situation to explore that of psychotherapy with the adult survivor of childhood sexual abuse.

Therapists also encounter this material at very different points in personal and professional development. One of the authors can recall, early in career development, being terrified and numbed by a client's story of childhood sexual abuse, and by the seemingly relentless nature of the flashbacks, nightmares, and intrusive images with which the client battled. Many hours of consultation and training, 15 years, and thousands of therapy sessions later, a similar experience with a client evokes feelings of warmth and compassion, and a sense of admiration for the capacity to cope in the face of terror. For some therapists, this scenario plays in reverse: early interest, almost fascination, with the phenomenon of dissociation, PTSD, and other aspects of delayed recall are followed by fatigue, withdrawal, and the inability to remain present to the client. For the therapist who has never personally confronted abuse, such stories from a client may evoke incredulity; for the therapist who has her- or himself survived this violation, it may be retraumatizing.

What we wish to emphasize at this point is the importance of therapist self-care in working with the client recovering memories of childhood trauma as another strategy for avoiding malpractice with clients. Therapists working with someone who is bombarded with the intrusions of delayed recall must have adequate professional and collegial support to prevent themselves from becoming overwhelmed. Professional consultation both with peers and more experienced clinicians can be essential; personal psychotherapy may also be a source of support. Therapists working with the client with recovered memories may also experience a sort of "survivor guilt" for having avoided this traumatic childhood experience; such guilt feelings may, if unnoticed and unchecked, become the nucleus of inappropriate heroics on the part of the therapist—such as permanently forgoing vacations—that are often a prelude to serious malpractice. Obtaining the support and care of consultation can be preventative measures that allow clinicians to remember that a part of our job description is to maintain our well-being so that we can offer containment for distress and tolerance for ambiguity.

## Changing Needs of the Client: How Can We Respond?

The questions and challenges that emerge in a therapist's office are not always what the therapist is prepared to deal with. A behavior therapist who specializes in working with people suffering from phobias, obsessions, and compulsions may take on what appears to be a simple treatment contract to address fear of snakes and find him or herself three sessions later with a client who is regressing on the office floor and reporting terrifying dreams of being sexually abused by a familiar-looking older man. Dissociative symptoms may begin to emerge in a person in treatment for an eating disorder (Torem, 1986; McCallum, Lock, Kullatoj, & Wetzel, 1992) or in alcohol and drug detoxification facilities. A graduate student in training may be assigned the care of a person who presents with symptoms of a major depression but begins to report delayed recollections of being raped as a child as treatment progresses.

Therapists in this situation have two often conflicting responsibilities. These are, first, not to practice outside their areas of intellectual and emotional competence, and second, not to abandon a client who is in crisis and in greater than ever need of stability. The desire to soothe a client should not, however, be an obstacle to a therapist's reasoned decision to transfer care if the clinician honestly assesses that she or he will be ultimately placing the client at risk by continuing as the treating therapist. There are a number of creative strategies for transferring care that do not convey a message of rejection, although they require careful planning by the therapist.

During a case in which one of the authors served as consultant, a therapist had been treating a woman for several years for seemingly intractable symptoms of depression and anxiety. There was a good working relationship, and the client expressed deep feelings of trust in the therapist. It was at this stage in treatment that the client began to actively dissociate and to present alter personalities during therapy sessions. A careful assessment of the client for dissociative disorders uncovered a lifelong history suggestive of dissociative identity disorder. The therapist felt completely beyond her depth, but the client was unwilling to cease treatment. The therapist then proposed to the client a treatment team of the original therapist and a second person, highly skilled in working with DID, who was known to the client as one of the therapist's consultation resources. The client was amenable to this, and the two therapists devised a joint treatment plan in which the original therapist focused on issues of containment and self-care, and the specialist worked on specific issues relating to dissociation. The client improved rapidly, and within 2 years of this joint therapy was able to terminate treatment with the original provider, at her own time and on her own speed.

When approached by people in need, therapists need to evaluate whether the anticipated issues fall within their realm of competence or expertise. To use an extreme example, an Anglo therapist who speaks only English and has never learned about or conducted clinical work with abuse victims should evaluate carefully whether he or she is the best person to work with a Hispanic patient who speaks very little English and who has recently recovered memories of childhood sexual abuse. Even when therapist and client speak the same basic language, it can be important to attend carefully to possible regional cultural or language differences that could lead to potentially problematic confusions of meaning. In one instance, a woman born in Puerto Rico walked into her office and found someone rifling through her purse. The potential thief ran off in the midst of an emotional confrontation, although no one was touched. Later, the woman described this event in Spanish to a social worker who had been born in Cuba. She used the word *asalto* to mean a "confrontation." The social worker, however, understood this term to refer to a physical assault (G. Koocher, personal communication, June 12, 1995) because the term was used differently in Cuban Spanish than in Puerto Rican Spanish.

## How Large a Treatment Team?

Case examples on pages 153–154, page 179, and elsewhere in this book bring up the question of how many providers are optimal. Whereas in an inpatient setting there commonly are a large number of professionals working on a treatment team, when possible clients can be offered options regarding the setting and the number of therapists by whom they will be treated. There is no general answer to the question of how many helpers there should be. Some clients may need the privacy, stability, and consistency of a single therapist. Trust may emerge gradually. Knowing that the therapist alone will hear their words, clients may slowly loosen what seem like immutable bonds holding a secret in. Other clients may heal and prosper best when many therapists are involved. The presence of a variety of clinicians may help clients to feel that they have more than one lifeline, that material they could not disclose to one clinician they may be able to disclose to another, and—crucially for some clients—that the potential intensity and privacy of an exclusively one-on-one therapeutic relationship may terrify some clients who fear that the therapist will be able to molest or otherwise hurt them. In the last instance, the client can be reassured by the protective presence and involvement of other clinicians, even though they are not physically present in the consulting room. For some clients, a range of providers who work in different modalities—talk therapy, movement therapy, art therapy, bodywork—may prove most helpful, allowing the expression and integration of experience in a range of ways. In such situations it is crucial that all members of the treatment team implement a well coordinated treatment plan, communicate clearly with each other (always with the client's informed consent), and avoid allowing turf issues, competition, or jealousy to stunt the team's ability to work together for the good of the client.

A woman in her late forties sought treatment from one of the authors, complaining of dissociative episodes of increasing frequency, nightmares, and what she described as "hallucinations" in which she felt her body become small and experienced being molested by her grandfather. The client became suicidal, requiring a period of inpatient therapy for purposes of safety and stabilization. While in treatment, she became quite insistent that all of her caregivers work together; she reported that it decreased her anxiety significantly to see her "team" in the conference room talking with one another. Later in the therapy, as more recollections emerged, the client was able to make sense of her strong need to see her caregivers working and talking together; she remembered how the various adults in her family communicated so poorly and were so distant from one another. When she had tried as a child to report what was being done to her, it had gotten lost in the general poverty of the family's communications. She realized that she did not trust caregivers to communicate with one another well enough to ensure her safety, nor did she believe that any one therapist alone was sufficient to contain her. Her primary therapist was able to frame this for her as an example of how the client knew important things about her self-care and had internal resources that she had never previously been aware of for meeting her own needs for safety.

However, when a client is required to deal with many therapists, rather than given options and choice about the therapy modality that is the best fit and most comfortable, the client runs the risk of feeling and being overpowered by the sheer force of authority of these many expert voices. Pasley (1994) and Gavigan (1994) have described how the abusive therapies that led to their false memories were characterized by multiple therapists who supported one another in hammering home the message that unfounded memories of abuse must be hunted down and dug out for healing to occur, leading each of these women into what they ultimately considered extremely destructive misadventures. Both of the authors have encountered similar examples in our forensic practices in which clients have been the target of multiple pressures from an array of therapists who were insistent on a treatment strategy in which the client had little or no say.

Care must be taken when considering the possible array of helpers, the settings in which they provide services, and the general services to be provided. For each client who believes him- or herself to be recovering memories of past trauma, the therapist must carefully address such questions as the following and ensure that none is answered by default (i.e., the therapist simply failed to consider it), prejudice, or convenience to the therapist:

- ☐ Are there considerations such as risk for suicide or threats from a third party that require special resources on either an outpatient basis or perhaps an inpatient basis?
- ☐ Has an adequate assessment been conducted at this point to enable questions about potential danger to self or others, danger from others, grave disability, impending crises, medical emergencies, and so on to be identified? If not, what other steps should the clinician take immediately to address those questions?
- ☐ What interventions are most likely to draw on and enhance the client's strengths?
- ☐ What interventions are least likely to place the client at risk for unintended harmful side-effects or consequences?
- ☐ Even if both therapist and client agree that the memories that the client has recovered are to be a primary focus of therapy, does the client have other special needs to be addressed? Do these needs, if any, require specialists, additional personnel, or other settings?
- ☐ Does the therapist feel any need for additional support, consultation, or supervision? If so, how is this need best met? What characteristics constitute those of the most helpful possible consultant or supervisor?
- ☐ Has the client received other mental health services? If so, why is he or she now seeking services from you, as opposed to the previous professionals? (There may, of course, be a variety of good reasons for seeking a new source of help, such as a prior therapist's moving away, ill-

ness, retirement, death, or simply wishing a therapist of a different gender or approach than that of the prior therapist. Some reasons, such as the prior therapist's continual suggestions that the client must be an incest victim or a sexual relationship with a prior therapist, may be extremely difficult for a client to discuss or even acknowledge.)

☐ What helpers, settings, and services does the *client* believe would be most helpful? This does not, of course, mean that therapists must grant a client's every wish. It is not uncommon for clients to wish for sexual contact with the therapist, medications that would be harmful for them, or other "interventions" that must not be implemented. However, asking about and understanding what the client wants can be extremely valuable. In some instances, the client may actually come up with an intervention that the therapist had not considered but ultimately agrees makes sense. In other instances, the therapist may be able to suggest acceptable variations or substitutes; this can be an important aspect of informed consent. In many instances it fosters greater communication between client and therapist. It emphasizes from the start that the client is to be an active participant in his or her own therapy.

## Containment and Flooding

As this manuscript was being prepared, a consensus appeared to be emerging among many who work with trauma survivors that an approach to treatment in which containment and self-care constitute the initial focus of intervention is the preferred strategy and one which best reduces risks of harm to the client (Alpert et al., 1996; Courtois, 1988; Frank, 1996; Harvey, 1996; Harvey & Herman, 1994; Herman, 1992; see also chapter 2). Therapists must continuously address concerns about the potential for memories to overwhelm and overpower their clients so that the experience of remembering itself does not become a retraumatizing event, but rather can be used in a controlled manner to provide optimal exposure of the sort useful for reintegration of traumatic affects and images.

Perhaps one consideration is the realization that memory is not completely under conscious control. There is no magical technique by which a client can learn to open and shut the spigot to particular memories as if memories were water in a pipe. At times, people who have experienced intrusive recall of trauma describe the sense that they are walking on eggs, wondering when some new, previously neutral environmental stimulus of smell, sight, sound, or touch will suddenly lead to an overpowering sense of being transported to a frightening past.

There are, however, factors that may influence an individual to be more or less vulnerable to frightening, aversive, or otherwise unwanted memories surging into consciousness as intrusive fragments, unbidden images, or dissociative flashbacks. One factor likely to intensify a client's fears of becoming overwhelmed by recovered memories is if the therapist adds pressure by saying something like "You will never get well until you remember whatever it was that happened to you" or "You will never get well until you let go of this focus on the past and get on with your life."

Therapists may sometimes use techniques that evoke intense affect or a catharsis without adequate assessment, planning, knowledge of the empirical literature, or demonstrable competence. Whereas the notion that catharsis per se is curative still pervades the popular culture of psychotherapy, it is a notion that seems to lack empirical data. Therapists may wish to consider strategies with a client for titration of affect, giving clients opportunities to move at their own pace and working to create and enhance feelings of safety at each step. Stage- and phase-oriented approaches to treatment that are emerging as the most commonly suggested strategies for working with this population also emphasize the importance of integrating affect and cognition, giving the client ample time to digest and make meaning of what is being remembered (Briere, 1996; Courtois, 1988; Harvey, 1996; Harvey & Herman, 1994). Empirical data suggest that controlled exposure to affect and memory in which titrated exposure to trauma-related material is used to metabolize and integrate previously fragmentary memories into more coherent cognitive narratives may be specifically helpful in addressing intrusive symptoms of PTSD (Carbonell & Figley, 1995; Foa, Rothbaum, Riggs, & Murdock, 1991, Shapiro, 1995). Such exposure can be differentiated from uncontrolled catharsis of the sort that was popularized in the early 1970s in the encounter movement, but which has not been shown to be effective in accomplishing much of anything except destroying pillows.

In some instances, a client may already be experiencing flooding upon entering therapy. The client may be experiencing what seem to her or him to be indications of abuse in the form of recovered memory fragments, intrusions, or flashbacks. Van der Hart, Brown, and van der Kolk (1989; see also Brown & Fromm, 1986; van der Hart, 1993) suggest that "People with acute posttraumatic reactions . . . first of all needed stabilization of symptoms. This consisted mostly of rest (including hospitalization), simplification of life style, and forming a therapeutic relationship" (p. 383).

Questions about how to work toward stabilization, when that is a part of the treatment plan, are difficult and complex. Stereotypical and unexamined views of what factors are most likely to decrease the flooding must be avoided. Although some clients have found various forms of solitary, silent contemplation or meditation soothing, these techniques should be considered with great caution for clients who are flooded with flashbacks, intrusive images, unbidden thoughts, and so on. Pope (1994) cited an example of unintended consequences of some meditative techniques:

> One patient who had learned meditation when quite young decided to resume the practice to help relieve the turmoil she suffered as a result of sex. . . . Meditation, however, seemed to evoke a dissociative state during which she felt lost and made incomprehensible sounds. She emerged from her repeated attempts to meditate in a state of panic. Discussing this experience with her . . . therapist, she discovered that the sounds were recreations of the noises that [the perpetrator] made when he was having sex with her. That so seemingly gentle, safe, and effective a technique as meditation can, under certain circumstances, leave a patient more vulnerable to distress underscores the importance of matching carefully each potential intervention to the individual patient's needs and situation with alertness to unintended side effects. (pp. 155–156)

Though at times contraindicated for patients who are flooded with intrusive images or flashbacks, methods of silent contemplation or meditation are examples of interventions that tend to promote autonomy, self-confidence, and the ability to care for oneself. They are methods that the therapist can teach to the patient or suggest that the patient learn on his or her own. The patient is then empowered to use the method as needed and is not dependent on the therapist for each administration. Like many of the other methods mentioned in this book, these encourage patients to participate actively in their therapy and to use therapy to heal, grow, and learn techniques that they can later continue without the direct help of the therapist.

Whereas interventions from the therapist to help calm and stabilize patients who are flooded with images may be necessary at the beginning of therapy or during crises, helping patients to begin to learn to calm and stabilize themselves at the earliest possible point in therapy can be extremely useful. Salter (1995), for example, discusses how, in working with some clients, the therapist can

> teach methods of self-soothing and not assume that the client will sooner or later simply internalize the therapist and thus let go. A nonabused 5-year-old, whose parents had divorced, once drew for me a picture of her in her dad's house and one of her in her mom's house. In each one, she drew inside her head a picture of the missing parent. She held each one in her head, she said, when she was in the other's house so that she would not miss them. It was a simple trick for a nontraumatized 5-year-old with object constancy, a trick no one had to teach her. It is an achingly difficult one for a traumatized adult, one someone needs to teach her. (p. 292)

As Salter noted, for some clients, the capacity to maintain an internal mental representation of either the therapist or any soothing person or object may itself have been impaired by prior negative experiences in the client's life. Therapists need to carefully assess the degree to which this capacity may have been damaged and then work with the client to develop those skills. Some people who are excellent at caring for others (because this was a survival need in a hostile childhood environment) may be almost completely incapable of accepting such caring, and may be remarkably unable to assist in their own containment for a period of time when being overwhelmed by intrusive traumatic images and sensations.

A final concern about approaches that calm, stabilize, or soothe patients: It is crucial to question what is causing the patient's agitated or distressed state and to develop useful working hypotheses about possible causes of the distress. Such hypotheses should not be cast in concrete (and, consistent with a major theme of this book, should be continually questioned), but may provide a helpful initial position from which to approach therapy. The reasons for questioning in this area are many, but three are particularly important.

First, as clear an understanding as possible about what one does and does not know about the patient and the patient's circumstances and background may be crucial. Thus, containment can be structured so as to clarify, rather than obscure, what the client has experienced. Containment strategies can move the client towards the integration of affect and intellect, helping make sense of the experience for both client and therapist.

Second, developing a working hypothesis about causality can be helpful in the patient's understanding of the actual causes of distress. A woman who is in agony over intrusive images that seem consistent with incest may think she is simply crazy. However, if she discovers that the flashbacks are the result of a prior therapist's malpractice or that they actually are the result of her having experienced incest as a child, then what she views as the "symptoms" of her craziness may begin to seem to her less manifestations of her "mental illness" and more a reasonable, understandable, and perhaps even healthy response to an injurious act—an attempt on her part to work through the trauma. Alternatively, if she learns that these images are due to untreated obsessive–compulsive disorder (OCD), and that serotonergic medications and cognitive therapy can treat this condition, she may similarly feel empowered with self-knowledge and less frightened of herself.

Third, the agitation or distress may (*or may not*) represent a source of important information and motivation. To use the two possibilities in the previous paragraph, which, of course, are but two possibilities (i.e., that the intrusive images are due to a prior therapist's malpractice or to actual incest), if the client had begun to experience the images only when she was in the presence of the prior therapist or only when her incestuous father was playing with her own daughter, the flashbacks and the agitation or distress might represent a danger signal that the prior therapist or her father represents a threat. This would clearly be the sort of data useful to the client. Obviously, any therapeutic approach whose sole purpose is to stop or soothe away responses that are alerting the patient to actual danger or abusive situations is, in and of itself, a danger and disservice to the patient. A possible analogy might be a woman who seeks therapy because she is nervous because her husband beats her, so the therapist's sole therapeutic focus is to teach her guided imagery to help her become less nervous or to prescribe anxiolytic medications (see Pope, Sonne, & Holroyd, 1993, p. 175). The patient, the patient's difficulties, and the possible interventions must never be taken out of adequate context. Some of the very earliest first-person literature by adult survivors of childhood sexual abuse describes the various silencing strategies employed by so-called "helpers" under the guise of soothing or relieving anxiety. A clinician must take care not to become intolerant of or impatient with a client's distress, so as to avoid creating containment strategies that are actually means of shutting the client up. The potential interventions, however, must be based on the clearest possible understanding of what needs to be addressed, thus underscoring the importance of assessment and questioning prior to and at all times during the process of intervention.

## Boundaries of the Therapy Process

Because sexual abuse constitutes such a severe violation of the emotional and physical boundaries of a child, the importance of boundaries in the therapy process with a person who may be recovering memories of such abuse is even more paramount than usual. The nature of such boundaries and the client's possession of the confidentiality privilege should be spelled out at the start of informed consent and informed refusal, and reinforced in various ways throughout the therapy experience. But the very fact that sexual abuse is under discussion may itself lead to apparently unavoidable breaches in the walls around therapy. There are times, of course, when the law requires clinicians to talk with third parties about specific individuals. When a delayed recall of abuse leads to the knowledge that an alleged perpetrator is now in inappropriate contact with other children, the standards mandating one to report suspected child abuse may come into play, requiring that a therapist make a report to a child protective agency.[6]

This sort of mandatory report constitutes a rare source of unavoidable breach of boundaries. But other breaks may emerge from the treatment plan or other factors. For example, a client may seek payment for therapy through a victim's compensation fund requiring that a perpetrator be identified to authorities and that the therapist write regular progress reports to the funding agency.

Whatever one's views on these issues, it is crucial that the therapist rethink and question each option and examine its implications and likely consequences. For instance, if along with calling the child protective agency, a therapist also calls other family members of a client to announce the presence of a sexual abuse perpetrator in their midst, is the therapist genuinely acting to protect children, or is this a malicious act? It is also crucial that therapists be fully aware of current criminal, civil, and administrative legislation and case law in the relevant jurisdiction governing mandated or discretionary disclosure of information to law enforcement personnel or others, actual or potential duties to third parties, and so on. We strongly recommend that therapists consult with competent and qualified attorneys who have expertise and experience in the relevant areas and who practice in the relevant state. (Legislation, case law, and administrative regulations vary from jurisdiction to jurisdiction.) It is also important to consider the clinical issues embedded in a manda-

---

[6]For a more detailed discussion of the relevant laws, see Kalichman (1993) and the books of mental health law for each state in the American Psychological Association Law and Mental Health book series (e.g., Caudill & Pope, 1995).

tory reporting process; that is, how will this affect a client's placement in the family system of origin to have the therapist file a Children's Protective Services report about an older family member? How will therapist and client plan to handle responses from the family of origin? If either therapist or client is considering going directly to the family with his or her concerns, what possible emotional, legal, or other risks are being taken?

More recently, some authors have suggested that anytime a client alleges sexual abuse, be it never forgotten or recently recalled, the therapist must engage in an investigative process to determine the validity of what is being reported (McHugh, 1994; Yapko, 1993; chapter 3, this volume). According to this view (see chapter 3), therapists supposedly must call members of the family—including, if necessary, the person alleged to have perpetrated the abuse—into the therapy office and inquire of them as to the reality of what the client says. Therapists who are considering this strategy need to consider the impact of such an intervention on the sense of safety and boundaries that the client obtains from therapy. There is some question in our minds of why this particular report of personal history should be more scrutinized than others. For instance, no one to our knowledge has suggested that clients who report overuse of alcohol must present lists of their drinking buddies so that the therapist may bring them to the office and query them, nor has anyone suggested that therapists respond to a client's report of having been robbed or raped but not notifying the police by going into the field to interview potential witnesses to verify the alleged rape or robbery.

## Is Confrontation Helpful?

Some therapists have found it helpful to arrange for clients who have recovered memories of childhood sexual abuse to confront the alleged perpetrator. At times, this has been done in the therapist's office, with the therapist present to provide support and validation for the survivor. However, therapists contemplating this strategy must, as always, carefully consider risks and benefits for the client, and attend to issues of timing. The therapist and client need to consider together carefully how and when such an encounter will take place, so that an important goal of treatment, that of empowering the client, will be embedded in any such meeting. Therapist and client also need to consider the rationale for this strategy: What does it intend to accomplish? Are there other ways in which to meet this end? What effect will the presence of an alleged perpetrator in the therapy office have on the client's future sense of the safety and boundaries of therapy? What possible beneficial and harmful consequences may result from such a meeting? Whose needs are being met by this intervention—the client's needs or the therapist's?

In some cases, a therapist may focus inappropriately on anger and confrontation, and may push a client to enact these feelings when they fit badly with the client's own personal worldview and values. This constitutes a violation in several ways—first, it is a violation of the client, who has become an object for the enactment of the therapist's own needs, and second, this inappropriate focus violates the therapy process itself in that containment and safety are no longer assured. During a case in which one of the authors was a consultant, a client sought a second opinion because she was uncomfortable with her therapist's insistence that she meet with and confront her father, who she had come to believe had sexually abused her. The therapist explained to her his belief that when people "held onto anger," they were at risk for developing a variety of physical illnesses and that the client had a responsibility to herself to call her abuser to account. The therapist had urged regular behavioral rehearsals on the client, using an "empty chair" model. The client told the consultant that she simply did not feel comfortable yelling and screaming at the empty chair, but wanted to do what was necessary to get better. The consultant suggested that there were a variety of ways to heal from abuse, and worked with the client in attending more carefully to issues of informed refusal.

However, for some clients, the expression of anger and confrontation can feel profoundly empowering. One individual evaluated by one of the authors shared how he and the members of his male survivors support group would come together for "anger parties," where people would take turns tearing up old telephone books. The man, who had been severely beaten and raped for many years by a boarding school teacher and who had begun to experience intrusive recall of the abuse in his thirties after achieving sobriety from alcohol and drug abuse, also found it helpful to take self-defense classes in which he could kick vigorously at an instructor dressed in a padded suit, imagining that it was the teacher who had harmed him. The client described a significant decrease in his depression resulting from these activities. What is notable is that these were not prescribed by his therapist; rather, they emerged from his and his peers' creative attempts to find safe (e.g., not harmful to other people) outlets for the rage they felt at their abusers. It is important to note that some family members, when abuse is at issue, may become quite upset at any expression of anger on the part of the client, even if it involves only tearing up phone books. They may file an ethics or other formal complaint against the therapist, or take other steps.

Barrett (1995) describes a mediation model for encounters between survivors and their alleged perpetrators that can be distinguished from confrontation by its emphasis on attempting to create communication and some form of coexistence between the parties. Regardless of the model, therapists must adequately understand the clinical, ethical, and legal implications of inviting someone else into the therapist–client relationship. As part of informed consent, the therapist should also ensure that the client has any information about such encounters that might affect his or her decision about participation. When the therapist invites a family member or other person in, the interaction may affect privilege and the duty of care, and may create subtle but destructive conflicts of interest. We strongly recommend that therapists considering such interventions consult adequately with an attorney who is skilled and experienced in mental health law.

Therapist and patient can carefully discuss which, if any, approaches the client wishes to use in taking the new belief that the client has been sexually abused out of the privacy of the therapy office and into the glaring light of other interpersonal exchanges. It may be especially important to explore the client's goals and expectations. Since it is common even for people who have perpetrated abuse to deny or minimize it (as the father of one of our clients said to his daughter, "I thought you were too young for it to bother you very much"), clients need to consider whether they possess sufficient resiliency to deal with the possibility that their family or friends will not respond in a positive manner to the client's sharing the sexual abuse story, and to be certain that they have a many-faceted support system in place at the time of such a disclosure.

# The Function of Forgiveness and of Not Forgiving

The meeting with the alleged perpetrator brings up the related topic of the client's forgiveness of the alleged perpetrator. Like instructions that the client must cut off all contact with the family or at least with the perpetrator, the message that the client must forgive an abuser seems to be a form of intrusive advocacy (Pope, Sonne, & Holroyd, 1993). *Intrusive advocacy* is the therapist's "tendency to want to guide, direct, or determine a patient's decisions about what steps to take or what steps not to take in regard to a perpetrator" (p. 116). Olio's (1992) analysis of what she terms the three myths of mandated forgiveness are summarized next[7].

## Myth #1—"Forgiveness Makes You a Better Person"

Olio notes that

> This myth originates with the difficulties we all have in facing and acknowledging the ugly act of child abuse. Especially when we contemplate its possibility in our own homes, child abuse calls into question many of our hopes and beliefs of the world as a fundamentally decent and safe place. It is, of course, natural to want to do everything possible to make the hurt go away. It is a well-meaning mistake that is often made to hope that by encouraging the survivor not to think about the abuse, it will stop bothering him or her.
>
> . . . . In addition, I believe this myth reflects a fear and a misunderstanding of anger. In this myth anger, outrage, and

---

revenge, are all used interchangeably, with no distinction drawn between the emotion itself and the various options available to express it. It seems important to remember that anger is a feeling, and feelings themselves do not damage anyone. Feelings of anger are a natural response to abuse, and as Bass and Davis (1988) point out, anger can sometimes be the "backbone of healing" the damage caused by sexual abuse.

## Myth #2—"Forgiveness Must be All Encompassing"

Olio comments that

> I imagine this concept of linking self-forgiveness to the forgiveness of others comes from the belief that, if we can acknowledge both the good and evil in others and forgive their mistakes, then we can more easily accept the good and evil in ourselves, and thus achieve self-forgiveness. Although this idea has theoretical merit, it would seem to apply more to the general development of a capacity to forgive rather than to the decision to forgive in a particular situation. The recognition that forgiveness can be a valuable process does not necessarily lead to the conclusion that forgiveness must be given in all instances . . .
>
> Self-forgiveness, or what might be more aptly titled self-acceptance, is an essential step in the integration of the abuse experiences. Survivors may have to forgive/accept that they did have needs, that they were small and powerless, that they had feelings in response to the abuse (pain, fear, rage, and in some cases even pleasure), and that it has taken time to heal. However, the idea that this self-forgiveness is somehow contingent on forgiving the abuser is troublesome, as it suggests the necessity of a merging with the person who is to be forgiven . . .
>
> Adults whose physical and psychic boundaries have been violated by childhood sexual abuse have difficulty enough maintaining a healthy sense of separation from the abuser. Especially in those cases where the abuser is someone, perhaps the only one, by whom the child has felt loved, the child may feel sorry for and/or have a deep need to protect the abuser. . . .
>
> The belief that forgiveness must be total to be effective implies that there is only one kind of "good enough" forgive-

ness. In reality the meaning and degree of forgiveness varies from person to person. Each person, as he or she is able to reconnect to his or her own experiences without the use of denial and dissociation, must find the type of forgiveness that fits for that unique person. If forgiveness is to be meaningful, it must be given out of free choice, which necessarily implies the freedom not to give it.

## Myth #3 "Failure to Forgive Maintains Helplessness"

Olio comments that

> Myth #3, which addresses issues of helplessness and responsibility, has been heavily influenced by the recovery movement and 12 step programs. Faced with the powerlessness experienced by individuals who abuse alcohol and the resulting enmeshed, codependent relationships, recovery programs have stressed the importance of each person's taking responsibility for him or herself. This has provided individuals with an understanding of the need to take charge of changing their lives, regardless of others' behaviors. Many people have experienced a great relief with the realization that they don't need to change anyone else in order to get on with their own lives. Forgiveness has been a central component of this approach . . . .
> This issue of empowerment is a tremendously important one for survivors of sexual abuse. Empowerment develops as the individual is able to fully acknowledge the painful realities of childhood, while simultaneously integrating an updated reality of grown-up strength and options. Forgiveness may be part of this process for some individuals; for others it will not be. The fact remains, however, [that] although forgiveness may result in a shift in the experience of victimization for some survivors, there is no evidence to suggest that survivors cannot come to an experience of empowerment and effectiveness through other means as well.

The issue of forgiveness is one that also intersects with a variety of personal ethical and theological systems of which either therapist or client may take part. Therapists need to become aware of what their own ethic is about this matter and then be careful to differentiate that personal ethic from what is clinically useful for the client and from the client's own system of belief about the concept of forgiveness. As with the expression of anger and confrontation, the expression of forgiveness can be profoundly helpful for some people and completely disempowering for others. Salter (1995) notes that many of the requests for forgiveness that come from perpetrators are self-serving and designed, consciously or otherwise, to silence the victim and reduce the perpetrator's own distress over being exposed to the painful consequences of his or her acts. The therapist working with the client around the issue of forgiveness needs to question whether the client is not being hooked into a similar experience of revictimization. Additionally, when a client's memories of abuse are relatively new, the urge to forgive may represent an attempt at premature closure of the topic based on the hope that this will make the frightening symptoms disappear. But as one trauma survivor with whom one of the authors has worked said in a poem written midway through the recovery process, "wounds heal from the bottom up and the inside out." Persistently urging forgiveness on a client prior to the opportunity to know and integrate one's experiences may again serve as an antitherapeutic form of silencing, and may prematurely reify the intrusive materials as memories before the client is certain of their actual nature.

## Finding "Truth" About Delayed Recall

When Frank Fitzpatrick began to experience his delayed recall of being sexually abused by Father James Porter, he was in the unusual situation of being able to call upon scores of other people who he knew had been in contact with Father Porter when they were also young and to get corroboration for his memories of sexual abuse, which were further confirmed by Porter's own confession. Similarly, Marilyn Van Derbur Atler's delayed recall of incestuous abuse by her father was confirmed by the never-forgotten memories of her similarly victimized sister. In a recently published chart review of 34 patients with DID that he had treated, Kluft (1995) found that 56% (19) of these patients were able to obtain independent confirmation of recalled abuse from observers, covictims, or even the perpetrators themselves. Of the 19 patients, 13 obtained corroboration for memories that were recalled during the course of treatment. But not everyone who experiences delayed recall will have access to this sort of corroborating material. How can therapists approach the issue of corroboration and the accuracy or inaccuracy of material that emerges as a recovered memory of childhood abuse?

First, therapists must once again remember that they are not in a position to ultimately validate or ultimately reject anything that their clients say about their lives. After all, the therapist was not present and did not witness the events in question. Even when a therapist has heard one sibling tell of sexual abuse, it cannot automatically be assumed that another sibling has had similar experiences, although the likelihood may be increased. Our experience and that of many other people who have worked with adult survivors of childhood trauma is that it is extremely difficult for people to believe that they were sexually abused as children, even when the details have never left their memories. Consequently, questions of validity, reality, and corroboration become even more complex when the memory has been delayed or out of consciousness for many years.

Therapists can empower clients in a number of ways at this point in the therapy process. Clients can be reminded that they are free to make their own decisions about what appears to them in images or dreams or flashbacks, and that the therapist will not push them in particular directions. After all, even in a forensic evaluation, the examiner does not speak to the ultimate issue of truth or falsity; in therapy—the natural home of ambiguity—it becomes even more important to allow this fluidity and uncertainty. Therapists can offer support for coping with the anxiety that derives from not having instant or convenient answers.

The therapist can also support clients in searching for corroboration *if this is what the client chooses to do*. Several studies reporting on clients with delayed recall of childhood abuse (Herman & Schatzow, 1987; Pope & Tabachnick, 1995) suggest that substantial numbers of the clients in question obtained corroboration of their recovered memories. One woman in treatment with one of the authors returned to her childhood hometown and called several people with whom she had attended elementary school simply to make contact. However, in the course of reacquainting herself with old friends, she discovered that she had made comments to several of them 30 years earlier that had been striking and disturbing, and thus memorable to the school friends, because they described sexual activities between the woman and her father. The client, who had spent her adolescence and young adulthood in a fog of drugs and alcohol and whose memories of incest had begun to intrude on her in sobriety, was astonished to learn of these witnesses that she had unknowingly created for herself. Not every person with delayed recall will find such striking corroboration. However, some clients may choose to seek out material that may be relevant to their recovered memories, such as school reports, medical records, or contemporaneous diaries. In some instances, as described earlier, there are others who, for whatever reasons, did not lose access to their recollections. It is important to emphasize both the potential strengths and the potential weaknesses of particular forms of information or corroboration about particular events. For example, that a client discovers that she had written in her diary at age 7 about being raped by her father and had told one or two trusted friends about it does not establish beyond question that the incest occurred. However, it may may cast doubt on allegations that she had a happy childhood and had confabulated a history of incest only as an adult in response to a therapist implanting the false memory.

At times, however, no such material is available. As therapists, we must support our clients in the realization that they may never know with absolute certainty what has happened to them. In these, as in all cases, we must empower our clients to be the ultimate experts regarding what is real for them, including the reality of possibly never knowing. Even the most fantastic story, which seems beyond our capacity to comprehend, may be true and real, and the most seemingly credible account can be utterly confabulated. But it is not within the skills of a psychotherapist to determine which is which with utter certainty. In some instances, we may aide our clients in a process of informed exploration by offering data to them about how memory works and how the suggestibility of children can be used to create recollections or perceptions that are inaccurate in content but contain valuable information about what may have happened.

For instance, a person who "remembers" being forced to drink "blood" can be questioned in a highly respectful and open-minded manner, about what sorts of things might be labelled "blood" to a suggestible child and remembered as such. One client treated by one of the authors who had such a recall reported that the "blood" made her feel sleepy when she drank it. On further thought, she considered that perhaps the "blood" had been wine or some other sort of red alcoholic beverage. This consideration led, in turn, to an association between the "blood of Christ"— the wine that she had seen the pastor of her church consecrate at communion services—and her childhood beliefs that this had really been blood in the communion cup. This last association aided her in understanding, as an adult, how easy it is to suggest something to a child, particularly when the suggestion came from a powerful authority figure and comported with reality as she understood it during her childhood (e.g., she had believed when young that the pastor was indeed drinking blood). The client came, over time, to no longer believe that she had drunk blood, but to an enhanced certainty that she had been sexually abused and that some of the holes in her recollection resulted from the effects of the soporific drink that had accompanied many of the episodes of abuse. Through the use of open-ended questions, therapists can support clients in the engagement of their adult functions of critical thinking. If this, in turn, means that at some point the client decides that none of her or his recollections were accurate, this also becomes the client's belief about reality, not subject to the therapist' needs to decide what constitutes "truth."

Individuals who at one point believed themselves to have accurately recalled sexual abuse may come to decide that this is not true and retract their original statements. At times, this reflects a clear development of new understandings about the nature of what was recalled. In other instances, a client may be responding to pressure from family or friends to relinquish statements that are distressing to others. Whatever the apparent motivations, a therapist's task, at this point as at others, is to follow the lead of the client and not become overly invested in the truth of what was previously presented as "real" by the client.

Memory is always reconstructive; new information and new experiences may lead a person to a reversal of their previous beliefs about their life. When the therapist has already been responding to the client's production of delayed recall materials with support for the client's exploration, reflection, and decision, then further transformations in the client's perceptions of the truth should come more easily.

However, it is also possible to treat an individual who is retracting materials that emerged in a previous therapy that the client believes to have been the result of pressure or suggestion from the previous therapist. During a case in which one of the authors testified as an expert witness, a young woman had been in treatment with a therapist who insisted that she had been sexually abused in her childhood by family members and clergy figures. She eventually produced material that was pronounced to be a "repressed memory of abuse" by the therapist. The client eventually broke away from the therapist and, after several months of no treatment, came to the conclusion that her new "memories" were invalid and had only emerged because of inappropriate treatment.

Again, the hallmark of competent response to a client in this circumstance is respect for the client's thoughtful consideration, questioning, and choices. When another therapist is being targeted for critique, it is particularly important that, as colleagues, we do not immediately, either consciously or otherwise, spring to his or her defense, but rather be open to the possibility that professional bad judgment or even malpractice has occurred. Not infrequently, therapist malpractice in the form of coercion and manipulation of a client's beliefs about the family of origin will be accompanied by other forms of psychotherapeutic malpractice; for instance, in the case described in the previous paragraph, the therapist also had sex with the client and hired her to work in his office and care for his children. It is equally important not to reflexively assume that the targeted therapist must have done something wrong simply because the charge has been leveled. That someone has charged a therapist with incompetent or malevolent behavior is not a pathognomonic sign that the therapist *engaged* in the behaviors and is not a pathognomonic sign that the therapist *did not engage* in the behaviors.

# Bibliotherapy, Self-Help Groups, and Other Adjunctive Therapies

In the recent debate over delayed recall, questions have been raised about the possible risks entailed in the use of self-help materials. Books such as *The Courage To Heal* have been singled out as possible causes of a rash of pseudomemories, and participation in groups such as Adults Molested as Children (AMAC) or Incest Survivors Anonymous (ISA) has been blamed for leading adults to inappropriately cut off contact with their families of origin. But these accusations appear to us to be premature because no empirical evidence supports them. These assertions appear to arise from speculation based on illusory correlations, misplaced attributions, and other fallacious premises. However, there is a need for caution when a therapist suggests other resources to a client. As with any adjunct to treatment, therapists need to carefully assess what may help the specific person with whom they are working. Interventions and resources that may be therapeutic at one stage may be ineffective or even destructive at another stage of treatment. However, there are no empirical data available that would demonstrate that self-help books or participation in survivor groups per se will implant pseudomemories in a client. Neither are there data indicating that this sort of adjunct is a required part of successful treatment. Instead, as with every other aspect of of treatment, the unique needs of the client must be carefully assessed, in a collaborative process with the client. For example, although many adult survivors of childhood sexual abuse have found self-help books or autobiographical accounts helpful, many have also commented that, early in a process of recall, such materials felt retraumatizing because the survivor did not yet have sufficient integration of and distance from her or his own recall process.

As an example of the importance of assessing the correct timing for each intervention, consider a client evaluated by one of the authors who described how, after reading the first few pages, she tore up her copy of *The Courage to Heal,* which she had purchased at her family practitioner's suggestion when she began to have intrusive recalls after gynecological surgery. She then reportedly burned the fragments in the fireplace to ensure that she would not be tempted to glue them back together because "all of this stuff was too scary for me to read about just then." She did note that, 2 years later, she was able to purchase the book again on her own initiative and slowly read it without becoming upset. If a client has been assessed to be highly suggestible or fantasy-prone, such materials could also theoretically be confusing to the client, who may become uncertain about where a particular mental image has been derived from—a confusion that will likely not be helpful in making sense of her internal process or external reality.

Another client of one of the authors decided to use soothing audiotapes designed to help people relax. She was excited about the prospect of using the tape to learn how to soothe herself between sessions. The next session, she entered and threw the tape across the room. When she had gotten home, lain down on her bed, and heard the male voice on the tape talking softly into her ear, it had unintentionally re-created aspects of the incest she had experienced. Even listening to just a few seconds of the tape had disconcerted, frightened, and confused her. She wanted nothing more to do with it. A year later, however, when she had made substantial progress in therapy, she sought out such tapes and found them extremely helpful. The timing seemed crucial.

Group participation can provide essential additional support for a person dealing with the trauma of sexual abuse. However, groups can also be a source of unhelpful pressure to conform to group norms. A therapist must carefully consider the potential strengths and weaknesses of a group (either therapy or self-help), either as the sole intervention or as an adjunct to individual therapy for this client. Groups may provide more contact with others and social support. They may help someone who has been abused to feel less isolated and abnormal. On the other hand, some groups may encourage something approaching a "group consensus," perhaps embodying some of the rules or assertions listed earlier in this chapter. If everyone else is talking about being an incest survivor, a client may feel reluctant to voice her doubts about the validity of the incest images that began intruding into her awareness, that led her to seek therapy, and that originally seemed to be memory fragments. Timing and the assessment both of the client's readiness and of the specific group culture are important considerations in employing group treatment.

Clients whose therapy has been founded on principles in which the client is authorized and empowered as an expert are unlikely to tolerate the latter sort of group because it will conflict with their growing sense of trust in their own perceptions and the therapist's support to question and challenge. Therapists considering making referrals to a therapy or self-help group must obtain information about the training and perspective of group therapists or leaders, if any, or about the group culture if the group in question is a leaderless self-help group. Often, groups in the 12-step tradition, such as ISA, will have occasional "open" meetings that can be attended by a nonsurvivor. A therapist considering referrals to a particular ISA meeting may wish to consider attending an open meeting to get a feel for the nature of the group norms and culture prior to making client referrals. Twelve-step and similar groups may also have informative documents addressed to the professional.

## If the Accused Contacts the Therapist

Therapists may receive phone calls from the person who their client believes to have sexually abused him or her or from a family member who, in the client's perceptions, is allied with that person. In this instance, therapists find themselves walking the delicate line between respect for the feelings of an aggrieved third party and the client's right to confidentiality. Therapists are reminded that under the laws in many states, they are not free even to identify whether a person is in therapy with them, as this would constitute a violation of the client's privilege. Consequently, requests for contact from an accused third party must be met with respect and care, but clear boundaries. While the painful feelings of that person can be acknowledged, the therapist must be firm in insisting that the client cannot be identified as such, and that the therapist is not free to speak to this third party unless the person can provide the client's written informed consent for waiver of confidentiality. It is also important that the therapist not take a hostile or adversarial position to the caller.

Therapists may find it useful to anticipate that throughout their career they may get many calls from a variety of people seeking information about a client. Calls may come from relatives, previous therapists, employers, insurance personnel, managed care auditors, attorneys, friends, reporters, private investigators, and virtually anyone else. Sometimes such calls catch the therapist off guard. Callers may be quite likeable, persuasive, intimidating, threatening, or persistent. Unless arrangements (including obtaining written informed consent from the client for release of information to a particular person for a particular rationale) have been made in advance, therapists might consider replying to all such callers with some variation of "I'm sorry, but I can't disclose any information at all about anyone who might be my patient unless I have written informed consent for release of information. Would you be able to provide such a document?" Persistent callers may respond, "But all I want to know is whether [person's name] is a client of yours," or "But I just want to make sure that I have the right therapist." To answer either question in the absence of the client's informed consent for release of information may, however, under certain circumstances violate the client's trust, ethical principles, licensing provisions, and the legal standards of care. Whether a person has consulted a therapist, has been in contact with a particular therapist, is still in treatment, and so on generally fall within the client's zone of privacy (i.e., this is the client's business and no one else's) unless there are specific legal exceptions.

Therapists in this situation are advised to seek legal counsel to ensure that they are practicing within the laws of their particular jurisdiction. We also believe it to be clinically astute to inform the client of what has happened, so that no secrets are kept from the client, and then to support the client in assessing what she or he would like to do. It is especially important at this juncture to avoid intrusive advocacy for any one position, but rather to be present with the client as she or he responds to what has occurred. For many clients, this experience creates a crisis in which they fear that they will no longer be believed or cared for by their therapist; for others, it becomes a catalyst for examining the relationship to the accused person.

One increasingly frequent outcome of treatment is that the matter moves from the enclosed arena of therapy to the public openness of the courtroom. A national survey found that 73% of therapists reported that one or more of their patients claimed to have recovered previously forgotten memories of childhood sex abuse; 21% reported that for at least one patient, the memory was false; 50% reported that at least one patient had found external validation; and 12% reported at least one patient who later rejected his or her own memory as false (Pope & Tabachnick, 1995). In this study, almost one out of six (15%) reported that at least one such patient filed a civil or criminal complaint. Clinicians must ensure that they are fully prepared to participate competently in these legal proceedings, which constitute an ultimate form of breaking down the protective walls of the psychotherapy process, and to anticipate the possibility that legal issues may intersect with the treatment. This preparation and competence for forensic work are the topic of chapter 6.

# 6

# Forensic Issues for Therapists and Expert Witnesses

**M**any of this book's readers may have a hard time imagining themselves testifying in court. The therapist who enters the courtroom enters what is to many a strange and very different world. This chapter attempts to identify some special concerns of forensic practice when recovered memories are at issue. It addresses such topics as legal issues regarding record-keeping, content of notes, and the importance of distinguishing between the roles of treatment provider and forensic evaluator if one's client goes forward into the legal arena. Finally, it discusses special issues that a therapist needs to take into account should she or he become the target of a lawsuit or complaint, either by third parties or a former client, in relation to the topic of delayed recall of childhood sexual abuse.

Many therapists find the world of the courtroom distasteful, characterized as it is by an adversarial atmosphere that runs counter to therapeutic norms of consensus and reconciliation, and attempt find ways to avoid participating in legal exchanges. There are good reasons for this feeling of alienation. As linguistics Professor Robin Lakoff, noted,

> The witness stand is not a place for comfortable conversation. Usually, the giver of information holds power, but a witness does not. A witness cannot control topics or their interpreta-

tion and has no say when the conversation begins or ends. . . . The lawyer–witness repartee may seem to an outside observer like especially snappy but otherwise normal conversation. But as in therapeutic discourse, its purpose and therefore its rules are different. To the observer, the discourse seems a dyad between lawyer and witness. But in terms of its function in a trial, both are in fact acting together as one participant, the speaker, with the jury as hearer. Without this understanding, much about the examination procedure would be unintelligible. (1990, pp. 90–91)

## Vulnerability of the Therapist

Lakoff's observation that examiner and witness are "acting together as one participant," while valid, may be misleading to some who are unfamiliar with what a skilled, prepared cross-examiner can do to a witness who is incompetent, unprepared, or not telling the whole truth. Such "conversations" can be agonizing to watch, and even worse to be a participant in when one is being asked the questions. If the attacked witness does not seem to be lying or trying to mislead, but is simply incompetent or unprepared, those who have served as experts may watch with a mixture of pity and fear. One lawyer wrote about how he knew it was time "to uncoil and strike":

> Have you ever seen a "treed" witness? Have you ever had the experience of watching a witness's posterior involuntarily twitch? Have you ever seen them wiggle in their chairs? Have you seen the beads of perspiration form on their foreheads? Have you ever been close enough to watch their ancestral eyes dilating the pupil so that they would have adequate tunnel vision of the target that was attacking? (Burgess, 1984, p. 252)

The late trial attorney Louis Nizer (1961) described how the method by which a witness was made to "walk barefoot and blindfolded over red-hot plowshares laid lengthwise at unequal distances has been replaced by a stream of burning questions which a cross-examiner may hurl at the witness to drag from him [sic] the concealed truth" (p. 14).

However threatening such descriptions, most therapists seem to have come to understand that in the course of their work they may be required to testify in a legal setting whether or not this is what they want. While it is a possibility that any client can have the sort of experiences that lead to his or her therapist's appearance in a courtroom, the issues inherent in cases of recovered memories of childhood sexual abuse raise that likelihood significantly. The scenario of a client recovering memories raises its own risks for litigation against alleged perpetrators and therapists themselves.

Consider just a few of the possible scenarios evolving from a case in which one's patient recovers memories and alleges childhood sexual abuse, all of which might place the therapist and the therapy process under the scrutiny of the legal system. It is possible that a patient who reports recovered memories of abuse may file a civil or criminal complaint against the alleged perpetrator, and the therapist will be subpoenaed to testify. Although in many other circumstances there might be a therapist–patient privilege that the patient could assert to prevent the therapist from testifying, once the patient has placed his or her mental or emotional condition at issue before the court, she or he has taken a step that commonly constitutes a waiver of the privilege by the client. This leaves the therapist with few options but to be present in court. It is possible that a patient who reports recovered memories may file other claims, such as for worker's or crime victims' compensation or social security disability, in which the therapist may be required to testify. If the patient recovered memories during therapy with a prior therapist and now believes them to be confabulations arising from therapist suggestions, the patient may sue that therapist for malpractice; the subsequent therapist may be called to testify. If criminal charges are filed against the patient, the therapist may be required to testify in the trial if a defense is being raised alleging diminished capacity or impairment resulting from the effects of childhood sexual abuse.

Third parties, primarily accused parents, may bring lawsuits against the therapists who have treated their adult offspring. These suits may include claims that the therapist failed in her or his duty of care to the parent, that the therapist has slandered the parent, or that the therapist has failed to adequately investigate the sexual abuse allegations made by the client, among other potential causes of action. Parents and others may also file formal complaints with state licensing boards and with local, state, or national ethics committees of professional associations.

The False Memory Syndrome Foundation (FMSF; see chapter 3) informed accused parents that "the parent may take the legal position that the accusing child is incompetent and seek guardianship proceedings" ("Legal Aspects of False Memory Syndrome," 1992, p. 3), but also noted the possibility of a patient–parent suit. They suggested to their readers,

> The best course of action is by the child who realized the error of the accusations made, and recants and brings an action for malpractice, against the therapist. It would seem that there is a very real possibility that the parent could join in this action. . . . Therapists, medical institutions and insurance companies will be seriously threatened by such actions . . . ("Legal Aspects of False Memory Syndrome," 1992, p. 3)

## When the Therapist's Mental Health History Is an Issue

There is another forensic issue, in addition to whether the therapist is required to appear in court as a witness or defendant or to turn over patient records, that may cause therapists great concern no matter how unlikely the prospect seems. This is the possibility that records of the therapist's own treatment (i.e., when the therapist has received mental health services) may become evidence. Texas' Twelfth District Court of Appeals considered whether a counselor appointed by the court (pursuant to a divorce decree) to provide assessment and counseling services to three children should be forced to supply records of mental health services that she herself had received. An attorney representing one of the parents served her with a subpoena requiring her to produce "[a]ll psychological and/or psychiatric records in the custody of or subject to the control of [the counselor] . . . pertaining to the mental and/or emotional health of [the counselor] on which her examination is required" (*Cheatham v. Rogers*, 1992,

p. 233). The counselor contested the subpoena and asserted "that her personal mental health records are (1) confidential and not subject to disclosure . . ., (2) 'protected from discovery by [counselor's] right to privacy under the United States Constitution,' and (3) 'not relevant to any issue in dispute in this cause nor reasonably calculated to [lead] to the discovery of admissible evidence,'" (p. 233). The appellate court held against the counselor and concluded that the subpoena should be enforced. Justice Colley's opinion held that applicable law

> made a necessary intrusion upon the privacy rights of persons who become prospective expert witnesses in judicial proceedings involving the status, welfare, and interests of children. We are of the opinion that this vital and compelling state interest far outweighs [the counselor's] constitutional right of privacy with respect to her personal mental health records. (p. 236)

It is crucial that readers not overgeneralize from such examples. It is useful to be aware of evolving trends in case law, but each example applies to a particular set of facts informed by the case law of a specific jurisdiction; the case law of one jurisdiction may not inform that of another. Both legislation and case law change from time to time and jurisdiction to jurisdiction. Such particular illustrations are included here solely to alert readers to the range of potential legal issues for which they can obtain legal guidance from a local attorney (i.e., an attorney familiar with the legal standards and requirements in the reader's jurisdiction) who is skilled and experienced in mental health law. To avoid undue expense, practitioners in a specific area may consider pooling their resources, either through formal organizations such as a professional association or through more ad hoc groups, to retain an attorney to answer a specific set of questions.

As stated earlier, this book assumes basic familiarity with the principles and literature of assessment, therapy, and forensic work. The purpose of this chapter is not to provide a comprehensive guide to forensic work, but rather to highlight some of the more unique or salient forensic issues arising in the area of reports of delayed recall of childhood sexual abuse. Our comments are made primarily for the treating therapist rather than the forensic expert witness, assuming that the latter possesses a degree of familiarity with forensic practice beyond that of most mental health professionals. Those seeking a more general guide to forensic preparation (e.g., for depositions, rendering direct and cross-examination testimony in court, assessing malingering, writing forensic reports) are referred to Pope, Butcher, and Seelen (1993), which discusses in detail an outline for the expert witness' preparation that can be found in Appendix F in the current volume.

## Virtual Legal Reality: Preparing as If You Will Go to Court

As may be clear from the foregoing, we believe it may be useful for all therapists to enter the virtual reality in which going to court in some form or another is anticipated as a possibility. Asking yourself, "What if I were cross-examined about the intervention that I am considering?" as suggested in chapter 4, is yet another form of the constant questioning that we believe can be essential for all therapists who are striving to develop and maintain competency in this field. As the examples of the diverse ways that therapists may be suddenly drawn into court make clear, therapists need to make decisions from the start of treatment that will be useful should that virtual reality ever transform into physical reality. Therapists need to make the assumption that any case can end up in court, and should act in ways that will create preparation for that possibility. This does not mean practicing defensively or focusing solely on the problem of so-called risk management. Much of what we suggest tends to strengthen the therapeutic alliance and create the possibility of greater trust and openness in therapy because many of the strategies preparing one for the possibility of court are also paradigms for the empowerment of clients.

## Notes and Records

We have previously mentioned the importance of informed consent and informed refusal. We risk being repetitive by stating here that the presence of a clear, signed, written consent document in a client's file can be invaluable to client, therapist, and the integrity of the clinical process. It is also important to realize that a form is only one aspect of the continuing consent process. But what besides this should be in the client's file, which is, after all, a legal record of the treatment process?

Record-keeping guidelines created by various professional organizations can be helpful in preparing notes that will be accurate and useful under the glare of a legal spotlight (Committee on Professional Practice and Standards, 1993). These guidelines, some of which may have been incorporated into state laws regulating some mental health professionals, detail the sort of information which, at a minimum, should be present in a client's file.

What should such notes include and in what form? At a minimum, notes should include the problems addressed at a particular session and the kinds of interventions used. The notes should indicate who was present at the session; for instance, if you have requested that your client's partner or spouse attend a session as a collateral, this should be indicated in the file, along with documentation that you have given that third party informed consent to participate in this adjunctive capacity. Notes should be behaviorally descriptive of what your client said and did, with direct quotations when possible; there should be sufficient detail so that someone reading the record would have a basic comprehension of what occurred during that therapy session. Brevity is preferable when possible; meeting this level of note-taking does not require the inclusion of copious material.

For example, consider a hypothetical therapy session in which a client who has been recovering memories comes into the session with reports of a great deal of intrusive material happening since the last session. The therapist has a working diagnosis for the client of PTSD, and also has some concerns about possible borderline pathology that are still being assessed. The client tells the therapist that she is having flashbacks and intrusive thoughts, and that she has also been thinking a lot about killing herself. The therapist responds by first checking into whether the client has means and a plan for suicide and otherwise assesses the suicide risk. The therapist renews a prior contract that the client will do no harm to herself and will call the therapist immediately should she find it difficult to stay safe. The therapist also assesses the availability of other social support for the client and spends some time discussing with her the difficulties she faces in getting sufficient support from her partner. The remainder of the session is devoted to an exploration of ways to reduce intrusive materials and how to cope when they emerge, including relaxation exercises to do after a flashback has happened, self-nurturing exercises, and some physical activities that will increase the client's feelings of physical powerfulness and safety. A note of this session might go as follows:

> Client reported flashbacks, intrusive thoughts of rape episode by F. Affect upset, tearful, appeared to dissociate at times in session. Suicidal ideation; no plan or means. Worked on strategies to contain and care for self during these intrusive episodes. Checked on support system. No-self-harm contract renewed until next week. Still taking Zoloft 50 mg qd; some relief reported.

Notice what is present in this example and what is not included. The client's report of symptoms and problems, demeanor, and behavior during the session are all noted. The presence of suicidal ideation is noted, as is the information indicating that the therapist has explored for means and plan, which both increase the actual risk of harm to self; a contract to stay safe is also noted. The interventions are described in terms of their treatment goals.

What is *not* in this note are the therapist's unfiltered, careless speculations, fantasies, projections, or assumptions about what is happening. Such material is, unfortunately, very common in client files that both authors have reviewed in our roles as experts in a number of court cases over the years. Often, this other material appears in the form of process notes, scribbled on sheets of paper as the client speaks and representing ongoing impressions and attempts at quotation from the client. At other times, notes contain a large amount of interpretive materials in which the client and, at times, third parties are commented upon by the therapist. An example of this sort of note follows, using the same hypothetical therapy session as was described in the previous sample note:

Client reported flashbacks and intrusive thoughts, including suicidal ideation, with dramatic presentations of her distress. Appears to be reenacting borderline patterns of instability and threats to self in attempts to manipulate her family members and therapist into giving her more support. Also wearing very seductive clothes and doesn't realize she is trying to turn me on; will discuss transference next week. Could this be example of how she related to her father? Maybe repressed fantasy of seducing him; repressed fantasy of killing mother as rival and replacing her? Father seems to have been both punitive and seductive with her, which could account for her current style of interacting in therapy. She also discussed her upset that her boss at work [first and last name] is having an affair with her coworker [first and last name] and either they are embezzling from the payroll or client has need to make up lies. Some narcissistic elements beginning to emerge as well.

This session note presents a very interesting picture of the therapist's thoughts and musings about the client, as well as what may be subtle expressions of resentment contained in the description of the client as "dramatic," "manipulative," and "narcissistic." Describing the client's clothes as "seductive" may reflect nothing about the client or what she was wearing, but perhaps only the therapist's reaction to her (see Pope, Sonne, & Holroyd, 1993). The therapist's statement that the client "doesn't realize she is trying to turn me on" makes it appear that the therapist can read the client's mind. There is a little bit about what the client was complaining of that day. There are the therapist's speculations about the client's father, a third party whom the therapist has presumably never met. There are descriptions of two named individuals and the therapist's conclusion that either the allegations against them are true or the client is a liar. The client is described in terms that are pathologizing and pejorative.

What is absent from this note is any notion of what the therapist did or said, what interventions were used, or what goals of therapy were attended to; the reader of the note does not even know whether the therapist assessed the client's lethality in the face of suicidality, or what steps the therapist took to ensure safety. The reader has no idea if the client is on medication and, if so, whether it is helping. Readers mainly know that the therapist has many opinions, not all of them necessarily founded, and a willingness to describe people who have never been personally encountered.

The first sample note is useful in court because it attempts to record relevant facts and avoids the therapist's random free associations, wild leaps of inference, sloppy speculation, and other material that does not meet professional standards of care, rigor, and responsibility. The second is a playground for an opposing attorney. If this client goes on to sue her father for sexual abuse, the attorney will be certain to have the therapist's speculations made a part of the record. First, the records will serve to demonstrate how disturbed the client is, and second, they will  point out that the therapist had bias against the father and might have unconsciously encouraged the client to believe confabulations and take this action against an innocent man. The client will have also doubtless had the chance to read this note and others like it, and to learn perhaps for the first time of some of the hostile countertransference to her; this is unlikely to be helpful to the continuing working alliance in therapy. If the client's father decides to sue, the therapist's commentary on him—a person whom the therapist has never seen—will become central to the creation of a case that the therapist harmed him maliciously in some way. And if the client decides to recant and sue the therapist, the less-than-compassionate version of her distress will not help to resolve the situation amicably. The employer and co-worker may also be less than pleased, either because their actual affair is now public knowledge, or because they have been falsely accused in public of something they did not do but must now deal with.

It may be useful to consider how the client might react to the notes. In some states, clients have the right to see their files in any case; but if litigation ensues for whatever reason, the client is almost certain to gain access to and read his or her own records. Notes that can be shared with clients are most likely to be those that meet the tests of good documentation for legal purposes— those that are behaviorally descriptive, lacking in pejorative terminology, but possessing clear information about interventions and risk issues. In some states that have adopted forms of the Uniform Health Care Information Act, the law may allow clients to review and correct errors in their files; some therapists find that it is a helpful intervention to periodically go over files with clients as a means of summarizing, tracking progress together, and allowing for the chance to include any corrections. Both authors have had the experience, in reviewing prior treatment records for legal cases, of finding serious errors in files that had not been checked with the client, were never corrected, and now were creating problems for the client in litigation. Care for the client is thus maximized if the client becomes an active participant in the maintenance of his or her own records.

It may also be useful to consider notes in light of the golden rule: If your own therapist maintained documents about you as you maintain documents about your clients, would you find them acceptable? Would you have any complaints or concerns? If so, what are they, and do they indicate flaws in your procedures for taking notes?

Finally, the content of notes should reflect the therapist's awareness of the standards of care and the empirical science upon which treatment is founded. Whether the focus of a litigation is a complaint against an alleged sexual abuse perpetrator or one against the therapist her- or himself, the therapist's record should indicate that such information was taken into account in the development of the treatment plan. The most recent Supreme Court decision regarding the admissibility of scientific evidence into the courtroom, *Daubert v. Merrell Dow* (1993), separates the notion of the generic expert from the value of what is said and clarifies that experts must be able to address the research that both supports and refutes their positions in court. The therapist working with delayed recall, while not preparing to serve in the expert role, may wish to consider that when litigation occurs, decisions regarding the course of treatment will be subjected to a similar level of scrutiny, often by attorneys who have read much of the literature on this issue that we have analyzed and critiqued earlier in this volume. When the therapist has integrated this level of knowledge and awareness into the treatment from early on and has documented that reference to an empirical knowledge base, she or he is in a better position not only to offer the highest quality care to the client, but to withstand the slings and arrows of outrageous attorneys if need be.

Because a client's file is a legal document, however, other kinds of change or corrections are not generally permissible. Under no circumstances should "substitute" notes be rewritten to replace the original notes. Attempts to do this can lead to terrible difficulties for therapist and client alike. For example, in a case in which one of the authors served as a forensic expert, a prior treating therapist had minimal, but correct and concurrent, notes. However, as the client's case approached trial, he wrote a new set of notes, based entirely on recollections, in which various inaccurate materials were stated as facts; these materials were extremely harmful to the client, who then had to spend much time attempting to demonstrate that the therapist had made these things up. It is important to consult with your attorney or another qualified source of legal guidance to determine what kinds of corrections are permissible or mandatory in your jurisdiction and the form they should take. In some instances, for example, a therapist may wish to correct some of the original history months later (e.g., the therapist may have misunderstood the client, or the client may later have discovered an error in the original information provided to the therapist). One form that may be permitted or required in some jurisdictions is for the therapist to draw a single line through the error (so that the original passage remains legible), to write the correction in the margin, and then to sign and date the correction. Similarly, a therapist may wish to annotate earlier material in a chart; again, some jurisdictions permit or require the therapist to include such amendments in the margin or on an additional sheet of paper and to sign and date them. Aside from specific laws governing the maintenance of notes, what is essential is that a third party should be able to tell, about any word or words in the notes, (a) what the words say (i.e., they must be legible), (b) who wrote them, and (3) when they were written.

In cases in which recovered memories are at issue, therapists may feel a need to go back and change earlier records. A client may have entered therapy to discuss what she was experiencing as delayed memories but later during the course of therapy concluded were not valid memories of abuse. A client may have entered therapy claiming never to have experienced incest and later report recovered memories of incest. Whatever changes are legally permitted or required, the therapist must make it clear what the original notes were (including date and author), as well as the corrections, additions, or other changes (including date and author). A therapist is free to change note-taking style midstream as she or he becomes more sophisticated as to the possible legal implications of the therapy record. But old notes, no matter how problematic, must be preserved as is. Therapists who take notes on the computer should be reminded that most systems will attach a time and date stamp to your file, pointing the way to any signs of possible tampering with records. Even hard drives that were completely erased can often, if need be, be reconstructed so as to recover erased files, although the technology with which to accomplish this is expensive. But in one case of which the authors are aware, attorneys did spend the money for this sort of discovery activity. Therapists who believe that they will be able to evade these requirements easily may face quite a different scenario if they appear in court. The *subpoena duces tecum* (freely translated as "the subpoena to produce everything you have that even vaguely touches on this matter") is likely to be more detailed than the therapist anticipated and could ask for absolutely everything and anything that could have been in a file.

## A Sample Subpoena

An effective subpoena requests, both generally and specifically, all documents related to the case. It defines *document* to include all written material, correspondence, testing material, testing results (whether hand or computer scored or interpreted), memoranda, audio- or videotape recordings, computer recordings (whether printed, recorded electronically on disks, or otherwise stored), photographs, ledgers, and notes. The following model subpoena was presented as involving a hypothetical case in which Ms. Mary Smith is suing Dr. A. Acme, and Dr. Jones was retained by Dr. Acme's attorney to conduct a psychological evaluation of Ms. Smith. The subpoena included:

1. Dr. Jones' entire original file pertaining to the psychological examination (evaluation) of Mary Smith and any psychological testing, including but not limited to testing materials and results. . . .

2. All notes of conversations with any person, including Mary Smith or any person consulted in connection with this case or the examination (evaluation) of Mary Smith and any psychological testing. . . .

3. All scorings, computerized scorings, and hand scorings of any and all psychological tests or assessment instruments. . . .

4. All psychological testing documents for Mary Smith, including the original completed examinations (i.e., the actual answer form), score sheets, and notes written by Mary Smith or anyone else in connection with the testing.

5. All . . . testing documents for Mary Smith, including the original completed examination, score sheets, and notes.

6. All documents that were reviewed in connection with your examination (evaluation) of Mary Smith or any aspect of the case of *Smith v. Acme*.

7. All reports and drafts of reports prepared in connection with your examination (evaluation) of Mary Smith or your evaluation in the case of *Smith v. Acme*.

8. A list of all documents, including computer-scored or computer-generated information, that you reviewed or wrote or that you discussed with any person in connection with your examination (evaluation) of Mary Smith . . . whether these documents are still in your possession.

9. The original file folders in which any information regarding Mary Smith is or has been stored.[1]

10. All calendars that refer to appointments with Mary Smith or any person with whom you discussed the evaluation of Mary Smith or the case of *Smith v. Acme*.

11. All billing statements and payment records.

12. All correspondence with any person in any way relating to the case of *Smith v. Acme*.

13. All video tape recordings or audio tape recordings of or pertaining to Mary Smith.

14. The witness's curriculum vita vitae. . . .

15. The originals of all correspondence, notes of conversations, and documents between and among the expert wit-

---

[1]This is requested because short scribbled notes written on the file folder itself, either outside or inside, may be useful.

ness, attorneys (who retained the expert), representatives, and consultants of the attorneys in any way related to the case.
(Pope, Butcher, & Seelen, 1993, pp. 87–88)

The model also sets forth three sets of deposition questions to be posed to a mental health professional (asked by the attorney for the other side) to assess compliance with the subpoena:

☐ Has the therapist complied fully with each and every element of the subpoena to produce? Are there any items that were not made available?

☐ Were any of these documents altered in any way? Were any of them recopied, erased, written over, enhanced, edited, or added to in any way since the time each was originally created? Are the photocopies made available true and exact replicas of the original documents without any revision?

☐ Have any documents falling within the scope of the subpoena or otherwise relevant to the case been lost, stolen, misplaced, destroyed, or thrown away? Are any documents you made, collected, handled, or received that are within the scope of this subpoena or otherwise relevant to this case absent from the documents made available to me? (Pope, Butcher, & Seelen, 1993, pp. 140–141)

Psychologists whose files contain psychological test materials may wish to take special steps to preserve the security of those materials. There are several possible routes to take when this concern emerges. These include contacting the attorney who has sent the subpoena to request the name of his or her consulting psychologist, so that the tests may be forwarded directly to that person, and seeking a protective order from the court for the psychological test materials until such time as another psychologist is made available by the other attorney to examine the tests. The psychologist may also, with the advice of his or her own attorney, decide to contest this part of the subpoena and wait to see if the court will issue an order requiring production of the test materials, because a subpoena, unlike a court order, is issued not by the judge, but often by the clerk of the court at the request of an attorney, absent the scrutiny of a judge. Many major testing companies are willing to provide standard letters to therapists asserting a legal requirement for the psychologist not to turn tests over to unqualified individuals; these letters can be helpful to the psychologist in stating his or her case for the necessity of maintaining test security even in the legal context.

In summary, whatever is in a client's file, however apparently innocuous, may be among those items that a subpoena requires the therapist to produce. Therapists should thus ask themselves what belongs in a file and what criteria it should meet. As with other topics, this book has no set of easy answers that the therapist may unthinkingly apply to every situation of note-taking. There is no substitute for the process of constantly questioning what form of note-taking makes most sense in light of the task at hand, the individual client, the jurisdiction's legal standards, and possible future uses. Consultation with a forensically experienced colleague or one's own attorney can be of help in arriving at a working answer.

## When a Patient Becomes a Plaintiff

Rarely does a person begin treatment with the goal of creating a foundation for suing someone. For many clients who recover memories of childhood sexual abuse, either prior to or during therapy, legal battles are likely the furthest thing from their minds; surviving the onslaught of frightening intrusive recollections and making sense of their personal histories and family relationships in the light of this information seem to present more pressing concerns.

For those clients who wish to take legal action, the legislation and case law relevant to the jurisdiction become crucial. The relevant laws are worded differently in each jurisdiction (see Appendix B, this volume for a listing of the laws in each state). In some states in which laws have been written specifically to respond to the needs of adult survivors, the statute provides a special statute of limitations, both for delayed memory of sexual abuse and for delayed discovery that never-forgotten sexual abuse was the cause of problems. Other states cover only delayed memories. The period during which the person may bring a suit also varies from state to state. In some states that do not explicitly allow for such lawsuits, lawsuits may proceed on a case-by-case basis under the well-established legal theory of delayed discovery, in which the statute of limitations is presumed to toll from the time that the person should have reasonably discovered the damages done to them. It is crucial that the therapist, no matter how well intended or knowledgeable, avoid any temptation to "play attorney." He or she should never be a source of legal counsel and guidance, for which the state requires admission to the bar. Great damage can be done if a therapist tells the client such legal conclusions as "I'm sure the law allows you to sue your parents;" "The statute of limitations has obviously run out, so you can't take any legal action;" or "What happened to you doesn't give you something you can sue over." Clients can obtain such information from qualified lawyers. Clients asking for legal advice can be encouraged to search carefully for an attorney, looking for one who preferably has had some prior experience in this area of the law and who seems aware of and attentive to the psychological complexities of such lawsuits. In the absence of better referral sources, the client may wish to consult the local bar association or check with local sexual assault or domestic violence hotlines for names of attorneys who are familiar with the field of sexual abuse.

Motivations for bringing such lawsuits vary. One of the authors has conducted approximately 100 evaluations in cases of adult survivors—both women and men suing alleged perpetrators, both family members and nonfamily members—and has routinely asked during those evaluations about the plaintiff's goals and motivations in bringing their cases. Their answers appear to converge around several themes. First, almost every plaintiff speaks of the importance of having her or his story heard—"my day in court," to borrow a frequently used term. The "breaking silence" component of litigation seems to be important to many of the survivors who take the legal route. Many plaintiffs are also motivated by a desire for some sort of concrete amends from the person they believe to have harmed them, either through a frank admission of guilt or via a determination by triers of fact that the alleged abuse is likely to have occurred. Nearly every person speaks of seeking funds to pay for therapy; the desire to get healed is another strong motivator. Few seem interested in retributive justice or punishment, although many harbor the desire that their alleged perpetrator be forced into treatment and are often unhappy to learn that this cannot be accomplished through civil litigation. Many also speak of a desire to protect other potential victims by exposing the perpetrator through the lawsuit. Most of these plaintiffs express profound ambivalence about their decisions to sue and profound ambivalence about the party being sued who, in many cases, they once loved or still love. Rage and a desire for revenge have been singularly absent; fear of the alleged perpetrator is prominent. Sadness over alienation from other family members is another common theme.

On a few occasions, other motivations have emerged. At times, the plaintiff is suing to please a spouse or partner. At other times (although this is quite unusual in the authors' experience), the agenda appears to be that of the alleged offender's spouse. If a client is considering taking legal action so as to please and care for third parties, this might provide a focus of therapy and enter into assessments of readiness, described subsequently, that should be present in therapy while the client is making such a decision.

However, more problematic from our perspective have been those very rare occasions in which it appears as if the party motivating the lawsuit is the plaintiff's own treating therapist. Given most therapists' aversion to the courtroom, this is a somewhat unusual scenario, but it does occur and can create problems for the therapy, the client, and the therapist. Sonne and Pope (1991; see also Pope, Sonne, & Holroyd, 1993; chapter 5, this volume) have developed the concept of *intrusive advocacy* to describe those instances in which a therapist who is well meaning, but inattentive to issues of power and motivation, becomes overly active in attempts to persuade a client to bring or to not bring a lawsuit or a complaint. Therapists who engage in intrusive advocacy are putting their own needs and desires above the legitimate needs of the client and the responsibilities of psychotherapy. These needs and desires could include therapists' development of a polarizing stance in which they must represent the "good parent" and consequently encourage acting out against the "bad parent"; therapists' belief that healing will not happen unless the client takes legal action against her or his perpetrators; or, most problematic of all, therapists' desire to get paid more for their work by a client of otherwise limited means. However, we wish to stress that in our experience intrusive advocacy often takes the form of a therapist unduly influencing a client to take no formal action, which reflects the therapist's hesitance to appear in court.

What is an appropriate stance for a therapist to take? As with other forms of advocacy that may interfere with therapy, the therapist must confine her- or himself to what therapy is. Initially, a therapeutic stance includes working with the client to assess her or his readiness to embark on such an undertaking and perhaps assisting the client, if requested, to locate resources. The therapist must take care to enable the client to arrive at his or her own decision about what steps to take or not to take. The therapist's need or desire to be in or out of the legal system cannot be a consideration here; clients must get the message that their decisions will be supported, no matter what they may be, and that subsequent rethinking and changing decisions is also acceptable.

What issues are likely to emerge when clients begin to consider litigating? It may be useful for the therapist to invite clients at this point to consider the ways in which they are and are not prepared for this process (Brown, 1996). Such assessment might include careful examination of the client's own mental state and capacity for resilience; whereas the law may require that a case be filed within 2 years of recovery of memories, for example, a client may still be emotionally unready and too vulnerable to withstand the stresses of litigation. Therapists can help a client to weigh the sometimes conflictual tugs toward or away from litigation, all the time carefully avoiding trying to steer the client toward a decision that the therapist thinks is "right." The support that is available from others may be an important part of this deliberative process. In some states, the law is such that a nonoffending spouse must be sued conjointly for negligence for damages to be collected under insurance policies that exclude coverage for intentional acts or criminal behaviors. If a client's primary support comes from her or his mother, the possibility that it is the mother who will be sued and accused of negligence needs to be explored and clarified with an attorney. Unfortunately, we are aware of several cases in which an attorney failed to inform the plaintiff of this possibility, which left the treating therapist to deal with the extra distress engendered in the client by the loss of this previously supportive family member and the furor that ensued in the family.

This aspect of the law also intersects with a common therapeutic issue regarding the client's feelings towards the nonoffending spouse in cases in which the alleged perpetrator is a family member. Because it is also not unheard of for the survivor of abuse to be subjectively angrier at the nonoffending parent for a presumed failure to protect the survivor than at the offending parent for having committed the sexual violations, a therapist can help a client to clarify whether the lawsuit represents an enactment of that dynamic in a manner that might crystallize it beyond repair. This is not to say that there are no collusive or nonprotective, nonoffending parents—only that many nonoffending parents have been anything but inattentive and uncaring, and to require that they be labeled "negligent" in a court of law may compound the damage for the client.

A therapist can also encourage a client to gather good information prior to initiating a lawsuit. Such information, which can be obtained from an attorney, might include such things as how long the case will take, the degree to which the plaintiff will feel "put on trial" or exposed, and what a civil case can actually accomplish, as well as some reasonable estimation of what a damages award might be. The losses of confidentiality attendant upon claiming emotional distress damages should be made very clear so that a client is prepared for the alleged perpetrator's attorney (and thus possibly the alleged perpetrator) to read her or his therapy case file. None of this should be read as attempts to scare a client away from pursuing a lawsuit, should that be her or his goal; as one plaintiff said to one of the authors, "He's already violated me more than anyone can ever know. Who cares if he reads my therapy file?" Rather, this assessment of risks inherent in litigating is yet another aspect of the therapist's stance of asking questions, in this case helping empower a client to think clearly and carefully about this action and its many ramifications.

Therapists working with a client in litigation must also be aware of the impacts of the impending lawsuit on the therapy process. Clients are likely to become increasingly aware that everything said in therapy may be exposed and distorted in court, and may find themselves becoming more guarded and less able to fully participate in the therapy process. Therapists must be prepared to accommodate this possibility and to see it as a real response to the impending legal context rather than as evidence of client avoidance or resistance. Aspects of the litigation may be retraumatizing for the client, especially if the perpetrator's legal strategy is to blame or stigmatize the victim for her or his own difficulties or highlight the plaintiff's history of substance abuse, sexual acting-out, or other socially stigmatized symptoms of distress. The client may find her- or himself accused of being irresponsible, or unwilling to "grow up" or "forgive and let go." Dealings with the attorney, no matter how competent and caring, may sour, however temporarily; at some point in the litigation process, there may be a pull to split between "good therapist" (who is supportive and returns phone calls) and "bad attorney" (who is unavailable, is in court or unwilling to listen to the client tell her or his story yet again, or responds like an attorney and not a therapist to the client's distress). There may also be periods when the patient experiences the attorney as "good" (a committed and forceful advocate) and the therapist as "bad" (perhaps unwilling to provide certain testimony that the attorney believes would be helpful).

An important responsibility of a therapist whose client is a plaintiff is to take steps to protect the integrity of the therapy, beginning with the clear separation of the roles of therapist and forensic expert. This may include initiating discussions with the client about those aspects of the litigation process that are likely to be problematic for the client, and being clear with both oneself and one's client that the goal of therapy is the client's healing, recovery, and improved functioning, not the creation of materials for the lawsuit. This will also include the therapist having clear communications with his or her client's attorney about the role of the therapist in the case, so that misunder-standings are avoided and potential conflicts and triangles are identified and worked out in advance, and so that the attorney is aware from the earliest possible moment of the need to obtain an independent evaluator for the client. It may also prove necessary to spend time in therapy dealing with new revelations about the workings of the justice system and addressing the client's disillusionment with what may be possible there. The encounter with the litigation process can be transformed to become a useful catalyst for the questions of meaning-making and existential reevaluations that accompany the therapy process for most trauma survivors, whether or not court enters the picture.

When possible, the attorney should be encouraged not to rely upon the therapist as the sole or primary expert witness, but rather to engage an independent evaluator who can undertake tasks that might be problematic for the therapy relationship, such as assessing the plaintiff's credibility and issues of malingering or deception. We cannot overemphasize this point sufficiently, as it is one at which both attorneys and therapists routinely engage in the blurring of boundaries and role definitions to the ultimate detriment of all parties. Therapists do not commonly read all of the depositions in a case and conduct extensive interviews with collaterals or review all of a plaintiff's medical, work, and educational records; these are usually tasks for a forensic evaluator. The presence of an independent evaluator can further reduce the burden on the treating therapist to be the sole mental health voice, which frees the therapist to refocus on the task of providing treatment.

Finally, although we encourage all therapists to obtain regular consultation on their work no matter what the circumstances, when a client is a plaintiff the therapist will be in particular need of such support. It may be especially helpful to get consultation from a colleague who is forensically knowledgeable and able to help prepare a therapist for participation in such events as depositions and court testimony, and who can help make a therapist aware of when events in the case, however problematic, are within the norms for litigation or are actually cause for concern.

# Criminal Cases Based On a Client's Recovered Memories

It is relatively rare, but not unheard of, for a prosecuting attorney to undertake a criminal case based solely or primarily on recovered memories. Is it difficult to collect complete information on this type of case because such cases are often brought quietly at a local level and rarely appear in the appellate literture, but there appear to have been fewer than 100 such cases. Whitfield (1996; see also Whitfield, 1995) reports that the ratio of civil to criminal cases in this area is about 10 to 1. This is largely because the frequent standard of proof required in a criminal case—"beyond a reasonable doubt"—is so much higher than that of civil cases, which tend to require only a "preponderance of evidence." Additionally, for most crimes, the statute of limitation will have irrevocably expired long before an accusation is made based on delayed recall. The major exception to this is cases involving homicide charges, for which the statute of limitations is indefinite. In most such cases, evidence other than a person's report of delayed recall of a crime will be necessary for a prosecution to move forward.

The suggestions that we have made regarding prudent actions for the therapist whose client is a civil plaintiff carry even more weight when the matter being considered is a criminal complaint. Because in some states a person alleging recovered memories of childhood sexual abuse may gain access to victim's compensation funds through a timely police report, it is not unreasonable for therapists to consider the possibility that clients who choose this as a route to fund treatment may find themselves as witnesses in a criminal case. However, it appears that it is unusual for prosecutors even in the most victim-friendly jurisdictions to move on such cases, often because the criminal statutes have expired. But because so much is at stake, the importance of helping clients to assess their readiness to go forward in such a weighty undertaking and of clarifying therapists' potential role in the proceedings is tremendously increased. Therapists must, consequently, be especially attentive to the possibility of suggestion and intrusive advocacy when a client is considering embarking on a criminal complaint.

## When the Therapist Is the Defendant

A particularly unpleasant experience in the life of a therapist is to receive a letter from an attorney or state licensing authority stating that a lawsuit or complaint is about to be filed against her or him. Even if one is certain that this action has no merit and that one will ultimately be vindicated, being the target of a complaint is a personally unsettling, and potentially time-consuming and demoralizing, experience. Every complaint, no matter how unfounded it may appear, must be taken seriously and responded to in a straightforward and timely manner. A therapist's assessment of the seriousness of the problem and the validity of the complaint may or may not be accurate; no matter what the outcome of a complaint process, it is important to engage in a self-care process on several different dimensions.

We are using the term *complaint* in the broadest possible fashion, to encompass civil suits against therapists for malpractice and complaints to regulatory agencies such as licensing boards and professional ethics committees. Each of these settings has its own sets of rules and procedures with which therapists should become familiar, but certain issues transcend the setting for the professional who is the target of the complaint.

Therapists who receive a complaint are likely to be upset, angry, and perhaps frightened. These are reasonable responses. These feelings may persist during the amount of time the complaint is in process, placing therapists at risk in their work and personal life. To survive the complaint process and protect the quality of their work, their clients' well-being, and their personal relationships, therapists may need several different kinds of support. First, an attorney should be contacted immediately. If complaints are in the form of a civil lawsuit, therapists should immediately contact their malpractice insurance carrier, who will engage an attorney. However, therapists may wish to also engage their own attorney, because the attorney assigned by the insurance carrier is the carrier's attorney, not the therapist's, and may act in the best interests of the client (the insurance carrier) in ways that may not always be compatible with the wishes or well-being of the therapist. Some insurance coverage also extends to representation at licensing board hearings; others do not. But therapists, not being attorneys, should not attempt to represent themselves in the legal or quasi-legal settings in which a complaint is adjudicated, even (or perhaps especially) when the therapist believes the complaint to have little or no merit.

Second, a therapist should consider seeking professional consultation and personal therapy. We suggest seeking a consultant who will be able to objectively review the work that is being complained about and who can give the therapist honest feedback about what she or he has done. Such consultation can be enormously relieving because it often provides validation for the actions the therapist has taken or may inform a therapist of the need to begin now to take steps to remedy problems in her or his work. Whichever is the case, consultation may need to continue until the complaint is resolved, so as to ensure the quality of the therapist's work during a stressful period because personal distress may be a risk factor for professional impairment (Pope & Vasquez, 1991). Personal therapy is another strategy for managing the distress engendered by being the target of a complaint, and provides a confidential setting in which an accused therapist can deal with the affects evoked by this difficult experience. It may be important for the therapist to consult the attorney about issues of privacy, confidentiality, and privilege in regard to all conversations (e.g., with the attorney, with a consultant, with a therapist, and with others).

The therapist who is the target of a complaint should carefully gather all records related to the matter at hand. As mentioned above, no attempts should *ever* be made to alter written records. No attempt should *ever* be made to destroy or conceal materials. If a record does not exist, attempts should not be made to create one for purposes of responding to the complaint.

When the complainant has not been a client and instead is the client's parent, grandparent, or other alleged perpetrator, the therapist may feel a strong urge to involve the client in the defense against the complaint by attesting to the client's satisfaction with what has been done by the therapist. At times, the client may actively wish to do so, feeling that an important source of support is under attack. However, the therapist must be extremely cautious at this juncture. First, the opportunity exists for the therapist to emotionally exploit the client in a defense against a third party who is often the person that the client believes to have sexually abused him or her. This appearance of having developed a "common enemy" can in turn lead to serious treatment errors as the therapist loses emotional boundaries with the client or the client engages in emotional role-reversal and attempts to protect or take care of the therapist. The therapist in this circumstance must be extremely careful in considering whether to list the client as a witness on the therapist's behalf and take whatever steps are possible to avoid this outcome because of its negative effects on the therapy. Obviously, any decisions that might affect confidentiality, privilege, or the treatment plan should be made only after adequate consultation with an attorney. The therapist must continually ask, How will this affect the therapy? Another continuing question is, in light of these events or decisions, does the treatment plan need to be revised, and do additional steps need to be taken to ensure full informed consent or informed refusal? Should the client be offered a referral to another therapist so as to more fully reduce the risk of becoming embroiled in the dispute between the therapist and a third party?

The therapist must also be in a heightened state of awareness regarding the potential for the development of hostile or resentful feelings towards the client. Conversely, this experience as the target of a client's parents' wrath may offer the therapist profound insight into the client's experiences with that same person, which may, in turn, be used in a highly effective manner in therapy. Frequent professional consultation increases the probability that positive use will be made of the experience of a complaint from a third party who is also perceived as hostile by the client.

Complaints against a therapist by a former client for alleged malpractice regarding recovered memories are relatively new, although increasing almost exponentially in number (Margaret Bogie, personal communication, March, 1995). We can understand the desire to respond to such a complaint with all available defenses, but we encourage therapists in this situation to work with their attorney to avoid a defense of demonizing the former client. Instead, emphasis should be put on obtaining expert testimony addressing the standard of care for similarly trained persons during the times at which the alleged malpractice took place. Although there is a powerful popular myth that people who bring lawsuits against health professionals are making easy money, the reality is that less than 10% (Vidmar, 1992) of all court cases against health care providers are won by the plaintiff if the case proceeds into the courtroom and is not settled prior to trial. This does not negate the importance of a careful and thorough defense strategy. However, we believe that whatever good the client still believes that she or he has received from the now-complained-about therapy will be preserved, and the former client's future capacity to feel safe in therapy enhanced, if the defense strategy is not an attack on that client.

Accusations against therapists by those who have been harmed can paint a picture of such horror that it is difficult to believe that such events actually occurred. We encourage our readers to take this information seriously, because in our collective experience as expert witnesses in cases involving therapy malpractice, almost nothing has been too horrific or absurd that some therapist has not admitted to engaging in it under the rubric of treatment. Some therapists have subjected their patients to vile and degrading practices (Pope, 1994; Pope & Bouhoutsos, 1986). Intentionally or unintentionally, therapists may place their patients at risk for deep and lasting harm, or may push their patients remorselessly toward suicide. Both authors are well aware from our work in the area of psychotherapy malpractice that there are far too many therapists whose practices are dangerous and in need of remediation, or even of being stopped. Why has the field allowed those who practice dangerously or harmfully to continue in this way? Perhaps one reason is a tragic, unjustified, and arrogant sense of entitlement among some in the mental health professions. As noted in *Sexual Involvement With Therapists: Patient Assessment, Subsequent Therapy, Forensics*, "This entitlement places the professional beyond the mechanisms of accountability and responsibility applicable to others who hold regulated (e.g., through governmental licensure) positions of great trust" (Pope, 1994, p. 36; see also for other factors that may enable therapists to continue perpetrating serious malpractice without genuine accountability). The reality of abusive psychotherapy makes it doubly important that complaints about improper handling of recovered memories be taken seriously by individual therapists and the mental health professions as a whole.

Nowhere is the responsibility to continue questioning even the most long-standing theories, assumptions, and conclusions more difficult and important. Even if the accusing client seems psychotic, vengeful, or untruthful, even if the therapist has a lifelong career of exemplary behavior, even if the therapist has always meant well and done his or her best, even if the correct answer would seem fatal to defending the case, the therapist must repeatedly and seriously ask him- or herself this question: Despite all other factors, is it possible that I have done something wrong for which I should be honest and responsible? The answer that comes from within may be the most difficult news that the therapist has ever had to endure. Temptations to shunt it aside are likely numerous (e.g., no one will ever really know, I can prove it never happened, the client doesn't know how to tell that what I did was wrong, I'll never get anymore referrals if I admit I did something like this, I'll lose my job). To disclose such an answer to others can be all but impossible, but can in fact have quite positive consequences in the long run, preserving the therapist's self-image as a healer. Often it is one of the most private and conflictual decisions that therapists can make about their integrity, honesty, sense of justice, and willingness to affirm that other people and their rights are real.

## The Forensic Evaluator in Recovered Memory Cases

The role of the forensic evaluator in a case involving allegations of recovered memory is in many ways not different from that of a forensic evaluator in any sort of personal injury lawsuit. That is, the evaluator's job is to assist the triers of fact by presenting information about a person's mental state that will inform the decision-making process in the litigation. It is clearly not the job of the treating therapist. We assume that individuals who are reading this volume with an eye to serving in the forensic evaluator role in recovered memory cases will be thoroughly familiar with the standards for forensic practice, and refer readers to several texts on the topic (Bersoff, 1995; Melton, Petrila, Poythress, & Slobogin, 1987; Weiner & Hess, 1987), as well as to the *Specialty*

*Guidelines for Forensic Psychologists* (Committee on Ethical Guidelines for Forensic Psychologists, 1991; Pope, Butcher, & Seelen, 1993, Appendix C-1), for an extensive discussion of the roles and norms for forensic practice. We heartily encourage therapists who are considering this option to move carefully and obtain the neccessary training and experience prior to offering themselves as a forensic expert. There is little more damaging to a plaintiff's cause than to offer an expert who is not truly versed in the rules of forensic mental health practice.

However, as with the treatment of clients with recovered memories, evaluations within this context require the acquisition of some specialized domains of knowledge that may lie outside the ken of the usual forensic evaluator. We suggest that, similar to child custody evaluations, which require that the evaluator have a broad information base in a number of topic areas, in this field the evaluator must be familiar with specialized knowledge. This is equally true whether the expert is retained by the plaintiff's or the defendant's attorney or appointed by the court.

Parallel to what we have suggested regarding necessary domains of knowledge for clinical competence, forensic evaluators should have familiarity with the field of child sexual abuse broadly, and any topics specific to the client in question (e.g., male survivors, survivors of color, sexual minority survivors); trauma, particularly the field of interpersonal violence; memory and suggestibility; and developmental psychopathology. It may be helpful for evaluators to also be familiar with the literature on perpetrators of sexual abuse, simply so that a framework exists within which to examine the plausibility of what is being alleged by a plaintiff or defendant. Knowing, for instance, that some pedophiles "trade" children between families may make it easier to accord credence to a plaintiff who tells a story of being handed over by a father or stepfather to male friends for the purpose of further sexual abuse. The evaluator should be prepared to offer testimony that meets the standards for admissibility of evidence in that particular jurisdiction and to be aware of whether Frye, Daubert, or other standards are applicable in the court where this case is being heard.

The evaluator must also be familiar with the criticisms made of concepts such as repression, dissociation, forgetting, and amnesia, as well as other factors that may lead to delayed recall—especially as they relate to traumatic experiences. She or he should be be prepared to testify whether information on this topic meets the applicable standards of admissibility (e.g., Frye or Daubert), depending upon the jurisdiction. The courts have not spoken with unanimity on this question. Forensic evaluators should be prepared to offer to the court information about the scientific and clinical foundations upon which the topic of delayed recall for trauma could be considered scientifically acceptable, and should not assume that courts will a priori either accept or reject this sort of information.

# Conclusion

That any clinical case is potentially a forensic case is a sharp reminder of the contexts that envelop, color, influence, and sometimes intrude on our work as therapists. Therapist and patient may see each other only in the seemingly private consulting room. The patient may have little actual realization that the therapist lives between sessions in the midst of a family, friends, and the social flow of everyday life. The therapist may have remarkably little detailed knowledge about the other people in the patient's life, the habitual encounters that the patient may no longer notice, and the concentric circles of people in whose midst the patient's life is lived. Even if they meet an hour each day, there is relatively little time to describe what happens the other 23 hours. Therapist and patient meet in a provisional cocoon of relative privacy, confidentiality, and privilege. But it is the society through its legal system that licenses therapists, establishes the rules of confidentiality and privilege, and accords a provisional, limited privacy to the work of therapy. The interdependence, interactions, and conflicts among therapy, forensics, and the larger society pose questions that are among the most important and relatively neglected in our scientific research, clinical training programs, and ethics codes (Pope & Bajt, 1988; Pope & Vasquez, 1991). They provide an array of contexts for the struggle to understand what people report as delayed memories of childhood sex abuse. As one takes the witness stand, one takes an oath to tell the truth, the whole truth, and nothing but the truth. Part of that truth, surely, is how much is not known in this area in which new data regarding trauma, memory, and suggestibility are emerging almost daily. Knowing that, therapists must not only honestly acknowledge how much we do not know and that much of what we do know must be greatly qualified, but also continue the constant process of questioning. Questioning ourselves, questioning the field, and questioning that which already appears to be certain are among our essential and most useful responsibilities.

*H = In my Library*

# References

*H* Alpert, J. L. (1995). *Sexual abuse recalled: Treating trauma in the era of the recovered memory debate*. Northvale, NJ: Jason Aronson.

Alpert, J. L., Brown, L. S., & Courtois, C. A. (1996). Symptomatic clients and memories of childhood abuse: What the trauma and child sexual abuse literature tells us. In J. Alpert, L. S. Brown, S. J. Ceci, C. A. Courtois, E. F. Loftus, & P. A. Ornstein, *Final report of the working group on investigation of memories of childhood abuse*. Washington, DC: American Psychological Association.

American Psychiatric Association. (1994). *Diagnostic and statistical manual of mental disorders* (4th ed.). Washington DC: American Psychiatric Press.

American Psychological Association (1992). Ethical principles of psychology and code of conduct. *American Psychologist, 47,* 1597–1611.

American Psychological Association approves FMSF as a sponsor of continuing education programs. (1995, November–December). *False Memory Syndrome Foundation Newsletter* (e-mail edition).

American Psychological Association Task Force on Violence in the Family (1996). *Violence and the Family: Report of the American Psychological Association Task Force on Violence in the Family*. Washington, DC: American Psychological Association.

Anderson, L. R. (1995, August). *Resources used and problems faced by successful survivors of sexual abuse*. Poster session presented at the 103rd Annual Convention of the American Psychological Association, New York, NY.

Arkes, H. R., Saville, P. D., Wortmann, R. L., & Harkness, A. R. (1981). Hindsight bias among physicians weighing the likelihood of diagnoses. *Journal of Applied Psychology, 66,* 252–254.

Armstrong, L. (1994). *Rocking the cradle of sexual politics: What happened when women said incest*. Reading, MA: Addison Wesley.

Author target of false-memories lawsuit. (1994, May 4). *Sacramento Bee*, p. B3.

Baker, K. (1996). Child sexual abuse: The recovered memory/false memory debate. *Treating Abuse Today, 5*(6), 25–30.

239

Barach, P. (1996, April). Adventures in the memory zone. Invited lecture presented at the Eleventh Regional Conference on Trauma and Dissociation, Akron, OH.

Barnier, A. J., & McConckey, K. M. (1992). Reports of real and false memories: The relevance of hypnosis, hypnotizability, and context of memory test. *Journal of Abnormal Psychology, 101*, 521–527.

Barrett, M. J. (1995). Out of the box: A family therapist's approach to the "False Memory Syndrome." *Treating Abuse Today, 5*(2), 6–15.

Bartlett, F. (1932). *Remembering: A study in experimental and social psychology.* New York: Macmillan.

Bauer, P. J. (1996). What do infants recall of their lives? Memory for specific events by one- to two-year-olds. *American Psychologist, 51*, 29–41.

Becker, D., & Lamb, S. (1994). Sex bias in the diagnosis of borderline personality disorder and post-traumatic stress disorder. *Professional Psychology: Research and Practice, 25*, 55–61.

Beitchman, J., Zucker K., Hood, J., daCosta, G., & Ackman, D. (1991). A review of the short-term effects of childhood sexual abuse. *Child Abuse and Neglect, 16*, 101–118.

Berliner, L., & Williams, L. M. (1994). Memories of child sexual abuse: A response to Lindsay and Read. *Applied Cognitive Psychology, 8*, 379–388.

Bernstein, E. M., & Putnam, F. W. (1986). Development, reliability and validity of a dissociation scale. *Journal of Nervous and Mental Disease, 174*, 727–735.

Bernstein, E., & Putnam, F. (1993). An update on the Dissociative Experiences Scale. *Dissociation, 6*, 16–28.

Bersoff, D. N. (Ed.) (1995). *Ethical conflicts in psychology.* Washington, DC: American Psychological Association.

"Biography." (1995). *American Psychologist, 50*, 242–243.

Bird, C. (1927). The influence of the press upon the accuracy of report. *Journal of Abnormal and Social Psychology, 22*, 123–129.

Blume, E. S. (1990). *Secret survivors: Uncovering incest and its aftereffects in women.* New York: Wiley.

Borys, D., & Pope, K. S. (1989). Dual relationships between therapist and client: A national study of psychologists, psychiatrists and social workers. *Professional Psychology: Research and Practice, 20*, 283–293.

Boss, K. (1994, September 25). Into the past imperfect: Elizabeth Loftus challenges our total recall. *Seattle Times*, pp. 8–13, 24.

Bower, G. H. (1981). Mood and memory. *American Psychologist, 36*, 129–148.

Bower, G. H. (1990). Awareness, the unconscious and repression: An experimental psychologist's perspective. In J. L. Singer (Ed)., *Repression and dissociation: Implications for personality theory, psychopathology and health* (pp. 209–231). Chicago: University of Chicago Press.

Bowers, K. S. (1994). Dissociated control, imagination, and the phenomenology of dissociation. In D. Spiegel (Ed.), *Dissociation: Culture, mind and body* (pp. 21–40). Washington, DC: American Psychiatric Press.

Bowman, C. G., & Mertz, E. (1996). A dangerous direction: Legal intervention in sexual abuse survivor therapy. *Harvard Law Review, 109*, 549–639.

Braude, S. E. (1995). First person plural (revised edition). Lanham, MD: Rowman & Littlefield.

Breland, K., & Breland, M. (1961). The misbehavior of organisms. *American Psychologist, 16,* 681–684.

Bremner, J. D., Randall, P., Scott, T. M., Bronen, R. A., Seibyl, J. P., Southwick, S. M., Delaney, R. C., McCarthy, G., Charney, D. S., & Innis, R. B. (1995). MRI-based measurement of hippocampal volume in patients with combat-related posttraumatic stress disorder. *American Journal of Psychiatry, 152,* 973–981.

Brewin, C. R., Andrews, B., & Gotlib, I. A. (1993). Psychopathology and early experience: A reappraisal of retrospective reports. *Psychological Bulletin, 113,* 82–98.

Briere, J. N. (1996). *Therapy for adults molested as children: Beyond survival* (rev. 2nd ed.). New York: Springer.

Briere, J. N. (1992). Methodological issues in the study of sexual abuse effects. *Journal of Consulting and Clinical Psychology, 60,* 196–203.

Briere, J. N. (1995). *Trauma Symptom Inventory*. Odessa, FL: Psychological Assessment Resources, Inc.

Briere, J. N. (in press). *Psychological assessment of adult posttraumatic states*. Washington DC: American Psychological Association.

Briere, J. N., & Conte, J. (1993). Self-reported amnesia for abuse in adults molested as children. *Journal of Traumatic Stress, 6,* 21–31.

Briere, J., & Zaidi, L. Y. (1989). Sexual abuse histories and sequelae in female psychiatric emergency room patients. *American Journal of Psychiatry, 146,* 1602–1606.

Brown, D. (1995a). Pseudomemories: The standard of science and standard of care in trauma treatment. *American Journal of Clinical Hypnosis, 37,* 1–24.

Brown, D. (1995b). Sources of suggestion and their applicability to psychotherapy. In J. L. Alpert (Ed.), *Sexual abuse recalled* (pp. 61–100). Northvale, NJ: Jason Aronson.

Brown, D., & Fromm, E. (1986). *Hypnotherapy and hypnoanalysis*. Hillsdale, NJ: Lawrence Erlbaum.

Brown, L. S. (1994). *Subversive dialogues: Theory in feminist therapy*. New York: Basic Books.

Brown, L. S. (1995, October 20). Recovered memory panel discussion. Discussion presented at the fall meeting of the Washington Psychological Association, Tacoma, WA.

Brown, L. S. (1996a). Your therapy client as plaintiff: Clinical and legal issues for the treating therapist. In J. L. Alpert (Ed.), *Sexual abuse recalled: Perspectives for clinicians* (pp. 337–362). New York: Jason Aronson

Brown, L. S. (1996b, March). *Theory in feminist therapy: Where do we go from here.* Invited address presented at the Annual Conference of the Association for Women in Psychology, Portland, OR.

Brown, R. (1958). *Words and things*. Glencoe, IL: The Free Press.

Bruhn, A. R. (1995). Early memories in personality assessment. In J. N. Butcher (Ed.), *Clinical personality assessment* (pp. 278–301). New York: Oxford University Press.

Bryer, J. B., Nelson, B. A., Miller, J. B., & Krol, P. A. (1987). Childhood sexual and physical abuse as factors in adult psychiatric illness. *American Journal of Psychiatry, 144*, 1426–1430.

Burgess, A. W., Hartman, C. R., & Baker, T. (1995). Memory presentations of childhood sexual abuse. *Journal of Psychosocial Nursing, 33*, 9–16.

Burgess, J. A. (1984). Principles and techniques of cross-examination. In B. G. Warschaw (Ed.), *The trial masters: A handbook of strategies and techniques that win cases* (pp. 249–255). Englewood Cliffs, NJ: Prentice-Hall.

Burnam, M. A., Stein, J. A., Golding, J. M., Siegel, J. M., Sorenson, S. B., Forsythe, A. B., & Telles, C. A. (1988). Sexual assault and mental disorders in a community population. *Journal of Consulting and Clinical Psychology, 56*, 843–850.

Butler, K. (1994, September 6). Self-help authors freed from liability; suit involving incest claims continues. *San Francisco Chronicle*, p. A16.

Butler, K. (1995, March–April). Caught in the cross fire. *The Family Therapy Networker*, pp. 25–34, 69–78.

Butler, S. (1978). *Conspiracy of silence: The trauma of incest*. San Francisco: New Glide Publications

Butters, N., & Cermak, L. S. (1986). A case study of the forgetting of autobiographical knowledge: Implications for the study of retrograde amnesia. In D. C. Rubin (Ed.), *Autobiographical memory* (pp. 253–272). Cambridge: Cambridge University Press.

Cahill, L., Prins, B., Weber, M., & McGaugh, J. L. (1994). B-adrenergic activation and memory for emotional events. *Nature, 371*, 702–704.

Calof, D. (1996, June 2). Notes from a practice under siege. Paper presented at the Eighth Annual Eastern Regional Conference on Abuse, Trauma, and Dissociation, Washington, DC. (Audiotape available from Audiotape Transcripts, LTB, 800-338-2111)

Campbell, T. W. (1994). *Beware the talking cure: Psychotherapy may be hazardous to your mental health*. Boca Raton, FL: Upton Books.

*Canterbury v. Spence.* (1972). United States Court of Appeals, District of Columbia Circuit. 464 F.2d 772.

Caplan, P. J. (1995). *They say you're crazy: How the world's most powerful psychiatrists decide who's normal*. Reading, MA: Addison Wesley.

Carbonell, J. L., & Figley, C. R. (1995, August). Active ingredient in short-term treatments for PTSD. In C. R. Figley & J. L. Carbonell (Chairs), *Innovations in short-term treatment for traumatic stress*. Symposium presented at the 103rd Annual Convention of the American Psychological Association, New York, NY.

Carlson, E. B., & Putnam, F. W. (1993). An update to the Dissociative Experiences Scale, *Dissociation, 6*, 16–27.

Carlson, E. B., Putnam, F. W., Ross, C. A., Torem, M., Coons, P., Dill, D., Lowenstein, R. J., & Braun, B. G. (1993). Validity of the Dissociative Experiences Scale in screening for multiple personality disorder: A multicenter study. *American Journal of Psychiatry, 150*, 1030–1036.

Carstensen, L., Gabrieli, J., Shepard, R., Levenson, R., Mason, M., Goodman, G., Bootzin, R., Ceci, S., Bronfenbrenner, U., Edelstein, B., Schober, M., Bruck,

M., Keane, T., Zimering, R., Oltmanns, T., Gotlib, I., & Ekman, P. (1993). Repressed objectivity. *APS Observer*, March, p. 23.

Caudill, O. B., & Pope, K. S. (1995). *Law and mental health professionals: California*. Washington, DC: American Psychological Association.

Ceci, S. J., & Bruck, M. (1995). *Jeopardy in the courtroom: A scientific analysis of children's testimony*. Washington DC: American Psychological Association.

Ceci, S. J., Huffman, M. L. C., Smith, E., & Loftus, E. F. (1994). Repeatedly thinking about a non-event: Source misattributions among preschoolers. *Consciousness and Cognition, 3*, 388–407.

Ceci, S. J., Ross, D. F., & Toglia, M. P. (1987). Suggestibility of children's memory: Psycholegal implications. *Journal of Experimental Psychology: General, 116*, 38–49.

*Cheatham v. Rogers*. (1992). 824 S. W. 2d 231.

Christianson, S-A. (1992). Emotional stress and eyewitness memory. *Psychological Bulletin, 112*, 284–309.

Chu, J. A., Matthews, J., Frey, L. M., & Ganzel, B. (in press). The nature of traumatic memories of childhood abuse. *The Harvard Review of Psychiatry*.

Clark, D. A. (1988). The validity of measures of cognition: A review of the literature. *Cognitive Therapy and Research, 12*, 1–20.

*Cobbs v. Grant* (1972). Supreme Court of California, 502 P.2d 1, 8 Cal.3d 229.

Coles, R. (1973). Shrinking history. *New York Review of Books, Part I*, pp. 15–21 (February 22); *Part II.*, pp. 20, 25–29 (March 8).

Committee on Ethical Guidelines for Forensic Psychologists (1991). Specialty guideline for forensic psychologists. *Law and Human Behavior, 15*, 655–665.

Committee on Professional Practice and Standards. (1993). Record keeping guidelines. *American Psychologist, 18*, 984–986.

Connors, M. E., & Morse, W. (1993). Sexual abuse and eating disorders: A review. *International Journal of Eating Disorders, 13*, 1–11.

Cooper, & Cooper. (1991). How people change inside and outside therapy. In R. C. Curtiss & G. Stricker (Eds.), *How people change: Inside and outside therapy* (pp. 173–189). New York: Plenum.

Courtois, C. (1988). *Healing the incest wound: Adults survivors in therapy*. New York: W. W. Norton.

Crews, F. (1995). *The memory wars: Freud's legacy in dispute*. New York: New York Review of Books.

Crews, F. (1996). The verdict on Freud. *Psychological Sciences, 7*, 63–68.

Dalenberg, C., Coe, M., Reto, M., Aransky, K., & Duvenage, C. (1995, January). *The prediction of amnesiac barrier strength as an individual difference variable in state-dependent learning paradigms*. Paper presented at a conference, Responding to Child Maltreatment, San Diego, CA.

Danieli, Y. (1985). The treatment and prevention of long-term effects and intergenerational transmission of victimization: A lesson from Holocaust survivors and their children. In C. Figley (Ed.), *Trauma and its wake* (pp. 293–313). New York: Brunner/Mazel.

*Daubert v. Merrell Dow Pharmaceutical*. (1993). 113 S. Ct. 2786.

Davidson, J. R. T., & Fairbank, J. A. (1993). The epidemiology of post-traumatic stress disorder. In J. R. T. Davidson & E. B. Foa (Eds.), *Posttraumatic stress disorder: DSM-IV and beyond* (pp. 147–172). Washington DC: American Psychiatric Press.

Dawes, R. M. (1994). *House of cards: Psychology and psychotherapy built on myth.* New York: Free Press.

Dawes, R. M. (1995). Book review of "Return of the Furies: An Investigation into Recovered Memory Therapy" by Hollida Wakefield and Ralph Underwager. *FMS Foundation Newsletter,* January, pp. 11–13.

de Rivera, J. (1994). Impact of child abuse memories on the families of victims. *Issues in Child Abuse Accusations, 6,* 149–155.

Doe, J. [Pamela Freyd] (1991). How could this happen? Coping with a false accusation of incest and rape. *Issues in Child Abuse Accusations, 3,* 154–165.

Doe, J. [Pamela Freyd] (1994). How could this happen? In E. Goldstein & K. Farmer (Eds.), *Confabulations: Creating false memories, destroying families* (pp. 27–60). Boca Raton, FL: Upton Books.

Doris, J. (Ed.). (1991). *The suggestibility of children's recollections.* Washington DC: American Psychological Association.

Drajer, N. (1988). *Seksueel misbruik van meisjes door verwanten. Een landlijke onder-zoek naar de omvang, de aard, de gezinsachtergroden, de emotionele betenkis en de psychiatrische gevolgen* [Sexual abuse of girls by family members: A national study of incidence, prevalence, family history, emotional meaning, and psychiatric consequence]. The Hague, The Netherlands: Ministerie van Social Zaken en Werkgelegenheid.

Duvenage, C., & Dalenberg, C. (1993, January). *Dissociation, child abuse history and amnesiac barrier strength in a non-clinical population.* Paper presented at a conference, Responding to Child Maltreatment, San Diego, CA.

Elliott, D. M., & Briere, J. N. (1994, November). Trauma and dissociated memory: Prevalence across events. In L. Berliner (Chair), *Delayed trauma memories: Victim experiences and clinical practice.* Symposium presented at the Tenth Annual Meeting, International Society for Traumatic Stress Studies, Chicago, IL.

Elliott, D. M., & Briere, J. N. (1995). Post traumatic stress associated with delayed recall of sexual abuse: A general population study. *Journal of Traumatic Stress, 8,* 629–647.

Enns, C. Z., McNeilly, C., Corkery, J., & Gilbert, M. (1995). The debate about delayed memories of child sexual abuse: A feminist perspective. *The Counseling Psychologist, 23,* 181–279.

Erdelyi, M. (1990). Repression, reconstruction and defense: History and inte-gration. In J. L. Singer (Ed)., *Repression and dissociation: Implications for per-sonality theory, psychopathology and health* (pp. 1–31). Chicago: University of Chicago Press.

Evans, F. J. (1967). Suggestibility in the normal waking state. *Psychological Bulletin, 67,* 114–129.

Evans, J. (1989). *Bias in human reasoning: Causes and consequences.* Hillsdale, NJ: Lawrence Erlbaum.

Every, M. (1993). Child abuse: Does memory serve? *Sarasota Herald-Tribune,* January 20, pp. 1E & 8E.

False Memory Syndrome Foundation. (1992a). Information needed in assessing allegations by adults of sex abuse in childhood. *False Memory Syndrome Foundation Newsletter*, November 5, p. 5.

False Memory Syndrome Foundation. (1992b). *Legal aspects of False Memory Syndrome*. Philadelphia: Author.

False Memory Syndrome Foundation. (1992c, October 5). What can families do? *False Memory Syndrome Foundation Newsletter*, p. 4.

False Memory Syndrome Foundation. (1993, May 3). Important organizational notice. *False Memory Syndrome Foundation Newsletter*, p. 7.

False Memory Syndrome Foundation. (1994, July/August). How does a person know that memories of abuse were false? *False Memory Syndrome Foundation Newsletter*, pp. 3–4.

False Memory Syndrome Foundation. (1995). *Amicus Curiae Brief filed with the Supreme Court for the State of Rhode Island in the cases of Heroux v. Carpentier (Appeal No. 95-39) and Kelly v. Marcantonio (Appeal No. 94-727)*.

False Memory Syndrome Foundation. (1996a, February 1). FMS Foundation Scientific and Professional Advisory Board. *False Memory Syndrome Foundation Newsletter* (e-mail edition).

False Memory Syndrome Foundation. (1996b). Information sheet and order form for "False Memory Syndrome" video. Philadelphia: Author.

Feldman-Summers, S., & Kiesler, S. B. (1974). Those who are number two try harder: The effect of sex on attributions of causality. *Journal of Personality and Social Psychology, 30*, 846–855.

Feldman-Summers, S., & Pope, K. S. (1994). The experience of "forgetting" childhood abuse: A national survey of psychologists. *Journal of Consulting and Clinical Psychology, 62*, 636–639.

Fernberger, S. W. (1932). The American Psychological Association: A historical summary, 1892–1930. *Psychological Bulletin, 29*, 1–89.

Fernberger, S. W. (1943). The American Psychological Association, 1992–1942. *Psychological Review, 50*, 33–60.

Fidell, L. S. (1970). Empirical verification of sex discrimination in hiring practices in psychology. *American Psychologist, 25*, 1988–1994.

Fischoff, B. (1982). For those condemned to study the past: Heuristics and biases in hindsight. In D. Kahneman, P. Slovic, & A. Tversky (Eds.), *Judgment under uncertainty: Heuristics and biases* (pp. 335–351). Cambridge: Cambridge University Press.

Fitzpatrick, F. (1994). Isolation and silence: A male survivor speaks out about clergy abuse. *Moving Forward, 3*, 4–8.

FMSF Advisory Board Meeting: Where Do We Go From Here. (1993). *FMS Foundation Newsletter*, December, p. 3.

Foa, E. B., & Riggs, D. S. (1993). Post traumatic stress disorder in rape victims. In J. M. Oldham, M. B. Riba, & A. Tasman (Eds.) *American Psychiatric Press Review of Psychiatry* (pp. 273–303), Volume 12. Washington DC: American Psychiatric Press.

Foa, E. B., Rothbaum, B. O., Riggs, D. S., & Murdock, T. B. (1991). Treatment of posttraumatic stress disorder in rape victims: A comparison between cognitive-behavioral procedures and counseling. *Journal of Consulting and Clinical Psychology, 5*, 715–723.

Fox, R. (1995). The rape of psychotherapy. *Professional Psychology: Research and Practice, 26*, 147–155.

Frank, R. A. (1996). Tainted therapy and mistaken memory: Avoiding malpractice and preserving evidence with possible adult victims of childhood sexual abuse. *Applied and Preventive Psychology, 5*, 135–164.

Fredrickson, R. (1992). *Repressed memories: A journal to recovery from sexual abuse.* New York: Simon and Schuster.

Freyd, J. J. (1983). Representing the dynamics of a static form. *Memory and Cognition, 11*, 342–346.

Freyd, J. J. (1993, August). Theoretical and personal perspectives on the delayed memory debate. Paper presented at a conference, Controversies around recovered memories of incest and ritualistic abuse, Ann Arbor, MI.

Freyd, J. J. (1994) Betrayal-trauma: Traumatic amnesia as an adaptive response to childhood abuse. *Ethics and Behavior, 4*, 307–329.

Freyd, J. J. (1996). *Betrayal trauma theory: The Logic of Forgetting Abuse.* Harvard University Press.

Freyd, J. J., & Finke, R. A. (1984) Representational momentum. *Journal of Experimental Psychology: Learning, Memory and Cognition, 10*, 126–132.

Freyd, J. J., & Finke, R. A. (1985). A velocity effect for representational momentum. *Bulletin of the Psychonomic Society, 23*, 443–446.

Freyd, J. J., & Gleaves, D. H. (1996). "Remembering" words not presented in lists: Relevance to the current recovered/false memory controversy. *Journal of Experimental Psychology: Learning, Memory, and Cognition, 22*, 811–813.

Freyd, J. J., & Johnson, J. Q. (1987). Prolonging the time course of representational momentum. *Journal of Experimental Psychology: Learning, Memory and Cognition, 13*, 259–268.

Freyd, J. J., Kelly, M. H., & DeKay, M. T. (1990). Representational momentum in memory for pitch. *Journal of Experimental Psychology: Learning, Memory and Cognition, 16*, 1107–1117.

Freyd, J. J., & Miller, G. F. (1992, November). *Creature motion.* Paper given at the 33rd annual meeting of the Psychonomic Society, St. Louis, MO.

Freyd, J. J., Pantzer, T. M., & Cheng J. L. (1988). Representing statics as forces in equilibrium. *Journal of Experimental Psychology: General, 117*, 395–407.

Freyd, P. [writing as Jane Doe]. (1991). How could this happen? Coping with a false accusation of incest and rape. *Issues in Child Abuse Accusations*, vol. 3 (3), pp. 154–165.

Freyd, P. (1992a, February 29). Dear Friends. *False Memory Syndrome Newsletter*, p. 1.

Freyd, P. (1992b, February 29). How do we know we are not representing pedophiles? *False Memory Syndrome Newsletter*, p. 1.

Freyd, P. (1993). Editorial *False Memory Syndrome Foundation Newsletter, 2* (7), 1–3.

Freyd, P. (1994a). Editorial *False Memory Syndrome Foundation Newsletter, 3* (6), 1–3.

Freyd, P. (1994b) False Memory Syndrome Foundation. Paper presented at

Conference Current Topics in the Law and Mental Health, Seattle, WA, Nov. 4–6.

Freyd, P. (1996). Dear Friends. *False Memory Syndrome Foundation Newsletter* (e-mail edition), March 1.

Freyd, P. [writing as Jane Doe] (1994). How could this happen? In E. Goldstein & K. Farmer (Eds.), *Confabulations: Creating false memories, destroying families* (pp. 27–60). Boca Raton, FL: Upton.

Freyd, P., Roth, Z., Wakefield, H., & Underwager, R. (1993, April). *Results of the FMSF Family Survey.* Paper presented at a conference, Memory and Reality, sponsored by the False Memory Syndrome Foundation, Valley Forge, PA.

Fried, S. (1994, January). War of remembrance: How the problems of one Philadelphia family created the False Memory Syndrome Foundation and triggered the most controversial debate in modern mental health. *Philadelphia*, 66–71, 149–157.

Friedman, N. (1967). *The social nature of psychological research: The psychological experiment as a social interaction.* New York: Basic Books.

Gardner, M. (1993). The False Memory Syndrome. *Skeptical Inquirer, 17*, 370–375.

Gardner, R. A. (1993). A theory about the variety of human sexual behavior. *Issues in Child Abuse Accusations, 5*, 105.

Gardner, R. A. (1992). *True and false accusations of child sex abuse.* Cresskill, NJ: Creative Therapeutics.

Garry, M., & Loftus, E. F. (1994, January). Repressed memories of childhood trauma: Could some of them be suggested? *USA Today, 122* (2584), pp. 82–83.

Gavigan, M. (1994). My recovery from "recovery". In E. Goldstich and K. Farmer (Eds.), *True Stories of False Memories* (pp. 251–283). Boca Raton, FL: SIRS.

Geller, J. D., Colley, R. S., & Hartley, D. (1981). Images of the psychotherapist. *Imagination, Cognition and Personality, 1*, 123–146.

Geise, A. A., Adler, L. E., Mongomery, P., Nagamoto, H., Gerhardt, G., McRae, K., Hoffer, L. (1994, November). Sensory physiology and catcholamines in PTSD. Poster presented at the Tenth Annual Meeting of the International Society for Traumatic Stress Studies, Chicago, IL.

Gidycz, C. A., & Koss, M. P. (1989). The impact of adolescent sexual victimization: Standardized measures of anxiety, depression and behavioral deviancy. *Violence and Victims, 4*, 139–149.

Gleaves, D. H. (1996a). The evidence for "repression": An examination of Holmes (1990) and the implications for the recovered memory controversy. *Journal of Child Sexual Abuse, 5*, 1–19.

Gleaves, D. (1996b). The sociocognitive model of dissociative identity disorder: A re-examination of the evidence. *Psychological Bulletin, 120*, 42–59.

Goffman, E. (1961). *Asylums: Essays on the social situation of mental patients and other inmates.* Garden City, NY: Anchor.

Goldstein, E., & Farmer, K. (Eds.). (1993). *True Stories of False Memories.* Boca Raton, FL: SIRS Books.

Goldstein, E., & Farmer, K. (Eds.). (1994). *Confabulations: Creating false memories, destroying families.* Boca Raton, FL: SIRS Books.

Goodman, G. S., Bottoms, B. L., Schwartz-Kenney, B., & Rudy, L. A. (1991). Children's memory for a stressful event: Improving children's report. *Journal of Narrative and Life History, 1,* 69–99.

Goodman, G. S., Quas, J. A., Batterman-Faunce, J. M., Riddlesberger, M. M., & Kuhn, J. (1994). Predictors of accurate and inaccurate memories of traumatic events experienced in childhood. *Consciousness and Cognition, 3,* 269–294.

Goodyear-Smith, F. (1993). *First do no harm: The child sexual abuse industry.* Auckland, NZ: Benton-Guy Publishing.

Guthiel, T. G., Bursztajn, H. J., Brodsky, A., & Alexander, V. (Eds.). (1991). *Decision-making in psychiatry and the law.* Baltimore: Williams and Wilkins.

Guthrie, H. (1976). *Even the rat was white: A historical view of psychology.* New York: Harper & Row.

Gynther, M. D., Fowler, R. D., & Erdberg, P. (1971). False positives galore: The application of standard MMPI criteria to a rural, isolated, Negro sample. *Journal of Clinical Psychology, 27,* 234–237.

Hammond, D. C., Garver, R. B., & Mutter, C. D. (1995). *Clinical hypnosis and memory: Guidelines for clinicans and forensic hypnosis.* Des Plaine, IL: American Society for Clinical Hypnosis.

Harvey, M. R. (1996). An ecological view of psychological trauma and trauma recovery. *Journal of Traumatic Stress, 9,* 3–24.

Harvey, M. R., & Herman, J. L. (1994). Amnesia, partial amnesia and delayed recall among adult survivors of childhood trauma. *Consciousness and Cognition, 3,* 295–306.

H Hassan, S. (1990). *Combating cult mind control.* Rochester, VT: Park Street Press.

Henderson, D. J. (1975). Incest. In A. M. Freedman, H. I. Kaplan, & B. J. Sadock (Eds.), *Comprehensive textbook of psychiatry* (pp. 1530–1539). Baltimore: Williams & Wilkins.

Herman, J. L. (1981). *Father-daughter incest.* Cambridge, MA: Harvard University Press.

H Herman, J. L. (1992). *Trauma and recovery.* New York: Basic Books.

Herman, J. L. (1994). Presuming to know the truth. *Neiman Reports, 48,* 43–45.

Herman, J. L., & Schatzow, E. (1987). Recovery and verification of memories of childhood sexual trauma. *Psychoanalytic Psychology, 4,* 1–14.

Hernandez-Peon, R., Scherrer, H., & Jouvet, M. (1956). Modification of electrical activity in the cochlear nucleus during "attention" in unanesthetized cats. *Science, 123,* 331–332.

Hilgard, E. R. (1977). *Divided consciousness: Multiple controls in human thought and action.* New York: John Wiley & Sons.

Hoffer, E. (1989). *The true believer.* New York: HarperPerennial. (Original work published 1951)

Hollingshead, A., & Redlich, F. C. (1958). *Social class and mental illness: A community study.* New York: Wiley.

Holmes, D. S. (1990). The evidence for repression: An examination of sixty years of research. In J. L. Singer (Ed.), *Repression and dissociation:*

*Implications for personality theory, psychopathology and health* (pp. 85–102). Chicago: University of Chicago Press.

Homans, L. A. (1995). WSPA and concerns regarding the new Value Behavioral Health contract. *Washington Psychologist, 49*, 1–2.

Horowitz, M. (1986). *Stress response syndromes*. New York: Jason Aaronson.

Horowitz, M., Wilmer, N., & Alvarez, W. (1979). Impact of Event Scale: A measure of subjective stress. *Psychosomatic Medicine, 41*, 209–218.

Howe, M. L., & Brainerd, C. J. (1989). Development of children's long term retention. *Developmental Review, 9*, 301–340.

Howe, M. L., Courage, M. L., & Peterson, C. (1994). How can I remember when "I" wasn't there: Long-term retention of traumatic experiences and emergence of the cognitive self. *Consciousness and Cognition, 3*, 327–355.

Hubel, D. H., & Wiesel, T. N. (1962a). Cortical and callosal connections concerned with the vertical meridian of visual fields in the cat. *Journal of Neurophysiology, 30*, 1561–1573.

Hubel, D. H., & Wiesel, T. N. (1962b). Receptive fields, binocular interaction, and functional architecture in the cat's visual cortex. *Journal of Physiology, 160*, 106–154.

Hubel, D. H., & Wiesel, T. N. (1979). Brain mechanisms of vision. *Scientific American, 241*, 150–162.

Hyman, I. E., Jr., Husband, T. H., & Billings, F. J. (1995). False memories of childhood experiences. *Applied Cognitive Psychology, 9*, 181–197.

Jacobson, A., & Richardson, B. C. (1987). Assault experiences of 100 psychiatric inpatients: Evidence of the need for routine inquiry. *American Journal of Psychiatry, 144*, 434–440.

Jacobson, A., Koehler, J. E., & Jones-Brown, C. (1987). The failure of routine assessment to detect histories of assault experienced by psychiatric patients. *Hospital and Community Psychiatry, 38*, 386–389.

James, W. (1890). *The principles of psychology* (Vol. 1). New York: Dover.

Janoff-Bulman, R. (1992). *Shattered assumptions: Toward a new psychology of trauma*. New York: Free Press.

Kahn, J. P. (1994, December 14). Trial by memory: Stung by daughters' claims of abuse, a writer lashes back. *Boston Globe*, p. 80.

Kalichman, S. C. (1993). *Mandated reporting of suspected child abuse: Ethics, law, and policy*. Washington, DC: American Psychological Association.

Kazdin, A. E. (1978). Covert modeling: The therapeutic application of imagined rehearsal. In. J. L. Singer and K. S. Pope (Eds.), *The power of human imagination: New methods in psychotherapy* (pp. 255–278). New York: Plenum.

Kendall-Tacket, K., Williams, L. M., & Finkelhor, D. (1993). Impact of sexual abuse on children: A review and synthesis of recent empirical studies. *Psychological Bulletin, 113*, 164–180.

Kihlstrom, J. (1995a). Inferring history from symptoms. Internet posting, January 24.

Kihlstrom, J. (1995b). On checklists. Internet posting, January 24.

Kihlstrom, J. (1996). False memory syndrome. *FMS Foundation Brochure* (e-mail version). Philadelphia: FMSF.

Kihlstrom, J. F., & Harackiewicz, J. (1982). The earliest recollection: A new survey. *Journal of Personality and Social Psychology, 50*, 134–138.

Kihlstrom, J. & Hoyt, I. (1990). Repression, dissociation, and hypnosis. In J. L. Singer (Ed.), *Repression and dissociation: Implications for personality theory, psychopathology, and health* (pp. 181–208). Chicago: University of Chicago Press.

Kluft, R. P. (1995). The confirmation and disconfirmation of memories of abuse in DID patients: A naturalistic clinical study. *Dissociation, 8*, 253–258.

Kluft, R. P. (1990). Incest and subsequent revictimization. In R. P. Kluft (Ed.), *Incest-related syndromes of adult psychopathology* (pp. 263–288). Washington DC: American Psychiatric Press.

Koffka, K. (1935). *Principles of Gestalt psychology*. New York: International Library of Psychology, Philosophy and Scientific Method.

Koslyn, S., & Koenig, O. (1992). *Wet mind: The new cognitive neuroscience*. New York: Free Press.

Koss, M. P., Goodman, L. A., Browne, A., Fitzgerald, L. F., Keita, G. W., & Russo, N. F. (1994). *No safe haven*. Washington, DC: American Psychological Association.

Koss, M. P., Tromp, S., & Tharan, M. (1995). Traumatic memories: Empirical foundations, forensic and clinical implications. *Clinical Psychology: Science and Practice, 2*, 111–132.

Kristiansen, C. M. (1994). Bearing witness to the patriarchal revictimization of survivors. *Newsletter of the Canadian Psychological Association Section on Women and Psychology, 20 (2)*, 7–16.

Kristiansen, C. M., Haslip, S. J., & Kelly, K. D. (in press). Scientific and judicial delusions of objectivity in the recovered memory debate. *Feminism and Psychology*.

Krivacska, J. J. (1994). Child sexual abuse: Cause and effects. A social constructionist view. *Journal of Sex Research, 31*, 157–159.

Krystal, J. (1996, June). *The neurobiology of dissociation*. Plenary lecture presented at the Second International Conference of the ISTSS, Jerusalem, Israel.

Lakoff, R. T. (1990). *Talking power: The politics of language*. New York: Basic Books.

Landsberg, M. (1996a, February 11). Beware of false prophets. *Toronto Star*, p. A2.

Landsberg, M. (1996b, February 4). Incest. *Toronto Star*, p. A2.

Langer, E. J. (1989). *Mindfulness*. Reading, MA: Addison-Wesley.

Langer, E. J., & Abelson, R. P. (1974). A patient by any other name . . . : Clinician group differences and labeling bias. *Journal of Consulting and Clinical Psychology, 42*, 4–9.

Lanktree, C., Briere, J., & Zaida, L. (1991). Incidence and impact of sexual abuse in a child outpatient sample: The role of direct inquiry. *Child Abuse and Neglect, 15*, 447–453.

Lashley, K. (1988). In search of the engram. In J. A. Anderson & E. Rosenfeld (Eds.), *Neurocomputing: Foundations of research* (pp. 59–63). Cambridge, MA: MIT Press. (Originally published 1950)

Lebowitz, L., Harvey, M. R., & Herman, J. L (1993). A stage-by-dimension model of recovery from sexual trauma. *Journal of Interpersonal Violence, 8*, 387–391.

Levi, P. (1988). *The drowned and the saved*. New York: Vintage. (Translated by R. Rosenthall)

Levinson, A. (1995). Some Facts on Child Abuse. Associated Press wire report, October 7.

Li, C. K., West, D. J., & Woodhouse, T. P. (1993). *Children's sexual encounters with adults: A scientific study*. Buffalo, NY: Prometheus Books.

Liem, J., James, J., & O'Toole, J. (1994, November). Assessing resilience in adult female survivors of childhood sexual abuse. In F. K. Grossman (Chair), *Resiliency: Research and reflections*. Symposium presented at the Tenth Annual Meeting, International Society for Traumatic Stress Studies, Chicago, IL.

Lightfoot, L. (1993). Child abuse expert says paedophilia part of "God's will"; Dr. Ralph Underwager. *London Times*, December 19, p. 2.

Lindsay, D. S. (1995a). Backlash: Comments on Enns, McNeilly, Corkery, and Gilbert. *Counseling Psychologist, 23*, 280–289.

Lindsay, D. S. (1995b, August 14). Letter to Karen Olio.

Lindsay, D. S., & Poole, D. A. (1995). Remembering childhood sexual abuse in therapy: Psychotherapists' self-reported beliefs, practices, and experiences. *Journal of Psychiatry and Law*, Fall, 461–476.

Lindsay, D. S., & Read, J. D. (1994). Psychotherapy and memories of childhood sexual abuse: A cognitive perspective. *Applied Cognitive Psychology, 8*, 281–338.

Loftus, E. F. (1979). *Eyewitness testimony*. Cambridge, MA: Harvard University Press.

Loftus, E. F. (1988). *Memory: Surprising new insights into how we remember and why we forget*. New York: Ardsley House. (Originally published 1980)

Loftus, E. F. (1992). When a lie becomes memory's truth: Memory distortion after exposure to misinformation. *Current Directions in Psychological Science, 1*, 121–123.

Loftus, E. F. (1993). The reality of repressed memories. *American Psychologist, 48*, 518–537.

Loftus, E. F. (1995a, June). Realities and myths of the repressed memory controversy. Paper presented at the annual convention of the American Psychological Society, New York, NY.

Loftus, E. F. (1995b). Remembering dangerously. *Skeptical Inquirer, 19*(2), 20–30.

Loftus, E. F., & Davies, G. M. (1984). Distortions in the memory of children. *Journal of Social Issues, 40*, 51–67.

Loftus, E. F., Garry, M., & Feldman, J. (1994). Forgetting sexual trauma: What does it mean when 38% forget? *Journal of Consulting and Clinical Psychology, 62*, 1177–1181.

Loftus, E. F., & Hoffman, H. G. (1989). Misinformation and memory: The creation of new memories. *Journal of Experimental Psychology: General, 118*, 100–104.

Loftus, E. F., & Ketcham, K. (1994). *The myth of repressed memory: False memories and allegations of abuse*. New York: St. Martins Press.

Loftus, E. F., & Loftus, G. (1980). On the permanence of stored information in the human brain. *American Psychologist, 35*, 409–420.

Loftus, E. F., Milo, E., & Paddock, J. (1995). The accidental executioner: Why psychotherapy must be informed by science. *Counseling Psychologist, 23,* 300–309.

Loftus, E. F., & Pickrell, J. E. (1995). The formation of false memories. *Psychiatric Annals, 25,* 720–725.

Loftus, E. F., Polonsky, S., & Fullilove, M. T. (1994). Memories of childhood abuse: Remembering and repressing. *Psychology of Women Quarterly, 18,* 67–84.

Loftus, G. R., & Loftus, E. F. (1976). *Human memory: The processing of information.* Hillsdale, NJ: Lawrence Erlbaum.

Luth, S., & Zigler, E. (1991). Vulnerability and competence: A review of research on vulnerability in childhood. *American Journal of Orthopsychiatry, 61,* 6–22.

Lynn, S., & Nash, M. (1994). Truth in memory. *American Journal of Clinical Hypnosis, 36,* 194–208.

Marmar, C. R., Weiss, D. S., Schlenger, W. E., Fairbank, J. A., Jordan, B. K., Kulka, R. A., & Hough, R. L. (1994). Peritraumatic dissociation and posttraumatic stress in male Vietnam theater veterans. *American Journal of Psychiatry, 151,* 902–907.

Masson, J. M. (1984). *The assault on truth: Freud's suppression of the seduction theory.* New York: Farrar, Straus & Giroux.

Masten, A. S., Best, K. M., & Garmezy, N. (1991). Resilience and development: Contributions from the study of children who overcame adversity. *Development and Psychology, 2,* 425–444.

McCallum, K. E., Lock, J., Kulla, M., Rorty, M., & Wetzel, R. D. (1992). Dissociative symptoms and disorders in patients with eating disorders. *Dissociation, 5,* 227–235.

McCann, I. L., & Pearlman, L. A. (1990). *Psychological trauma and the adult survivor: Theory, therapy and transformation.* New York: Brunner/Mazel.

McCloskey, M., & Zaragoza, M. A. (1985). Misleading postevent information and memory for events: Arguments and evidence against memory impairment hypotheses. *Journal of Experimental Psychology: General, 114,* 1–16.

McConkey, K. M., Labelle, L., Bibb, B. C., & Bryant, R. A. (1990). Hypnosis and suggested pseudomemory: The relevance of test context. *Australian Journal of Psychology, 42,* 197–205.

McGaugh, J. L. (1992). Affect, neuromodulatory systems, and memory storage. In S-A. Christianson (Ed.), *Handbook of emotion and memory* (pp. 245–268). Hillsdale, NJ: Lawrence Erlbaum.

McGrath, E., Keita, G. P., Strickland, B. R., & Russo, N. F. (Eds.). (1990). *Women and depression: Risk factors and treatment.* Washington, DC: American Psychological Association.

McHugh, P. (1993a, May 3). Procedures in the diagnosis of incest in recovered memory cases. *FMS Foundation Newsletter,* p. 3.

McHugh, P. (1993b, October 1). To treat. *FMS Foundation Newsletter,* p. 1.

McMillen, C., Zuravin, S., & Rideout, G. (1995). Perceived benefit from child sexual abuse. *Journal of Consulting and Clinical Psychology, 63,* 1037–1043.

Meacham, A. (1993, April). Presumed guilty. *Changes*, pp. 71–82.

Mednick, M. T. (1989). On the politics of psychological constructs: Stop the bandwagon, I want to get off. *American Psychologist, 44*, 1118–1123.

Meichenbaum, D. (1994). *A clinical handbook/practical therapist manual for assessing and treating adults with post-traumatic stress disorder*. Waterloo, Ontario: Institute Press.

Melton, G. B., Petrila, J., Poythress, N. G., & Slobogin, C. (1987). *Psychological evaluations for the courts: A handbook for mental health professionals and lawyers*. New York: Guilford.

Merskey, H. (1992). The manufacture of personalities: The production of multiple personality disorder. *British Journal of Psychiatry, 160*, 327–340.

Middlebrook, D. W. (1991). *Anne Sexton: A biography*. New York: Houghton Mifflin.

Miller, G. A. (1956). The magic number seven, plus or minus two: Some limits on our capacity for processing information. *Psychological Review, 63*, 81–97.

Mitchell, J. (1993, August 8). Memories of a disputed past. *Oregonian*, pp. L1, L6–7.

Morrow, S. L., & Smith, M. L. (1995). Constructions of survival and coping by women who have survived childhood sexual abuse. *Journal of Consulting and Clinical Psychology, 42*, 23–44.

Müensterberg, H. (1908). *On the witness stand: Essays of psychology and crime*. New York: McClure.

Murdock, B. B. (1974). *Human memory: Theory and data*. Potomac, MD: Erlbaum.

Murdock, B. B. (1995). Human memory in the twenty-first century. In R. L. Solso & D. W. Massaro (Eds.), *The science of the mind* (pp. 109–122). New York: Oxford University Press.

Murphy, J. M. (1976). Psychiatric labeling in cross-cultural perspective. *Science, 191*, 1019–1028.

Myers, J. E. B. (1994). *The backlash: Child protection under fire*. Thousand Oaks, CA: Sage.

Nathan, D. (1992, October). Cry incest. *Playboy, 39*(10), 84–89.

Neisser, U. (Ed.). (1982). *Memory observed: Remembering in natural contexts*. San Francisco: Freeman.

Nethaway, R. (1993, August/September). Whining about abuse is an epidemic. *FMS Foundation Newsletter*, p. 6.

Nizer, L. (1961). *My life in court*. Garden City, NY: Doubleday.

Ochberg, F. (Ed.). (1988). *Post-traumatic therapy and victims of violence*. New York: Brunner/Mazel.

Ofshe, R., & Singer, M. (1994). Recovered memory therapy and robust repression: Influence and pseudo-memories. *International Journal of Clinical and Experimental Hypnosis, 42*, 391–410.

Ofshe, R., & Watters, E. (1993). Making monsters. *Society, 30*, 4–16.

Ofshe, R., & Watters, E. (1994). *Making monsters: False memories, psychotherapy, and sexual hysteria*. New York: Scribner's.

Olio, K. (1992). Recovery from sexual abuse: Is forgiveness mandatory? *Voices: The Art and Science of Psychotherapy, 28*, 73–79.

Olio, K. (1993). Comparing apples and oranges. *Raising Issues, 1*, 3–4.

Olio, K. (1994). Coping with ritual abuse reports. Paper presented at the annual meeting of the American Psychological Association, Los Angeles.

Olio, K. (1995a, August 14). Conscientious Trauma Treatment in a Contentious Climate. Paper presented at the annual convention of the American Psychological Association, New York, NY.

Olio, K. (1995b, July 20). Delayed recall of traumatic events: Politics, validity, and clinical implications. Paper presented at the Conference on Delayed Recall of Traumatic Events: Implications for Mental Health Professionals. Burlington, VT.

Olio, K. (1995c). Het voorschrift van Kihlstrom; over de verdenking van seksueel misbruik bij kinderen aan de hand van hun symptomen [Kihlstrom's prescription: On the suspicion of sexual abuse of children on the basis of their symptoms]. *Directieve Therapie, 15,* 194–195.

Olio, K. (1995d, September 30). Symposium. 6th Annual Conference on Abuse, Trauma & Dissociation, Austin, TX.

Olio, K. (in press). Are 25% of clinicians using potentially risky therapeutic practices? A review of the logic and methodology of the Poole, Lindsay, et al. study. *Journal of Psychiatry and Law.*

Olio, K., & Cornell, W. (1993). The therapeutic relationship as the foundation for treatment with adult survivors of sexual abuse. *Psychotherapy, 30,* 512–523.

Olio, K., & Cornell, W. (1994). The Paul Ingram case: Pseudomemory or pseudoscience? *Violence Update, 4* (10), 3–5.

Orlinsky, D. E., & Geller, J. D. (1993). Patients' representations of their therapists and therapy: New measure. In N. E. Miller, L. Luborsky, J. Barber, & J. P. Docherty (Eds.), *Psychodynamic treatment research: A handbook for clinical practice* (pp. 432–466). New York: Basic Books.

Ornstein, P. A., Ceci, S. H., & Loftus, E. F. (1996). The science of memory and the practice of psychotherapy. In J. Alpert, L. S. Brown, S. J. Ceci, C. A. Courtois, E. F. Loftus, & P. A. Ornstein, *Final report of the working group on investigation of memories of childhood abuse.* Washington, DC: American Psychological Association.

Pankratz, L. (1995). Ethics as a lifetime commitment. *Oregon Psychological Association Newsgram, 14,* 3, 8.

Pasley, L. E. (1994). Misplaced trust. In E. Goldstein & K. Farmer, *True stories of false memories* (pp. 347–365). Boca Raton, FL : SIRS Books.

Pavlov, I. P. (1927). *Lectures on conditioned reflex.* London: Martin Lawrence. (Translator: W. H. Gantt)

Pearlman, L. A., & Saakvitne, K. (1995). *Trauma and the therapist.* New York: W. W. Norton.

Pendergrast, M. (1995). *Victims of memory: Incest accusations and shattered lives.* Hinesburg, VT: Upper Access.

*People v. Shirley.* (1982). 31 Cal.3d 18.

Peterson, J. (1995, November). Therapists under fire: Harassment of clinicians. In R. Geffner (Chair), *Clinical issues and professional dilemmas in working with abuse victims and survivors.* Symposium presented at the Eleventh Annual Meeting, International Society for Traumatic Stress Studies, Boston, MA.

Pezdek, K. (1995, November). What types of false childhood memories are not likely to be suggestively implanted? Paper presented at the annual meeting of the Psychonomic Society, Los Angeles, CA.

Pezdek, K., Finger, K., & Hodge, D. (1996, November). False memories are more likely to be planted if they are familiar. Paper to be presented at the annual meeting of the Psychonomic Society, Chicago, IL.

Pezdek, K., & Roe, C. (1994). Memory for childhood events: How suggestible is it? *Consciousness and Cognition 3*, 374–387.

Pittman, R. K., Orr, S. P., & Lasko, N. B (1994, November). Hormonal modulation of traumatic memory consolidation and retrieval. In R. Yehuda & A. C. McFarlane (Chairs), *Biological basis of traumatic memory regulation.* Symposium presented at the Tenth Annual Meeting, International Society for Traumatic Stress Studies, Chicago IL

Polusny, M. A., & Follette, V. M. (1995). Long-term correlates of child sexual abuse: Theory and review of the empirical literature. *Applied and Preventive Psychology, 4*, 143–166.

Polusny, M., & Follette, V. (1996). Remembering childhood sexual abuse: A national survey of psychologists' clinical practices, beliefs, and personal experiences. *Professional Psychology: Research and Practice, 27*, 41–52.

Poole, D. (1996, February 2). Letter to Karen Olio.

Poole, D., Lindsay, D., Memon, A., & Bull, R. (1995). Psychotherapy and the recovery of memories of childhood abuse. *Journal of Clinical and Consulting Psychology, 63*, 426–438.

Pope, H. G., & Hudson, J. I. (1995a). Can individuals "repress" memories of childhood sexual abuse? An examination of the evidence. *Psychiatric Annals, 25*, 715–719.

Pope, H. G., & Hudson, J. I. (1995b). Can memories of childhood sexual abuse be repressed? *Psychological Medicine, 25*, 121–126.

Pope, K. S. (1978). How gender, solitude, and posture influence the stream of consciousness. In K. S. Pope & J. L. Singer (Eds.), *The stream of consciousness: Scientific investigations into the flow of human experience* (pp. 259–299). New York: Plenum.

Pope, K. S. (1990). Ethical and malpractice issues in hospital practice. *American Psychologist, 45*, 1066–1070.

Pope, K. S. (1994). *Sexual involvement with therapists: Patient assessment, subsequent therapy, forensics.* Washington DC: American Psychological Association.

Pope, K. S. (1995). What psychologists better know about recovered memories, research, lawsuits, and the pivotal experiment. *Clinical Psychology: Science and Practice, 2*, 304–315.

Pope, K. S., & Bajt, T. R. (1988). When laws and values conflict: A dilemma for psychologists. *American Psychologist, 43*, 828.

Pope, K. S., & Bouhoutsos, J. C. (1986). *Sexual intimacies between therapists and patients.* New York: Praeger/Greenwood.

Pope, K. S., Butcher, J. N., & Seelen, J. (1993). *The MMPI, MMPI-2, & MMPI-A in court: A practical guide for expert witnesses and attorneys.* Washington, DC: American Psychological Association.

Pope, K. S., & Feldman-Summers, S. (1992). National survey of psychologists' sexual and physical abuse history and their evaluation of training and competence in these areas. *Professional Psychology: Research and Practice, 23*, 353–361.

Pope, K. S., & Garcia-Peltoniemi, R. E. (1991). Responding to victims of torture: Clinical issues, professional responsibilities, and useful resources. *Professional Psychology: Research and Practice, 22*, 269–276.

Pope, K. S., Simpson, N. H., & Weiner, M. F. (1978). Malpractice in psychotherapy. *American Journal of Psychotherapy, 32*, 593–602.

Pope, K. S., & Singer, J. L. (1978a). Regulation of the stream of consciousness: Toward a theory of ongoing thought. In G. E. Schwartz & D. Shapiro (Eds.), *Consciousness and self-regulation: Advances in research and theory, vol. 2* (pp. 101–137). New York: Plenum.

Pope, K. S., & Singer, J. L. (Eds.) (1978b). *The stream of consciousness: Scientific investigations into the flow of human experience*. New York: Plenum.

Pope, K. S., & Singer, J. L. (1980). The waking stream of consciousness. In J. M. Davidson & R. J. Davidson (Eds.), *The psychobiology of consciousness* (pp. 169–191). New York: Plenum.

Pope, K. S., Sonne, J. L., & Holroyd, J. (1993). *Sexual feelings in psychotherapy: Explorations for therapists and therapists-in-training*. Washington, DC: American Psychological Association.

Pope, K. S., & Tabachnick, B. (1993). Therapists' anger, hate, fear and sexual feelings: National survey of therapists' responses, client characteristics, critical events, formal complaints and training. *Professional Psychology: Research and Practice, 24*, 142–152.

Pope, K. S., & Tabachnick, B. G. (1994). Therapists as patients: A national survey of psychologists' experiences, problems, and beliefs. *Professional Psychology: Research and Practice, 25*, 247–258.

Pope, K. S., & Tabachnick, B. (1995). Recovered memories of abuse among therapy patients. A national survey. *Ethics and Behavior, 5*, 237 248.

Pope, K. S., Tabachnick, B. G., & Keith-Spiegel, P. (1987). Ethics of practice: The beliefs and behaviors of psychologists as therapists. *American Psychologist, 42*, 993–1006.

Pope, K. S., & Vasquez, M. J. T. (1991). *Ethics in psychotherapy and counseling: A practical guide for psychologists*. San Francisco: Jossey-Bass.

Pride, M. (1986). *The child abuse industry: Outrageous facts About child abuse and everyday rebellions against a system that threatens every North American family*. Westchester, IL: Crossway Books.

Putnam, F. (1989). *Diagnosis and treatment of multiple personality disorder*. New York: Guilford.

Putnam, F. (1994, November). Sexual abuse as a biologically altering experience. In C. W. Portney (Chair), *Psychophysiological effects of childhood trauma and their influence on development*. Symposium presented at the Tenth Annual Meeting, International Society for Traumatic Stress Studies, Chicago, IL.

Putnam, F., & Tricket, P. (1993). Impact of child sexual abuse on females: Toward a developmental psychobiological integration. *Psychological Science, 4,* 81–87.

Reisberg, D., & Heuer, F. (1992). Remembering the details of emotional events. In E. Winograd and U. Neisser (Eds.), *Affects and accuracy in recall: Studies of "flashbulb" memories* (pp. 162–190). New York: Cambridge University Press.

Reiser, D. E., & Levenson, H. (1984). Abuses of the borderline diagnosis: A clinical problem with teaching opportunities. *American Journal of Psychiatry, 141,* 1528–1532.

Roediger, H. L., III, & McDermott, K. B. (1995). Creating false memories: Remembering words not presented in lists. *Journal of Experimental Psychology: Learning, Memory, and Cognition, 21,* 803–814.

Root, M. P. P. (1992). Reconstructing the impact of trauma on personality. In L. S. Brown & M. Ballou (Eds.), *Personality and psychopathology: Feminist reappraisals* (pp. 229–266). New York: Guilford.

Rosenhan, D. L. (1973). On being sane in insane places. *Science, 179,* 250–258.

Ross, C. A. (1990). *Multiple personality disorder.* New York: John Wiley & Sons.

Ross, C. A. (1992). Anne Sexton: Iatrogenesis of an alter personality in an undiagnosed case of MPD. *Dissociation, 5,* 141–149.

Ross, C. A., Norton, C. R., & Fraser, G. A. (1989). Evidence against the iatrogenesis of multiple personality disorder. *Dissociation, 2,* 61–65.

Roth, S., & Lebowitz, L. (1988). The experiences of sexual trauma. *Journal of Traumatic Stress, 1,* 79–108.

Russell, D. E. H. (1986). *The secret trauma: Incest in the lives of girls and women.* New York: Basic Books.

Russell, D. E. H. (1989). *Lives of courage: Women for a new South Africa.* New York: Basic Books.

Salter, A. (1995). *Transforming trauma: A guide to understanding and treating adult survivors of child sexual abuse.* Thousand Oaks, CA: Sage.

Scarr, S. (1988). Race and gender as psychological variables: Social and ethical issues. *American Psychologist, 43,* 56–59.

Sgroi, S. M. (1989). Stages of recovery for adult survivors of child sexual abuse. In S. M. Sgroi (Ed.), *Vulnerable Populations (Vol. 2): Sexual abuse treatment for children, adult survivors, offenders, and persons with mental retardation* (pp. 111–130). Lexington, MA: Lexington Books.

Shalev, A., & Peri, T. (1994, November). A biopsychological perspective on memory in PTSD. In R. Yehuda & A. C. McFarlane (Chairs), *Biological basis of traumatic memory regulation.* Symposium presented at the Tenth Annual Meeting, International Society for Traumatic Stress Studies, Chicago, IL.

Shapiro, F. (1995). *Eye movement desensitization reprocessing.* New York: Guilford.

Sheehan, P. (1988). Confidence, memory and hypnosis. In H. Pettinati (Ed.), *Hypnosis and memory.* New York: Guilford.

Sherril, M. (1995, September 1). Warriors in waiting. *Washington Post,* p. F1.

Shiffrar, M., & Freyd, J. J. (1993). Timing and apparent motion path choice with human body photographs. *Psychological Science, 4,* 379–384.

Siegel, R. J. (1990). Turning the things that divide us into the strengths that unite us. In L. S. Brown & M. P. P. Root (Eds.), *Diversity and complexity in feminist therapy*. New York: Haworth Press.

Siegel-Itzkovich, J. (1996). You must remember this . . . *Jerusalem Post*, May 19, p. 7.

Sifford, D. (1991). Accusations of sex abuse, years later. *Philadelphia Inquirer*, November 24, pp. 11–12.

Sifford, D. (1992). Perilous journey: The labyrinth of past sexual abuse. *Philadelphia Inquirer*, February 13, p. D-6.

Singer, J. L. (1980). The scientific basis of psychotherapeutic practice: A question of values and ethics. *Psychotherapy: Theory, Research and Practice, 17*, 372–383.

Singer, J. L. (Ed.). (1990). *Repression and dissociation: Implications for personality theory, psychopathology and health*. Chicago: University of Chicago Press.

Skinner, B. F. (1975). The steep and thorny way to a science of behavior. *American Psychologist, 30*, 42–49.

Slovenko, R. (1993). False memories/Broken families. *AAPL Newsletter, 18*, p. 39.

Social political movement. (1996, May). *FMSF Newsletter* (electronic version).

Sonne, J. L., & Pope, K. S. (1991). Treating victims of therapist-patient sexual involvement. *Psychotherapy: Theory, Research, Practice, Training, 28*, 174–187.

Soreson, S. B., & Golding, J. M. (1990). Depressive sequelae of recent criminal victimization. *Journal of Traumatic Stress, 3*, 337–350.

Southwick, S. M., Krystal, J. H., Bremner, J. D., Morgan, C. A., & Charney, D. S. (1994, November). Traumatic memory and noradrenergic systems. In R. Yehuda & A. C. McFarlane (Chairs), *Biological basis of traumatic memory regulation*. Symposium presented at the Tenth Annual Meeting, International Society for Traumatic Stress Studies, Chicago, IL.

Spanos, N. P., & McLean, J. M. (1986). Hypnotically created pseudomemories: Memory distortions or reporting biases? *British Journal of Experimental and Clinical Hypnosis, 3*, 155–159.

Spanos, N. P., (1994). Multiple identity enactments and multiple personality disorder: A sociocognitive perspective. *Psychological Bulletin, 116*, 143–165.

Spence, D. P. (1993, August). Narrative truth and putative child abuse. APA Division 24 presidential address delivered to the annual meeting of the American Psychological Association, Toronto, Ontario, Canada.

Spiegel, D. (1994, November). *Out of sight but not out of mind: Dissociation in acute and post-traumatic stress disorders*. Keynote address delivered at the Tenth Annual Meeting of the International Society for Traumatic Stress Studies, Chicago, IL.

Spielberger, C. D., Syderman, S. J., Ritterband, L. M., Reheiser, E. C., & Unger, K. K. (1995). Assessment of emotional states and personality traits: Measuring psychological vital signs. In J. N. Butcher (Ed.), *Clinical personality assessment: Practical approaches* (pp. 42–58). New York: Oxford University Press.

Standing, L. (1973). Learning 10,000 pictures. *Quarterly Journal of Experimental Psychology, 25*, 195–210.

Stanton, M. (1995, May 7). Bearing witness: A man's recovery of his sexual abuse as a child. *Providence Journal*, pp. A1, A18–19.

*State v. Warnberg*. (1994, March 24). No. 93-2292-CR, Court of Appeals of Wisconsin, District 4.

Steinberg, M. (1995). *Interviewer's guide to the Structured Clinical Interview for DSM–IV Dissociative Disorders*. Washington, DC, American Psychiatric Press.

Steinem, G. (1995, August 11). Opening address. Annual meeting of the American Psychological Association, New York.

Stigler, S. M. (1978). Some forgotten work on memory. *Journal of Experimental Psychology: Human Learning and Memory, 4*, 1–4.

Stricker, G. (1992). The relationship of research to clinical practice. *American Psychologist, 47*, 543–549.

Szasz, T. S. (1970). *The manufacture of madness*. New York: Harper & Row.

Szasz, T. S. (1994). *Cruel compassion: Psychiatric control of society's unwanted*. New York: John Wiley.

Tavris, C. (1992). *The mismeasure of woman*. New York: Simon & Schuster.

Tessler, M., & Nelson, K. (1994). Making memories: The influence of joint encoding on later recall by young children. *Consciousness and Cognition, 3*, 307–326.

Torem, M. (1986). Dissociative state presenting as an eating disorder. *American Journal of Clinical Hypnosis, 29*, 137–142.

Tsai, M., Feldman-Summers, S., & Edgar, M. (1979). Childhood molestation: Variables related to differential impacts on psychosexual functioning in adult women. *Journal of Abnormal Psychology, 88*, 407–417.

Tulving, E., & Thompson, D. (1973). Encoding specificity and retrieval processes in episodic memory. *Psychological Review, 80*, 352–373.

Tversky, A., & Kahneman, D. (1982). Judgment under uncertainty: Heuristics and biases. In D. Kahneman, P. Slovic, & A. Tversky (Eds.), *Judgment under uncertainty: Heuristics and biases* (pp. 3–20). Cambridge: Cambridge University Press.

Underwager, R., & Wakefield, H. (1991). Cur allii, prae aliis? [Why some, and not others?] *Issues in Child Abuse Accusations, 3*, 178–193.

Ussher, J. A., & Neisser, U. (1993). Childhood amnesia and the beginnings of memory for four early life events. *Journal of Experimental Psychology: General, 122*, 155–165.

Van de Hart, O. (1993). *Trauma, memory, and dissociation*. Lisse, The Netherlands: Swets & Zeitlinger.

Van der Kolk, B. A. (1992, June). PTSD, memory and noradrenergic dysregulation. In B. A. van der Kolk (Chair), *Biological aspects of trauma*, symposium presented at the First World Conference of the International Society for Traumatic Stress Studies, Amsterdam, The Netherlands.

Van de Hart, O., Brown, P., & Van der Kolk, B. (1989). Pierre Janet's treatment of posttraumatic stress. *Journal of Traumatic Stress, 2*, 379–395.

Van der Kolk, B. A., Brown, P., & van der Hart, O. (1989). Pierre Janet on Post traumatic stress. *Journal of Traumatic Stress, 2*, 365–378.

Van der Kolk, B., Fisler, R, and Vardi, D. (1994, November). Traumatic versus ordinary memory in traumatized subjects. In R. Yehuda & A. C. McFarlane (Chairs), *Biological basis of traumatic memory regulation*. Symposium presented at the Tenth Annual Meeting, International Society for Traumatic Stress Studies, Chicago IL.

Van der Kolk, B. A., & Fisler, R. E. (1994). Childhood abuse and neglect and loss of self-regulation. *Bulletin of the Menninger Clinic, 58*, 145–168.

Van der Kolk, B. A., & Kadish, W. (1987). Amnesia, dissociation and the return of the repressed. In B. A. van der Kolk (Ed.), *Psychological trauma* (pp. 173–190). Washington, DC: American Psychiatric Press.

Van der Kolk, B. A., & Saporta, J. (1991). The biological response to psychic trauma: Mechanisms and treatment of intrusions and numbing. *Anxiety Research, 4*, 199–212.

Van der Kolk, B. A., & van der Hart, O. (1991). The intrusive past: The flexibility of memory and the engraving of trauma. *American Imago, 48*, 425–454.

Vogel, M. L. (1994). Gender as a factor in the transgenerational transmission of trauma. *Women and Therapy, 15*, 35–47.

Wakefield, H., & Underwager R. (1993) Interview. *Paedika, 3*, pp. 2–12.

Wakefield, H., & Underwager, R. (1994). *Return of the furies: An investigation into recovered memory therapy*. Chicago: Open Court.

Walker, E. A., Katon, W. J., Harop-Griffith, J. et al (1988). Relationship of chronic pelvic pain to psychiatric diagnoses and childhood sexual abuse. *American Journal of Psychiatry, 147*, 75–80.

Walker, E. A., Katon, W. J., Roy-Byrne, P. P., Jemlka, R. P., & Russo, J. (1993). Histories of sexual victimization in patients with irritable bowel syndrome or inflammatory bowel disease. *American Journal of Psychiatry, 150*, 1502–1506.

Walker, L. E. A. (1994). *Abused women and survivor therapy*. Washington, DC: American Psychological Association.

Waller, N. (1994, November). Types of dissociation and dissociative types. In R. J. Loewenstein (Chair), *The nature of dissociation*. Symposium presented at the Tenth Annual Meeting, International Society for Traumatic Stress Studies, Chicago, IL.

Walz, J., & Berliner, L. (1994, November). Community survey of therapist approaches to delayed trauma memories. In L. Berliner (Chair), *Delayed trauma memories: Victim experiences and clinical practice*. Symposium presented at the Tenth Annual Meeting, International Society for Traumatic Stress Studies, Chicago, IL.

Wassil-Grimm, C. (1995). *Diagnosis for disaster: The devastating truth about false memory syndrome and its impact on accusers and families*. Woodstock, NY: Overlook.

Watson, J. B. (1939). *Behaviorism* (2nd ed.). Chicago: University of Chicago.

Weinberg, K. (1955). *Incest behavior*. New York: Citadel.

Weiner, J. B., & Hess, A. K. (Eds.) (1987). *Handbook of forensic psychology*. New York: Wiley-Interscience.

Werner, E. E. (1995). Resilience in development. *Current Directions in Psychological Science, 4*, 81–85.

Westen, D. (1996). *Psychology: Mind, brain, & culture*. New York: John Wiley & Sons.

Whitfield, C. (1996, July). Traumatic amnesia in the courts: Evolution of our understanding from a clinician's perspecive. In J. S. Dorado (Chair) *Forensic issues in adult memories of child sexual abuse.* Symposium presented at the Trauma and Memory Conference, Durham, New Hamsphire.

Whitfield, C. L. (1995). *Memory and abuse.* Deerfield Beach, FL: Health Communications.

Williams, L. M. (1992). Adult memories of childhood abuse: Preliminary findings from a longitudinal study. *The Advisor, 5,* 19–21.

Williams, L. M. (1994). Recall of childhood trauma: A prospective study of women's memories of child sexual abuse. *Journal of Consulting and Clinical Psychology, 62,* 1167–1176.

Williams, L. M. (1995). Recovered memories of abuse in women with documented child sexual abuse victimization histories. *Journal of Traumatic Stress, 8,* 649–673.

Woods, C. L. (1994) The Parental Alienation Syndrome: A dangerous aura of reliability. *Loyola of Los Angeles Law Review, 27,* 1367–1415.

Wright, L. (1994). *Remembering Satan: A case of recovered meory and the shattering of an American family.* New York: Knopf.

Wright, M., Wright, F., Hubbard, J., Northwood, A., Realmuto, G. M., & Masten, A. (1994, November). Startle reflect responses in Cambodian refugees traumatized as children. Poster presented at the Tenth Annual Meeting of the International Society for Traumatic Stress Studies, Chicago, IL.

Yapko, M. (1994). *Suggestions of abuse: True and false memories of childhood sexual trauma.* New York: Simon & Schuster.

Yates, J. L., & Nasby, W. (1993). Dissociation, affect and network models of memory: An integrative proposal. *Journal of Traumatic Stress, 6,* 305–326.

Yehuda, R. (1994, November). Stress hormones and memory disturbance in PTSD. In R. Yehuda & A. C. McFarlane (Chairs), *Biological basis of traumatic memory regulation.* Symposium presented at the Tenth Annual Meeting, International Society for Traumatic Stress Studies, Chicago, IL.

Yehuda, R. (1996, June). *The HPA axis and the neurobiology of trauma.* Plenary lecture presented at the Second International Conference of the ISTSS, Jerusalem, Israel.

Yehuda, R., Kahana, B., Binder-Byrnes, K., Southwick, S., Mason, J. W., & Giller, E. L. (1995). Low urinary cortisol excretion in Holocaust survivors with posttraumatic stress disorder. *American Journal of Psychiatry, 152,* 982–986.

Yuille, J. C. (1993). We must study forensic eyewitnesses to know about them. *American Psychologist, 48,* 572–573.

Yuille, J. C., & Cutshall, J. L. (1989). Analysis of the statements of victims, witnesses and suspects. In J. C. Yuille (Ed.), *Credibility assessment* (pp. 175–191). Norwell, MA: Kluwer Academic.

Zaragoza, M. S. (1991). Preschool children's susceptibility to memory impairment. In J. Doris (Ed.), *The suggestibility of children's recollections: Implications for eyewitness testimony* (pp. 27–39). Washington, DC: American Psychological Association.

Zaragoza, M. S., & Koshmider, J. W. (1989). Misled subjects may know more than their performance implies. *Journal of Experimental Psychology: Learning, Memory, and Cognition, 15,* 246–255.

Zaragoza, M. S., McCloskey, M., & Jamis, M. (1987). Misleading postevent information and recall of the original event: Further evidence against the memory impairment hypothesis. *Journal of Experimental Psychology: Learning, Memory and Cognition, 13,* 36–44.

Zeller, A. F. (1950). An experimental analogue of repression: Effect of individual failure and success on memory measured by relearning. *Journal of Experimental Psychology, 40,* 411–422.

# Appendixes

# Appendix A

# Useful Resources

It is important that clinicians and expert witnesses be as aware as possible of the full range of theory, research, and practice in this area. The present volume functions primarily as an introduction to the topic. This appendix lists various books and videos that present a range of views and information about memory, trauma, child abuse, clinical interventions, and forensic considerations. Two matters are crucial in using this appendix. *First, this list in no way indicates any endorsement of the works or the works' approach or contents.* Reading works outside one's specialties, orientation, and beliefs promotes professional development and growth; new ideas, information, and arguments challenge habitual ways of understanding an issue. Reading books from earlier eras—such as Bartlett's *Remembering*—enables the reader to view current research in historical context and note forgotten findings, recurrent patterns, and shifts in emphasis. Reading works with which one ultimately disagrees enables the reader to consider and articulate why certain ideas, evidence, or approaches are unconvincing, and thus set aside the works based on a full and fair firsthand engagement rather than prejudice. *Second, this is by no means an exhaustive list.* It presents only

a relatively small sample of diverse books relevant to delayed
memories of child sex abuse.

## Books

- *Autobiographical Memory* edited by David Rubin
- *The Best-Kept Secret* by Florence Rush
- *Betrayal Trauma* by Jennifer Freyd
- *Changing Our Minds* by Celia Kitzinger and Rachel Perkins
- *The Child Abuse Industry: Outrageous Facts about Child Abuse & Everyday Rebellions Against a System that Threatens Every North American Family* by Mary Pride
- *Come Here: A Man Overcomes the Tragic Aftermath of Childhood Sex Abuse* by Richard Berendzen and Laura Palmer
- *Conspiracy of Silence: The Trauma of Incest* by Sandra Butler
- *The Courage To Heal: A Guide for Women Survivors of Child Sexual Abuse* (third edition) by Ellen Bass and Laura Davis
- *Cults in Our Midst: The Hidden Menace in Our Everday Lives* by Margaret Singer with Janja Lalich
- *Father-Daughter Incest* by Judith L. Herman
- *First Do No Harm: The Sexual Abuse Industry* by Felicity Goodyear-Smith
- *Healing the Incest Wound: Adult Survivors in Therapy* by Christine Courtois
- *Human Memory: The Processing of Information* by Geoffrey Loftus and Elizabeth Loftus
- *I'm Dysfunctional, You're Dysfunctional* by Wendy Kaminer
- *Incest-Related Syndromes of Adult Psychopathology* edited by Richard Kluft
- *I Never Told Anyone* edited by Ellen Bass and Louise Thornton
- *In the Palaces of Memory* by George Johnson
- *Kiss Daddy Goodnight: A Speakout on Incest* by Louise Armstrong
- *Making Monsters* by Richard Ofshe and Ethan Watters
- *The Making of Memory: From Molecules to Mind* by Steven Rose
- *Memory and Abuse* by Charles Whitfield
- *Memory and Brain* by Lawrence Squire

- *Memory Observed: Remembering in Natural Contexts* by Ulric Neisser
- *Memory: Surprising New Insights Into How We Remember and Why We Forget* by Elizabeth Loftus
- *The Mind of the Mnemonist* by A. Luria
- *The Myth of Repressed Memory* by Elizabeth Loftus and Kathryn Ketcham
- *Neurocomputing: Foundations of Research* edited by James Anderson and Edward Rosenfeld
- *One Step Ahead of the Thought Police* by John Leo
- *On Trial: America's Courts and Their Treatment of Sexually Abused Children* by Billie Dziech and Charles Schudson
- *The Origin of Consciousness in the Breakdown of the Bicameral Mind* by Julian Jaynes
- *Principles of Learning and Memory* by Robert Crowder
- *Remembering* by F. C. Bartlett
- *Remembering Satan* by Lawrence Wright
- *Repression and Dissociation* edited by Jerome Singer
- *Return of the Furies: An Investigation Into Recovered Memory Therapy* by Holida Wakefield and Ralph Underwager
- *Rewriting the Soul: Multiple Personality and the Sciences of Memory* by Ian Hacking
- *Rituals in Psychotherapy: Transition and Continuity* by Onno van der Hart
- *Rocking the Cradle of Sexual Politics* by Louise Armstrong
- *Secret Survivors: Uncovering Incest and Its Aftereffects in Women* by E. Sue Blume
- *Secret Trauma: Incest in the Lives of Girls and Women* by Diana E. H. Russell
- *Suggestions of Abuse* by Michael Yapko
- *Synapses, Circuits, and the Beginnings of Memory* by Gary Lynch
- *Therapy for Adults Molested as Children* by John Briere
- *Transforming Trauma: A Guide to Understanding and Treating Adult Survivors of Child Sexual Abuse* by Anna Salter
- *Trauma and Recovery* by Judith Herman
- *True Stories of False Memories* by Eleanor Goldstein and Kevin Farmer
- *Unchained Memories* by Lenore Terr
- *Victims No Longer* by Mike Lew (for male survivors)
- *Victims of Memory: Incest Accusations and Shattered Lives* by Mark Pendergrast

- *Voices in the Night* edited by Toni A. H. McNaron and Yarrow Morgan
- *Wet Mind: The New Cognitive Neuroscience* by Stephen Kosslyn and Olivier Koenig

## Videos

- Making Memories: The Recovered Memory Movement by Berkely Creek Productions (1995)
- Trauma and Memory 1: The Dissociative Defense by Cavalcade Productions
- Trauma and Memory 2: The Intrusive Past by Cavalcade Productions
- True/Not True: When Memories Can be Trusted by Cavalcade Productions
- Divided Memories by Ofra Bikel, available from PBS Videos

## Legal Cases and Documents

- *Alleger v. Lewis*. (1993, August). Verbatim report for Case No. 91-2-00295-1, Findings of the Honorable James I. Maddock, Superior Court Judge, in and for the County of Kitsap in the State of Washington.
- *Crook v. Murphy*. (1994, March 4). Verbatim report of proceedings for Case No. 91-2-0011-2-5 before the Honorable Dennis D. Yule, Superior Court Judge, in and for the County of Benton of the State of Washington.
- *Doe v. LaBrosse*. 588 A.2d 605 (RI 1991).
- *Hoult v. Hoult*. (1995, May). Case No. 94-2034. Appeal from the United States District Court for the District of Massachusetts, Honorable Douglas P. Woodlock, U.S. District Judge.
- *Lemmerman v. Faulk*. 507 N.W. 2d 226 (Mich. App. 1993).
- *McCollum V. D'Arcy*. 638 A.2D 797 (NH 1994).
- *Ramona v. Isabella*. No. 61898 Cal. Super. Ct. May 13, 1994.
- *Singer & Ofshe v. American Psychological Association et al.* (1992, September 30). Amended Complaint. United States District Court, Southern District of New York, 92 Civ. 6082.
- *Singer & Ofshe v. American Psychological Association et al.* (1993, August 9). Memorandum and Order. United States District Court, Southern District of New York, 92 Civ. 6082.

□ *Singer & Ofshe v. American Psychological Association et al.* (1994a, January 31). Complaint for civil conspiracy, etc. Superior Court of the State of California in and for the County of Alameda, Case #730012-7.

□ *Singer & Ofshe v. American Psychological Association et al.* (1994b, June 17). Order. Superior Court of the State of California in and for the County of Alameda, Case #730012-8.

□ *Smith v. Smith.* (1993, January 18). Deposition of Elizabeth Loftus, PhD, in case #67-52-64 Superior Court of the State of California in and for the County of Orange.

□ *Tyson v. Tyson.* 727 P2d 226 (Wash. 1986).

□ *Underwager and Wakefield v. Salter.* (1994, April 25). U. S. Court of Appeals, Seventh Circuit.

## Legal Resource

□ *Repressed Memory PsychLaw Newsletter.* Available by subscription, 126 S. Grant, Denver, CO, 80209. This resource digests relevant civil and criminal case law, legislative initiatives, and psychological research and writing.

# Appendix B

# States With Delayed Discovery Laws

# Appendix B

## States With Delayed Discovery Laws

| State | Statute | Type 1 Delayed Realization | Type 2 Delayed Memory | Length of Statute |
|---|---|---|---|---|
| Alabama | — | | | |
| Alaska | ALASKA STAT. § 09.10.140(b) (1994) | — | ☑ | Within 3 years of majority or 3 years of discovery. |
| Arizona | — | | | |
| Arkansas | ARK. CODE ANN. § 16-56-130 (1994) | ☑ | ☑ | Within 3 years of discovery. |
| California | CA. CIV. PROC. CODE § 340.1 (1995) | ☑ | ☑ | Within 8 years of majority or 3 years of discovery. Certificate of Merit over age 26. |
| Colorado | COLO. REV. STAT. ANN. § 13-80-103.7 (1994) | ☑ | ☑ | Within 6 years of majority or 6 years of removal of disability. |
| Connecticut | CONN. GEN. STAT. ANN. § 52-577d (1994) | ☑ | ☑ | No discovery rule per se, but must bring action no later than 17 years from the age of majority. |
| Delaware | — | | | |

*Note:* Dashes in cells in table indicate no relevant laws in a given state. Information is current as of July, 1995. Some laws may have changed. Please check with your legal consultant.

| State | Citation | | | Limitation |
|---|---|---|---|---|
| Florida | FLA. STAT. ANN. § 95.11(7) (1994) | ☑ | ☑ | Within 7 years of majority, 4 years after leaving dependency of abuse, 4 years of discovery. |
| Georgia | GA. CODE ANN. § 9-3-33.1 (1994) | ☑ | ☑ | Within 5 years of majority. |
| Hawaii | *Considering Legislation* | | | |
| Idaho | IDAHO CODE § 6-1704 (1994) | ☑ | ☑ | Within 5 years of majority. |
| Illinois | ILL. ANN. STAT. CH. 735, ¶ 5/13-202.2 (1993) | ☑ | ☑ | Within 2 years of discovery, but no more than 12 years after age 18. |
| Indiana | | — | — | |
| Iowa | IOWA CODE ANN. § 614.8A (1995) | ☑ | ☑ | Within 4 years of discovery. |
| Kansas | KAN. STAT. ANN. § 60-523 (1994) | ☑ | ☑ | Within 3 years of majority or 3 years of discovery. |
| Kentucky | | — | — | |
| Louisiana | LA. REV. STAT. ANN. | ☑ | ☑ | Within 10 years of majority. |
| Maine | ME. REV. STAT. ANN. Tit. 14, § 752-C (1994) | ☑ | ☑ | Within 12 years of incident or 6 years of discovery. |
| Maryland | *Considering Legislation* | — | | |
| Massachusetts | *Considering Legislation* | | | |
| Michigan | | | | |
| Minnesota | MINN. STAT. ANN. § 541.073 (1994) | ☑ | ☑ | Within 6 years of discovery. (Provision for negligently permitting sexual abuse to occur.) |
| Mississippi | | — | | |
| Missouri | MO. ANN. STAT. § 537.046 (1994) § 9:2800.9 (1995) | ☑ | ☑ | Within 5 years of age 18 or 3 years of discovery. Certificate of Merit if over age 21. |

**Appendix B**   *(continued)*

| State | Statute | Type 1 Delayed Realization | Type 2 Delayed Memory | Length of Statute |
|---|---|---|---|---|
| Montana | MONT. CODE ANN. § 27-2-216 (1994) | ☑ | ☑ | Within 3 years of the event or 3 years of discovery. |
| Nebraska | *Considering Legislation* | — | — | |
| Nevada | NEV. REV. STAT. ANN. | ☑ | ☑ | Within 10 years of age 18 or 10 years of discovery |
| New Hampshire | — | — | — | |
| New Jersey | N.J. STAT. ANN. § 2A:61B-1 (1993) | ☑ | ☑ | Within 2 years of discovery. |
| New Mexico | N.M. STAT ANN. § 37-1-30 (1994) | ☑ | ☑ | By age 24, within 3 years of discovery, or within 3 years of beginning treatment. |
| New York | *Considering Legislation* | — | — | — |
| North Carolina | | — | — | — |
| North Dakota | *Considering Legislation* | — | — | — |
| Ohio | | ☑ | ☑ | |
| Oklahoma | OKLA. STAT. ANN. Tit. 12, § 95 (1995) | ☑ | ☑ | Within 2 years of the last act, 2 years of age 18, or 2 years of discovery of "objective, verifiable evidence," through 20 years from age 18. |
| Oregon | OR. REV. STAT. § 12.117 (1994) | ☑ | ☑ | Within 6 years of age 18 or 3 years of discovery, but no later than age 4. |

| State | Citation | | | Description |
|---|---|---|---|---|
| Pennsylvania | | — | — | |
| Rhode Island | R.I. GEN. LAWS § 9-1-51 (1994) | ☑ | ☑ | Within 7 years of the last act or 7 years of discovery. |
| South Carolina | *Considering Legislation* | | | |
| South Dakota | S.D. CODIFIED LAWS ANN. § 26-10-25 (1995) | ☑ | ☑ | Within 3 years of the act, 3 years of majority, or 3 years of discovery. |
| Tennessee | | — | — | |
| Texas | | — | — | |
| Utah | UTAH CODE ANN. § 78-12-25.1 (1994) | ☑ | ☑ | Within 4 years of age 18 or 4 years of discovery. (Provision for negligence.) |
| Vermont | VT. STAT. ANN. Tit. 12, § 560 (1994) | ☑ | ☑ | Within 6 years of the act or 6 years of discovery. |
| Virginia | VA. CODE ANN. § 8.01-249 (1994) | ☑ | ☑ | Within 10 years of the last act, 10 years of majority, or 10 years of removal of disability. |
| Washington | WASH. REV. CODE ANN. § 4.16.340(1) (1994) | ☑ | ☑ | Within 3 years of the act, 3 years of age 18, or 3 years of discovery. |
| West Virginia | | — | — | |
| Wisconsin | WIS. STAT. ANN. § 893.587 (1994) | ☑ | ☑ | Within 2 years of discovery. |
| Wyoming | | — | — | |

# Appendix C

# Sample Informed Consent Form for Forensic Assessment When Recovered Memories are at Issue

This appendix presents one example of a form that could be used for obtaining written informed consent for a forensic assessment when recovered memories are at issue. Although there are many possible approaches to informed consent for forensic assessment in this area, any consent form must be adapted to the purposes and procedures of a specific assessment, to the needs of the patient who is raising the issue of recovered memories, to the theoretical orientation or approach of the clinician conducting the assessment, to any unique circumstances of the assessment, and to the array of relevant legislation, case law, administrative regulations, and professional standards. To meet these requirements, clinicians conducting such assessments may find it useful to have a comprehensive form in their computer's data base. The form could have numerous statements relevant to the clinician's most common assessment situations, as well as reminders of other topics that may, however rarely, need to be addressed. When planning each forensic assessment, the clinician could duplicate the computer file containing this comprehensive form and then edit the duplicate so that it best addresses the elements of the next assessment.

It is essential that the clinician review such forms with his or her own attorney *before using the form*, to ensure that it is consistent with all applicable ethical, legal, administrative, and professional standards, as well as the approach and needs of the clinician planning the forensic assessments.

It is also essential that the clinician take adequate time to review an informed consent form with the patient who is to be assessed so that the patient understands all aspects of the planned assessments that might substantially affect the patient's decision regarding whether to proceed with the evaluation. It is important to give the patient adequate time to digest the information in the consent form, ask questions, and consider whether or not to consent to participate. Providing the form to the client by mail to read in the privacy of his or her home prior to meeting the clinician for the first time or scheduling sufficient time at the beginning of an evaluation to discuss the informed consent process can facilitate truly informed and full consent to the evaluation. It is especially important to clarify that this is not therapy and that confidentiality will not obtain.

Finally, such forms may play an essential role in the process of informed consent, but neither the clinician nor any one else should ever assume that the mere presence of the form constitutes or completes the process of consent. If the clinician has questions about the patient's capacity to give consent due to age, cognitive impairment, language difficulties, or other factors, competency to consent should first be established:

> Providing information in written form can be vital in ensuring that clients have the information they need. But the form cannot be a substitute for an adequate process of informed consent. At a minimum, the clinician must discuss the information with the client and arrive at a professional judgment that the client has adequate understanding of the relevant information.
>
> Clinicians using consent forms must ensure that their clients have the requisite reading skills. Illiteracy is a major problem in the United States; clinicians cannot simply assume that all of their clients can read. Moreover, some clients may not be well versed in English, perhaps having only rudimentary skills in spoken English as a second or third language. (Pope & Vasquez, 1991, p. 85)

Thus, the clinician should be prepared to provide informed consent in another form when the individual is print-impaired in some fashion. When necessary, the presence of a trained mental health interpreter for both the process of consent and the evaluation itself may be necessary.

## Sample Informed Consent for Forensic Assessment When Recovered Memory Is at Issue

Your attorney has asked that I conduct a psychological assessment in connection with your court case, which involves issues related to the recovered memories you have reported. This form was written to give you information about the assessment process. Although I am a mental health professional, this assessment is not therapy. While it may or may not be helpful to you, the goal of the assessment is to answer questions about you and the difficulties you may be having. The assessment will contain four main parts.

In the first part, which may take more than one session, I will be giving you several standardized psychological tests. [Add names and brief description of the tests you use.] We will discuss the instructions in detail when I give you the tests. It will be important that you understand the instructions for each test. If you do not understand the instructions for a test, it will be important for you to let me know immediately so that we can ensure that you understand.

In the second part, I will interview you. This interview is likely to take [fill in number] of hours. We will meet for approximately [fill in number] of sessions. During the interview, I will ask you questions about yourself and ask you to talk about yourself. Some of the questions will be about your memories and the way in which you came to believe that you recovered them. There may, of course, be areas that you are reluctant to talk about. If so, please be sure to tell me that the questions are making you uncomfortable or that you have reasons for not providing the information. We can then talk about your concerns. You can ask to take a break or end an assessment session earlier than planned if you feel unable to continue.

In the next part of the evaluation, I will be reviewing records and talking with people, such as family members, friends, coworkers, or a physician, clergy, or current therapist whose names I will obtain from you, to get more information about what has happened to you. This is to help me in finding materials that would give outside corroboration to what you have to tell me. A form asking for names and your release for me to contact those people is attached to this informed consent. I will only contact these people with your permission and will not share information about you during those contacts.

In the fourth part, I will describe my conclusions to you and will review with you the information from the interview and tests. You will have an opportunity to discuss any of the opinions or information that I review with you. I will invite you to comment on the information and on my opinions. This will give you an opportunity to call my attention to any errors in fact or conclusion that you believe I have made and any aspects that you believe are incomplete or misleading. (It is possible, of course, that we may disagree about certain conclusions or other aspects of this assessment.) I may do this orally or in writing, depending on whether the attorney has asked me to prepare a report. If I do prepare a report, I will ask you to review it to be certain that I have no factual errors in the report.

It is important that you be as honest as possible when responding to the items on the standardized tests, providing information during the interview, and writing your response to the assessment. Information that is withheld, incomplete, wrong, or misleading may be far more damaging than if I am able to find out about it now and put it in context in my report or testimony. It is important for us to discuss any concerns you have in this area.

Although I will try to be thorough when I interview you, I may not ask about some areas or information that you believe is important. If so, please tell me so that we can discuss it. I will also discuss with you the best way to recontact me if, once this evaluation is complete, you think of something that you believe it would be important for me to know.

I am a [psychologist, psychiatrist, or other professional title] licensed by the state of [name of state]. If you have reason to believe that I am behaving unethically or unprofessionally during the course of this assessment, I urge you to let me know at once so that we can discuss it. If you believe that I have not adequately addressed your complaints in this area, there are several agencies which you may consult, and, if you believe it appropriate, you may file a formal complaint against me. One agency is the state governmental board that licenses me to practice: [name, address, and phone number of the licensing board]. Other agencies are the ethics committees of my state professional association, [name, address, and phone number], and national professional association, [name, address, and phone number]. However, you have my assurance that I will endeavor at all times to conduct this assessment in an ethical and professional manner and will be open to discussing any complaints that you have in this area.

Please check each item below to indicate that your have read it carefully and understand it.

- □ I understand that Dr. _____ has been hired by my attorney, [fill in attorney's name], to conduct a psychological assessment for a case in which recovered memories have been reported.
- □ I understand that I will be asked to talk about the recovered memories, and I agree to do so.
- □ I understand that it is important for me to be honest and accurate when answering questions or providing information during this assessment.
- □ I understand that Dr. _____ may write a formal report about me based on the results of this assessment if my attorney so requests.
- □ I authorize Dr. _____ to send a copy of this formal report to my attorney and to discuss the report with him or her.
- □ I authorize Dr. _____ to speak to the following persons as information sources for this evaluation.
- □ I understand that Dr. _____ will provide me with this written report and that I may, if I choose, schedule an additional appointment with Dr. _____ to discuss the results of this assessment.
- □ I authorize Dr. _____ to testify about me and this assessment in depositions and trials related to my legal case.
- □ I understand that I may interrupt or discontinue this assessment at any time.

- ❏ I understand that even if I interrupt the assessment and it is not resumed, or if I discontinue the assessment, it is possible (depending on the applicable laws, on rulings by the court, and/or on decisions by the attorneys in this case) that Dr. _____ may be called to submit a report or testify about the assessment, even if the assessment is incomplete.
- ❏ I understand that if I disclose certain types of special information to Dr. _____, he/she may be required or permitted to communicate this information to other people. As previously discussed with Dr. _____, examples of such special information include reports of child or elder abuse and threats to kill or violently attack a specific person.
- ❏ I understand that the assessment will be audiotaped or videotaped to preserve an accurate record of what I have said.
- ❏ I understand that the audiotaped record of the assessment will be given to my attorney and may become evidence in the deposition or trial(s).
- ❏ I understand that the cost of this assessment will be _____ per hour. I understand that my attorney has already signed a contract to pay the fees for this assessment. I agree to these fees.

If you have read, understood, and checked off each of the previous sections, please read carefully the following statement, and if you are in agreement, please sign the statement. Do *not* sign if you have any questions that remain unanswered after our discussion of them or if there are any aspects that you don't understand or agree to; contact your attorney for guidance concerning how to proceed so that you fully understand the process and can decide whether you wish to continue.

*Consent Agreement*: I have read, agreed to, and checked off each of the previous sections. I have asked questions about any parts that I did not understand fully. I have also asked questions about any parts that I was concerned about. By signing below, I indicate that I understand and agree to the nature and purpose of this assessment, to the way(s) in which it will be reported, and to each of the points listed above.

Signature

_____

Name (please print)

_____

Date


The form and discussion that appear in this appendix have been adapted and amended, with permission from the publisher, from two prior forms (Pope, Butcher, & Seelen, 1993, pp. 197–199; Pope, 1994, pp. 205–210). © American Psychological Association.

# Appendix D

# Informed Consent Issues for Providing Therapy to a Patient When Recovered Memories are an Issue

Informed consent is best viewed as a process rather than a static formality. The process is likely to occur differently and to possess different content according to whether the therapy is, say, cognitive–behavioral, psychodynamic, feminist, existential, systems, or gestalt. Aside from differences of theoretical orientation and technique, each therapist, patient, and situation are unique, and the process of informed consent must be shaped to respect and take account of that uniqueness.

The process, both oral and written, will vary significantly from therapist to therapist, patient to patient, and setting to setting, but certain issues seem central to this process. What follows is a list of some of the most significant issues that tend to be a part of the informed consent process. It may be useful for the therapist to review this list periodically and consider the degree to which each issue may be essential to a particular patient's providing or withholding informed consent. Because both informed consent and therapy itself are processes, the list may be useful not only at the beginning of therapy but also in subsequent stages as the patient's situation, therapeutic needs, and treatment plan change.

□   Is there any evidence that the person is not fully capable of understanding the information and issues relevant to giving or withholding informed consent?

☐ Are there any factors that would prevent this person from arriving at decisions that are truly voluntary?

☐ Does the person adequately understand the type and nature of the services that the therapist is offering?

☐ Are their other methods (that might replace or supplement the therapy that you provide) that the person might use to effectively address the relevant issues of concern? If so, is the person adequately aware of them?

☐ If the degree of the therapist's education, training, or experience in the area of providing clinical or forensic services to patients reporting recovered memories would be relevant to the person's decision about whether to begin or continue work with the therapist, does the person have the relevant information?

☐ Does the person understand that the therapist is not an attorney and cannot provide legal counsel or representation?

☐ Does the person understand whether the therapist is licensed (or is, for example, an unlicensed intern); the nature of that license (e.g., psychology, psychiatry, social work); and how the license status may affect such issues as types of services provided (e.g., medications), confidentiality, privilege, etc.?

☐ If any information about the person or the treatment will be communicated to or will be in any way accessible to others in your setting (e.g., administrative staff, utilization review committees, quality control personnel, clinical supervisors) either orally (e.g., supervision, case conferences) or in writing (e.g., chart notes, treatment summaries, treatment reports), is the person adequately aware of these communications and modes of access and their implications?

☐ If information about the person or the treatment will be communicated to any payment source (e.g., an insurance company, a government agency), is the person adequately aware of the nature, content, and implications of these communications?

☐ Have any potential limitations in the number of sessions (e.g., a managed care plan's limitation of 10 therapy sessions, an insurance plan's limitation of payments for mental health services to a specific dollar amount) or length of treatment (e.g., if the therapist is an intern whose internship will conclude within 3 months, after which the therapist will no longer be available) been adequately disclosed to the person and the potential implications been adequately discussed?

☐ Does the person adequately understand the therapist's policy regarding missed or canceled appointments?

☐ Has there been adequate disclosure and discussion of any information about the therapist that might significantly affect the person's decision to begin or continue work with the therapist?

☐ Does the person adequately understand limits to accessibility to the therapist (e.g., will the therapist be available to receive or return phone calls during the day, during the evening, or on nights, weekends, or holidays)? Does the person adequately understand limits to the extent of such accessibility between regularly scheduled sessions (e.g., will phone contacts be limited to brief periods of 5 or 10 minutes, or will the therapist allow longer phone consultation)? Are fees for such services clearly defined?

☐ Does the person adequately understand what steps to take and what resources are (and are not) available in case of a crisis, emergency, or severe need?

☐ If the person or the treatment is to be used for teaching or related purposes, does the person adequately understand the nature, extent, and implications of such arrangements?

☐ If the person or the treatment is to be used for research or related purposes, does the person adequately understand the nature, extent, and implications of such arrangements?

☐ Does the person adequately understand limitations to privacy, confidentiality, and privilege, particularly those related to discretionary or mandatory reports by the therapist and to any legal actions?

☐ Does the person adequately understand the degree to which treatment notes and any other documents in the chart will be made available to the patient and/or to the patient's attorney?

☐ Does the client understand the implications of the use of such treatment modalities as hypnosis or amytal interviews, if these are contemplated? Are the effects of these treatments on a client's potential rights to pursue litigation outlined? Has the therapist considered the use of an additional, separate consent form for such techniques?

Because, as is often emphasized throughout this book, each patient, therapist, and therapy is unique, and no list can enumerate the relevant issues for all therapies, the therapist might consider what important issues the previous items in this list have missed in the following manner. As the therapist tries to identify empathically with the person seeking treatment, what would the therapist wish to know if he or she were in the patient's position? What information would the person wish to know that might significantly affect a decision about beginning therapy? What sort of information and what form of such information would be most empowering to a person's capacity to retain adult autonomy in the context of therapy on a difficult and painful topic?

# Appendix E

# Therapist's Outline for Frequent Review of Treatment and Treatment Plan When Recovered Memories Are an Issue

- Does the patient seem to be benefiting from the services that have been provided so far? What issues have been effectively addressed? What significant issues have not yet been addressed?
- Have the patient's strengths, abilities, and resources (personal or environmental) been adequately assessed? Does the current treatment plan adequately take account of these strengths, abilities, and resources?
- Have issues of informed consent been adequately addressed, particularly with regard to any recent changes in assessment strategy or treatment planning?
- Do the patient's descriptions of recovered memories or other matters raise any issues of either mandatory or discretionary reporting? If so, have these issues been adequately addressed?
- Have potential risks, if any, for violence, abuse, or life-threatening behaviors in regard to this patient been adequately assessed?
- Is there any evidence that the patient has medical needs that are not being met?
- If other professionals are also providing services to the patient, is there any evidence that any relevant issues related to coordination of services, miscommunications, turf issues, lines of responsibility, and so on have not been adequately addressed?

◻ Do the chart notes and documentation adequately reflect the current state of assessment, treatment, and treatment planning?

◻ Have any treatment issues emerged for which the therapist is not adequately competent or prepared? If so, have these issues been adequately addressed through such options as supervision by, consultation with, or referral to a colleague who possesses expertise in the relevant areas?

◻ Is the therapist experiencing, for whatever reasons, the type of reactions (e.g., boredom and disinterest in the case, an overwhelming urge to control the patient, a wish or tendency to avoid contact with the patient, extreme discomfort at the prospect that he or she might be called to testify in a legal proceeding, fear that he or she might be sued either for failing to recognize and address a history of abuse or for implanting false memories of abuse, overidentification with the patient, vicarious traumatization) that might constitute countertransference or some other phenomenon that might distort, block, or otherwise interfere with providing professional services? If so, have these reactions been adequately addressed (e.g., through consultation with a colleague)?

# Appendix F

# Outline of Topics for Forensic Preparation

The following outline contains a suggested list of topic areas that should be attended to by the mental health professional working in the forensic setting.

INITIAL CONTACT WITH THE ATTORNEY
  The task and the client
  Competence
  Conflicts of interest
  Additional aspects of adequate disclosure
  Scheduling
  Financial arrangements
  Communication, privilege, secrets, and surprises
  Other needs and expectations
CONDUCTING AN ASSESSMENT
  Reviewing the issues and the literature
  Choosing the tests to fit the tasks
  Choosing the tests to fit the individual
  Thinking about tests in context
  Informing the client
  Taking adequate notes
    Vision
    Hearing
    Mobility and access

Material in this appendix adapted with permission from Pope, Butcher, & Seelen, 1993, pp. 47–83. © American Psychological Association.

# Appendix G

# Therapist's Outline for Review Prior to Deposition and Cross-Examination

Ideally, a therapist will not be serving as the expert witness in her or his own patient's case. However, even when there is an expert evaluator, the treating therapist is likely to face being deposed and testifying if litigation emerges from the psychotherapy experience. Because this is an unfamiliar area for most psychotherapists, we offer the following questions that can be useful for a therapist to review prior to testifying. We strongly urge that the therapist meet with the attorney for his or her client prior to the deposition or courtroom appearance to review possible areas of testimony.

- Will the patient be present during the therapist's testimony? If so, have issues relating to the patient's encountering the therapist in a new setting and listing to testimony about the patient been addressed, as appropriate, with the patient?
- Have relevant published works presenting research, theory, and so on in the area of recovered memories of abuse (see, e.g., Appendix A) been reviewed?
- Is the therapist's curriculum vitae (c.v.) complete and up to date?
- Does the c.v. clearly reflect adequate education, training, and experience in providing assessment, therapeutic, and forensic services in this area (i.e., to patients for whom recovered memories are an issue) to constitute demonstra-

ble competence or expertise? If not, can the therapist address this issue of competence or expertise?

□   Have all chart notes and related documents been reviewed?

□   If a subpoena has been issued, has it been reviewed carefully to determine whether it directs the therapist to bring certain materials to the deposition or trial? If so, have all relevant issues regarding whether these materials should be made available been appropriately examined and resolved (e.g., in certain instances subpoenaed material may be protected by privilege)? If the therapist intends to bring the materials to the deposition or trial, have the materials been located and secured? Has the security of psychological tests, if in the record, been safeguarded?

□   Have possible time conflicts regarding testimony been discussed? For example, the therapist may be scheduled to testify Wednesday morning. The attorney calling the therapist to testify may have stressed that the direct examination will begin at 9:00 a.m. and should take no more than an hour. The attorney estimates that the cross-examination will also take no more than an hour. Accordingly, the therapist plans to complete testimony no later than noon and to see patients beginning at 1:30 in the afternoon. However, it is possible that there may be long delays before the court is called to order Wednesday morning. Numerous objections, unexpected rulings (i.e., unexpected by the attorney calling the therapist), and several recesses may stretch the direct examination to two or three times the estimated length. The attorney conducting the cross-examination may decide to question the therapist for—literally—2 or 3 days. The possibility that the therapist may not have completed testifying in time to see patients Wednesday afternoon needs to be adequately discussed and contingency plans created.

□   Have all payment arrangements regarding the therapist's deposition or trial testimony been clarified and agreed to by the relevant parties? Are all relevant parties complying with these arrangements?

□   Is there any need for (or benefit from) the therapist consulting with his or her own attorney? In many instances, therapists let themselves be guided by the attorney who calls them to testify. However, because the attorney is representing the interests of another person, it may be appropriate for a therapist preparing to appear as a witness in a case involving his or her patient to consult with independent counsel.

☐ Is the therapist aware of any bias, countertransference, or other personal reactions that might interfere with the ability to provide clear, truthful, and undistorted testimony? If so, how can these be effectively addressed?

# Appendix H

# Cross-Examination Questions for Therapists Who Testify About Recovered Memories of Abuse

Therapists providing clinical services to patients who have reported recovered memories and are now engaged in some sort of litigation are likely to face an extensive and probing deposition and a challenging cross-examination. The following questions are among those commonly asked.

Reviewing the questions below may help therapists to prepare for deposition and cross-examination. The questions will not come as a surprise (as they would if a therapist were encountering them for the first time while testifying), and the witness can have time to reflect upon their meaning, to review relevant information (e.g., treatment records, relevant publications), and to consider them from various perspectives prior to providing responses under oath. The witness can ensure that the answers to these questions are as informed, accurate, and clearly expressed as possible.

Reviewing these questions can not only help therapists to prepare to testify in a specific case but also provide opportunities to rethink and reevaluate the therapists' work more generally. Thinking about these questions and their implications may help therapists to identify weaknesses in their ways of practicing and to improve their resources and procedures for providing services to any patient for whom recovered memories of abuse are an issue.

Material in this appendix was adapted with permission from Pope, Butcher, & Seelen, 1993, and Pope, 1994. © American Psychological Association.

Although these questions are phrased for the treating therapist, they may also be helpful to other witnesses (expert or fact),
regardless of whether they are called by the prosecutor, plaintiff's attorney, defense attorney, or the court itself (e.g., when the
court appoints a clinician to conduct an independent psychological assessment of the patient).

# Therapist's Previous Work With Patients When Recovered Memories Are an Issue

□ How many patients have you seen clinically who have previously (i.e., previous to seeking services to you) reported
recovering memories of abuse?

□ How many patients have you seen clinically who, during
their work with you, have reported recovering memories
of abuse?

□ When you consider all the instances in which patients have
alleged to you that they have recovered memories of childhood sexual abuse, how many instances were there in
which you finally concluded that the allegations were
valid? In how many instances did you conclude that the
allegations were invalid? Were there any instances in
which you were unable to reach a final conclusion about
the validity of the allegations?

□ On what basis do you decide whether a patient's recovered
memories are true or false? That is to say, what does it take
for you to conclude that allegations are true? Are false?
Please list each type of evidence you take into account and
each element of your reasoning.

□ In assessing the validity of recovered memories, do you
rely on any checklists? If so, please provide information
about where the checklist was published and about the
availability of published information about the checklist's
validity, reliability, applicability, sensitivity and specificity, and so on. Please identify any sources that
represent peer-reviewed scientific and professional publications.

# Therapist's Knowledge of Relevant Research, Theory, and Current Practice

☐ Do you believe that a therapist working with a patient for whom recovered memories are an issue needs to be adequately aware of the current research, theory, and practice relevant to recovered memories of abuse? [This question is a foundation for the questions that follow. If the therapist answer's "no," it is likely that the attorney will elicit extensive testimony about the rationale and implications for this belief.]

☐ Are you adequately aware of the current research, theory, and practice relevant to recovered memories?

☐ What are the most recent research studies in this area that you are familiar with?

☐ What are the most recent publications regarding theory in this area that you have read and are familiar with?

☐ What are the most recent publications regarding practice in this area that you have read and are familiar with?

☐ Please provide citations for the articles, books, chapters, and other works about recovered memories that you have authored or coauthored. (Note: There is no reason to feel inadequate if, like the majority of mental health professionals, you have written nothing on this or any topic. But if you are prepared for this question, it may be easier to answer it calmly, rather than defensively or from a base of shame).

# Therapist's Sources of Knowledge About the Patient

☐ How many hours have you spent with the patient?

☐ Please describe your clinical training, identifying specifically your training in interviewing and assessing patients.

☐ Have you reviewed all relevant background documents? Please list those documents that you have reviewed. Would these include:

> prior medical records?
> prior records of psychological assessment or treatment?
> records of any hospitalizations?

> school records?
> prior records of employment?
> depositions and other legal documents? (NB: It is not usual for the treating therapist to have conducted this sort of extensive formal review. However, it is helpful to have at least a familiarity with prior mental health treatment records)

- In conducting your assessment of this patient, providing therapy to this patient, preparing to testify, or at any other time, have you ever made an effort to contact or interview any family member, friend, or acquaintance of this patient? Why or why not?
- Have you ever made an effort to contact or interview any teachers, employers, co-workers, or others involved in this patient's education or work? Why or why not?
- Have you made any effort to contact or interview any health care or mental health care professional who has provided assessment, treatment, consultation, or other services to the patient? Why or why not?
- Do you have a standard practice regarding contact with collateral sources? Why is that your standard practice? Did you apply that policy with this client? If not, what led you to act differently in this case? (NB: For a treating therapist, there is no set standard regarding whether or not to contact collaterals, and it is contraindicated in some theoretical orientations. It is simply important for you to have a clear rationale for what you have chosen to do.)
- Aside from those individuals previously mentioned, have you made any effort to contact or interview anyone else who might have information that would be relevant to your assessment of the patient, the therapy you provided to the patient, or your testimony here today? Why or why not?
- What sources of information have you sought or received about possible factors that might affect the patient's previous or current memory? Please address each of the following:

> blows to head, falls, etc.
> other trauma
> alcohol
> drugs
> neurological disorders

# Therapist's Use of or Reliance on Standardized Psychological Tests

- □ Was your therapy with this patient guided by an assessment that included the use of standardized psychological tests, regardless of whether you personally administered, scored, or interpreted the tests? Why or why not? (NB: Again, there is no set standard for the use of testing, and many treating therapists do not use formal psychometric assessment with their clients. Be sure to be able to give a rationale for your choices.)
- □ For each test, what are the reliability and validity when the test is used with this population?
- □ Are you aware of any standardized test that can reliably indicate whether a patient has been a victim of abuse, regardless of whether the abuse has never been forgotten, is not currently remembered, or is the subject of recovered memory?
- □ Are you aware of any research indicating that psychological test results can be misleading if interpreted in the absence of an adequate history?
- □ What aspects of this patient's characteristics and personal history were relevant to proper interpretation of the psychological tests?
- □ To what extent did any of the tests assess any aspect of memory function (e.g., Wechsler Memory Scale, Wechsler Adult Intelligence Scale, Halstead-Reitan Neuropsychological Assessment Battery)?
- □ To what extent did any of the tests rely on the patient's memory?

# Financial Issues

- □ How much are you charging for your testimony in this case? (NB: Of course, professionals do not charge for their testimony per se; they charge for their time and work.)
- □ When did you first discuss financial arrangements (e.g., how much the patient would pay per session) with the patient? What was the nature of those original arrangements? Were those arrangements part of the informed consent?

- Have the financial arrangements been changed in any way? If so, how?
- Have the financial arrangements, including changes, been fully documented?
- Did you, the patient, or any other relevant person ever depart in any way from these financial arrangements?
- Under these financial arrangements, how much money have you earned—whether or not the money has actually been paid to you—for your time and work in regard to this patient?
- Up to now, how much money, if any, has actually been paid to you?
- Currently, how much is owed to you? (Significant amounts will likely form the basis of numerous subsequent questions addressing such issues as the therapist's allowing a substantial debt to accumulate and the ways in which the likelihood of payment of this debt might hinge on the outcome of the trial, which in turn might be affected by the therapist's testimony. In the latter instance the therapist's possible bias is explored; the cross-examining attorney's questions may make clear that the therapist's testimony may significantly influence whether the therapist receives payment of moneys owed to him or her.)
- Have you ever sought a lien for any money that the patient owes to you?
- Have any of the attorneys in this case or those acting on the attorney's behalf offered you any money for your services or for other reasons?

## Compliance With Subpoena Duces Tecum

The three sets of questions in this section are taken verbatim from Pope, Butcher, & Seelen (1993, pp. 140–142). (NB: A subpoena duces tecum is a document produced by an attorney ordering you to appear in court or at a deposition. It is not a court order, which must be complied with. If you have concerns about complying with the terms of such a subpoena, which can be written by any lawyer, consult with your own attorney. In some states, a protective order can be obtained to maintain the confidentiality of files. Even when the court has ordered you to produce a document, you have the right to appear before the judge and present your case for why certain materials should remain confidential. Again, consult with your own attorney if this is the plan of action you intend to take.)

- Have you complied fully with each and every element of the subpoena to produce? Are there any items that you did not make available?
- Were any of these documents altered in any way? Were any of them recopied, erased, written over, enhanced, edited, or added to in any way since the time each was originally created? Are the photocopies made available true and exact replicas of the original documents without any revision?
- Have any documents falling within the scope of the subpoena or otherwise relevant to the case been lost, stolen, misplaced, destroyed, or thrown away? Are any documents you made, collected, handled, or received that are within the scope of this subpoena or otherwise relevant to the case absent from the documents made available to me?

## The Therapist's Forensic Experience When Recovered Memories Were at Issue

- Have you ever participated in civil, criminal, licensing, or any other forums in which reports of recovered memories were at issue?
- How many such cases involved patients to whom you had personally provided professional services?
- In how many such cases did you appear as a witness called by the plaintiff?
- In how many such cases did you appear as a witness called by the defense?
- In how many such cases did you appear in some other capacity than as a witness called by the plaintiff or defense?
- In how many such cases have you been allowed to testify as an expert witness (rather than in some other capacity, such as a percipient or fact witness)? Have you ever been barred from testifying? Have you ever failed to be qualified as an expert witness?

# Index

# About the Authors

**Kenneth S. Pope**, PhD, ABPP, received graduate degrees from Harvard and Yale, is a charter fellow of the American Psychological Society (APS), and has authored or coauthored over 100 articles and chapters in peer-reviewed scientific and professional journals and books. His 10 books include *The MMPI, MMPI-2 & MMPI-A in Court: A Practical Guide for Expert Witnesses & Attorneys* (with J. Butcher & J. Seelen); *Ethics in Psychotherapy and Counseling* (with M. Vasquez); and *The Stream of Consciousness: Scientific Investigations into the Flow of Human Experience* (with J. Singer). A psychologist in independent practice, he has served as chair of the Ethics Committees of the American Psychological Association (APA) and the American Board of Professional Psychology (ABPP), and was a recipient of the Frances Mosseker Award for Fiction, the Belle Meyer Bromberg Award for Literature, and the APA Division of Clinical Psychology Award for Distinguished Professional Contributions to Clinical Psychology. He received the 1994 American Psychological Association Award for Distinguished Contributions to Public Service, which included the following citation (*American Psychologist, 50*, pp. 241–243):

> For rigorous empirical research, landmark articles and books, courageous leadership, fostering the careers of others, and making services available to those with no means to pay. His works include 9 books and over 100 other publications on topics rang-

ing from treating victims of torture to psychometrics to memory to ethics. His pioneering research has increased our understanding of therapist–patient sex, especially in the areas of effects on patients, tendencies to deny or discount risks, factors enabling known perpetrators to continue or resume not only practicing but also abusing patients, and approaches to prevention . . . Pope's research frequently addresses concerns that are relatively neglected because they tend to cause anxiety, such as therapists' feelings of anger, hate, fear, or sexual attraction toward patients, or therapists own histories of sexual or physical abuse. He frequently declines compensation for his work to advance psychology in the public interest. This is evident in his recent book, *Sexual Involvement with Therapists: Patient Assessment, Subsequent Therapy, Forensics*, published by the American Psychological Association. Pope waived all royalties for the volume in order that it might be sold at reduced price and be more readily available and useful. His integrity, good will, humor, and tireless work in the public interest represent the finest ideals of our profession.

**Laura S. Brown,** PhD, ABPP, is a feminist clinical and forensic psychologist in independent practice in Seattle, WA, and clinical professor of psychology at the University of Washington. A fellow of the American Psychological Association and the American Psychological Society, she is a diplomate of the American Board of Professional Psychology. She was chosen by the American Psychological Association (APA) to present the Centennial Lecture on Women's Adult Development at the Smithsonian Institute. She has written and taught extensively— upwards of 70 book chapters or peer-reviewed scientific and professional articles—in the area of feminist therapy theory, ethics, and practice, and has testified in numerous court and regulatory matters on ethics and the standard of care in psychotherapy. She has also treated or evaluated several hundred people who have experienced delayed recall of traumatic events, and is frequently called by plaintiff and defense attorneys to serve as an expert witness in cases involving questions of recovered memories. She served on the APA's Working Group on Recovered Memories. She has won several awards from her colleagues, including the Distinguished Publication Award of the Association for Women in Psychology, the Leadership

Citation of the APA Committee on Women in Psychology, the Distinguished Contributions Award of the APA Committee on Lesbian and Gay Concerns, and the 1995 APA Award for Distinguished Professional Contributions to Public Service. Her most recent book is *Subversive Dialogues: Theory in Feminist Therapy* (Basic Books, 1994). Dr. Brown has also worked extensively toward the elimination of psychotherapeutic malpractice. Her testimony in the case of *Simmons v. U.S.*, cited by the judges of the Ninth Circuit Court of Appeals, has been extremely influential in creating a legal standard regarding sexual misconduct by psychotherapists. Dr. Brown has been president of two APA divisions and has served on the editorial boards of numerous scientific journals.